Progressive Business Plan for a Medical Equipment Rental Company

Copyright © 2017 by Progressive Business Consulting, Inc.
Pembroke Pines, FL 33027

Medical Equipment Rental Company Business Plan
_____ (date)

Business Name:
_____

Plan Time Period: 2017 - 2019

Founding Directors:
Name:
_____

Name:
_____

Contact Information:
Owner:
_____

Address:
_____

City/State/Zip: _____

Phone: _____

Cell: _____

Fax: _____

Website: _____

Email: _____

Submitted to: _____

Date: _____

Contact Info: _____

This document contains confidential information. It is disclosed to you for informational purposes only. Its contents shall remain the property of _____ (business name) and shall be returned to _____ when requested. This is a business plan and does not imply an offering of securities.

NON-DISCLOSURE AGREEMENT

_____ (Company)., and _____ (Person Name), agrees:

_____ (Company) Corp. may from time to time disclose to _____ (Person Name) certain confidential information or trade secrets generally regarding Business plan and financials of _____ (Company) corp.

_____ (Person Name) agrees that it shall not disclose the information so conveyed, unless in conformity with this agreement. _____ (Person Name) shall limit disclosure to the officers and employees of _____ (Person Name) with a reasonable "need to know" the information, and shall protect the same from disclosure with reasonable diligence.

As to all information which _____ (Company) Corp. claims is confidential, _____ (Company) Corp. shall reduce the same to writing prior to disclosure and shall conspicuously mark the same as "confidential," "not to be disclosed" or with other clear indication of its status. If the information which _____ (Company) Corp. is disclosing is not in written form, for example, a machine or device, _____ (Company) Corp. shall be required prior to or at the same time that the disclosure is made to provide written notice of the secrecy claimed by _____ (Company) Corp..
_____ (Person Name) agrees upon reasonable notice to return the confidential tangible material provided by it by _____ (Company) Corp. upon reasonable request.

The obligation of non-disclosure shall terminate when if any of the following occurs:
(a) The confidential information becomes known to the public without the fault of _____ (Person Name), or;
(b) The information is disclosed publicly by _____ (Company) Corp., or ;
(c) a period of 12 months passes from the disclosure, or;
(d) the information loses its status as confidential through no fault of

_____ (Person Name).

In any event, the obligation of non-disclosure shall not apply to information which was known to _____ (Person Name) prior to the execution of this agreement.

Dated: _____

_____ (Company) Corp.
_____(Person Name)

Business and Marketing Plan Instructions

1.	If you purchased this Business Plan Book via Amazon's Print-on-	Demand System, please send proof-of-purchase to	Probusconsult2@Yahoo.com and we will email you the file.

2.	Complete the Executive Summary section, as your final step, after	you have completed the entire plan.

3.	Feel free to edit the plan and make it more relevant to your strategic	goals, objectives and business vision.

4.	We have provided all of the formulas needed to prepare the financial	plan. Just plug in the numbers that are based on your particular	situation. Excel spreadsheets for the financials are available on the	microsoft.com website and www.simplebizplanning.com/forms.htm
		http://office.microsoft.com/en-us/templates/

5. Throughout the plan, we have provided prompts or suggestions as to what values to enter into blank spaces, but use your best judgment and then delete the suggested values (?).

6. The plan also includes some separate worksheets for additional assistance in expanding some of the sections, if desired.

7. Additionally, some sections offer multiple choices and the word 'select' appears as a prompt to edit the contents of the plan.

8. Your feedback, referrals and business are always very much appreciated.

Thank you

Nat Chiaffarano, MBA
Progressive Business Consulting, Inc.
Pembroke Pines, FL 33027
ProBusConsult2@yahoo.com

Medical Equipment Rental Company Business Plan:
Table of Contents

Section   Description   Page

1.0	**Executive Summary**
1.1.0	Tactical Objectives
1.1.1	Strategic Objectives
1.2	Mission Statement
1.2.1	Core Values Statement
1.3	Vision Statement
1.4	Keys to Success
2.0	**Company Summary**
2.1	Company Ownership
2.2	Company Licensing and Liability Protection
2.3	Start-up To-do Checklist
2.4.0	Company Location
2.4.1	Company Facilities
2.5.0	Start-up Summary
2.5.1	Inventory
2.5.2	Supply Sourcing
2.6	Start-up Requirements
2.7	SBA Loan Key Requirements
2.7.1	Other Financing Options

3.0	**Products and Services**
3.1	Service Descriptions
3.1.1	Product Descriptions
3.2	Alternate Revenue Streams
3.3	Production of Products and Services
3.4	Competitive Comparison
3.5	Sale Literature
3.6	Fulfillment
3.7	Technology
3.8	Future Products and Services
4.0	**Market Analysis Summary**
4.1.0	Secondary Market Research
4.1.1	Primary Market Research
4.2	Market Segmentation
4.3	Target Market Segment Strategy
4.3.1	Market Needs
4.4	Buying Patterns
4.5	Market Growth

Section	Description	Page
4.6	Service Business Analysis	
4.7	Barrier to Entry	
4.8	Competitive Analysis	
4.9	Market Revenue Projections	
5.0	**Industry Analysis**	
5.1	Industry Leaders	
5.2	Industry Statistics	
5.3	Industry Trends	
5.4	Industry Key Terms	
6.0	**Strategy and Implementation Summary**	
6.1.0	Promotion Strategy	
6.1.1	Grand Opening	
6.1.2	Value Proposition	
6.1.3	Positioning Statement	
6.1.4	Distribution Strategy	
6.2	Competitive Advantage	
6.2.1	Branding Strategy	

6.3	Business SWOT Analysis
6.4.0	Marketing Strategy
6.4.1	Strategic Alliances
6.4.2	Monitoring Marketing Results
6.4.3	Word-of-Mouth Marketing
6.5	Sales Strategy
6.5.1	Customer Retention Strategy
6.5.2	Sales Forecast
6.5.3	Sales Program
6.6	Merchandising Strategy
6.7	Pricing Strategy
6.8	Differentiation Strategies
6.9	Milestone Tracking
7.0	**Website Plan Summary**
7.1	Website Marketing Strategy
7.2	Development Requirements
7.3	Sample Frequently Asked Questions
8.0	**Operations**
8.1	Security Measures

9.0	**Management Summary**
9.1	Owner Personal History

Section	Description Page
9.2	Management Team Gaps
9.2.1	Management Matrix
9.2.2	Outsourcing Matrix
9.3	Employee Requirements
9.4	Job Descriptions
9.4.1	Job Description Format
9.5	Personnel Plan
9.6	RentalPlan
10.0	**Business Risk Factors**
10.1	Business Risk Reduction Strategies
10.2	Reduce Customer Perceived Risk Strategies
11.0	**Financial Plan**
11.1	Important Assumptions

11.2		Break-even Analysis
11.3		Projected Profit and Loss
11.4		Projected Cash Flow
11.5		Projected Balance Sheet
11.6		Business Ratios
12.0		**Business Plan Summary**
13.0		**Potential Exit Strategies**
		Appendix
		Helpful Resources

"Progressive Business Plan for a Medical Equipment Rental Company"

Copyright Notice

Copyright © 2017   Nat Chiaffarano, MBA
Progressive Business Consulting, Inc
All Rights Reserved.   ISBN: 9781521585573

This program is protected under Federal and International copyright laws.
No portion of these materials may be reproduced, stored in a retrieval system or transmitted in any manner whatsoever, without the written consent of the publisher.

Limits of Liability / Disclaimer of Warranty

The author and the publisher of "Progressive Business Plan for a Medical Equipment Rental Company", and all accompanying materials have used their best efforts in preparing this program. The author and publisher make no representations and warranties with respect to the accuracy, applicability, fitness or completeness of the content of this program. The information contained in this program is subject to change without notice and should not be construed as a commitment by the author or publisher.

The authors and publisher shall in no event be held liable for any loss or damages, including but not limited to special, incidental, consequential, or other damages. The program makes no promises as to results or consequences of applying the material herein: your business results may vary in direct relation to your detailed planning, timing, availability of capital and human resources, and implementation skills.

This publication is not intended for use as a source of legal, accounting, or professional advice. As always, the advice of a competent legal, accounting, tax, financial or other professional should be sought. If you have any specific questions about your unique business situation, consider contacting a qualified business consultant. The fact that an organization or website is referred to as a 'resource' or potential source of information, does not mean that the publisher or authors endorse the resource. Websites listed may also have been changed since publication of the book.

1.0 Executive Summary

Industry Overview

The Medical Equipment Rental industry provides healthcare institutions with an alternative to purchasing medical equipment. Over the past five years, the number of sophisticated diagnostic tests that require technologically advanced equipment at hospitals and medical centers has kept demand steady for leased equipment rather than outright purchases. Demographic shifts, such as an aging US population, and increases in healthcare funding will help demand for medical equipment rentals grow in the next five years. The rise in Medicare and Medicaid spending will continue to support demand for medical equipment rentals.

Over the past five years, the Medical Equipment Rental industry has exhibited growth, thanks to the rapid advent of high-cost equipment. As many healthcare providers have grappled with cuts in Medicare and Medicaid reimbursements they have shifted toward cost-saving strategies. In particular, many healthcare providers have rented, rather than purchased, medical equipment because they can access up-to-date technologies at a lower cost. In the coming years, in

response to the rapidly growing obese population, many healthcare providers will rent bariatric equipment, thus stimulating industry revenue growth. Over the time frame of 2015-2021, health spending is expected to grow at the rate of 6.2% annually. It reflects the net result of the aging of the population, Affordable Care Act, and generally improving socio-economic conditions.
Source: http://www.ibisworld.com/industry/medical-equipment-rental.html

The industry derives the majority of its revenue from supplying patient support systems. In 2013, IBISWorld estimates that patient support system rentals generate 53.0% of the industry's revenue. Patient support systems primarily include hospital beds and long-term care beds, though depending on design features, these systems can also provide patient data reporting and caregiver alerts. The demand for patient support systems is strongly tied to the number of patients at hospitals and nursing-care facilities. Typically, these healthcare establishments will rent patient support systems on a short-term basis, depending on fluctuations in the number of patient admissions. Generally, equipment is rented on a daily, monthly or pay-per-use basis.

Resource: www.transparencymarketresearch.com/medical-equipment-rental.html

Business Overview

_____ (company name) will sell, rent and service a wide range of medical supplies and equipment to patients needing specialty products to aid them in mobility and comfort.

_____ (company name) _____ was formed on _____ (date) to be a full-service Medical Equipment Rental Company in _____ (city), _____ (state). It will distinguish itself from the competition and capture market share by developing a reputation for absolute trustworthiness. It will follow the best practices of Medical Equipment Rental Companies, with particular emphasis on excellent customer service, convenient 24/7 hour online access, a deep selection of state-of-the-art and inspected Medical equipment, in-house skills development programs, a knowledgeable staff and competitive pricing.

We will assemble a National Sales Team to sell our solutions directly to hospital and healthcare facilities across the nation. This new initiative will allow hospitals and healthcare facilities to have a direct sales rep from our company, and allow us to offer customers the complete solution; whether it's equipment financing, rental, sales, biomedical services or asset management.

The Medical Equipment Rental Company will compete on the following basis:
1. Superior level of reliable medical equipment rental services.
2. Wraparound services, including home Medical Equipment maintenance service support.
3. Unique ability to help identify and match the medical equipment needs each client has with the 'right' Medical Equipment and operating support.
4. The most thorough and detailed Medical Equipment inspection and preparer service before rental.

We believe that we can become the Medical Equipment Rental Company of choice in the _____ area for the following reasons:
1. We will develop a training program to create a competent staff, dedicated to continuously improving their skill sets to better assist our customers in making informed medical equipment leasing arrangements.
2. We will develop a questionnaire to survey changing customer needs and wants, build a customer preference profile and enable customers to express their level of satisfaction.
3. We will become a one-stop destination for customers in need of medical equipment leasing and asset management services.
4. We will offer quality leasing services, using the latest customer profiling and needs matching software.

In order to succeed, _____ (company name) will have to do the following:
1. Conduct extensive market research to demonstrate that there

is a demand for a   Medical Equipment Rental Company with our aforementioned differentiation   strategy.
2.   Make superior customer service our number one priority.
3.   Stay abreast of developments in the Medical Equipment Rental Company   industry.
4.   Precisely assess and then exceed the expectations of all customers.
5.   Form long-term, trust-based relationships with clients to secure profitable   repeat business and referrals.
6.   Develop process efficiencies to achieve and maintain profitability.
7.   Thoroughly understand the client's need for quality, inspected medical   equipment delivered on-time and at reasonable rental rates.

Products and Services

The revenues of the Company will come from the rental and sale of durable medical equipment and soft medical supplies to a number of different consumers, doctors, outpatient centers, assisted living facilities, home healthcare providers, hospices and hospitals. The Company will specialize in the rental of standard durable medical equipment as well as computerized systems for healthcare management. In addition to the above products, the Company will have the ability to source any piece of medical equipment that it does not carry in its inventory lines. This can be especially lucrative for major medical equipment pieces such as X-Ray machines, CT scanners, MRI machines, and other computerized diagnostic equipment that the Medical Device Distributor can broker between manufacturers and buyers.

Target Market

The target market for our medical equipment rental service company will be home healthcare providers, hospitals, hospices, assisted living facilities, nursing homes, medical practices, outpatient clinics, geriatric care providers, rehabilitation centers and private families in the ____ area.

Marketing Strategy

The foundation for this plan is a combination of primary and secondary research, upon which the marketing strategies are built. Discussions and interviews were held with a variety of individuals and other agencies to develop financial and proforma detail. We consulted census data, county business patterns, and other directories to develop the market potential and competitive situation. We will make appointments with local Medical facilities to talk with the heads of purchasing departments, office managers and asset managers. We will introduce our company and its services through these meetings and hand out brochures highlighting the availability of our staff and specialties. We will set up a phone line to handle the requests for equipment rentals on a 24-hour basis and consider buying software that is designed for Medical Equipment Rental Companies that can help track equipment, record maintenance hours and client requests. We will also create a website that clients can use to enter rental requests and learn more about our company. Our market strategy will be based on a cost effective approach to reach this defined target market. The basic approach to promote our services will be through establishing relationships with key influencers in the medical community and then through referral activities, once a significant client base has been established.

_____ (company name) will focus on developing loyal client relationships by offering medical equipment need matching services based on the customer's need for time-saving convenience, selection recommendations, operational support and value-driven rental pricing. The newest equipment offerings, staff accessibility, timely deliveries and value-based pricing will all serve to differentiate our company from the other providers in the area. With the help of an aggressive marketing plan, _____ (company name) expects to experience steady growth.

_____ (company name) also plans to attract customers through the use of
the following methods:
1.	Internet banner ads	2.	Online classifieds
3.	Direct emails	4.	Newsletter
5.	Online job sites	6.	Ezine Advertising

7. Direct Mailers Recruiting
8. Telephone
9. Health Fairs Recruiting (WOM)
10. Word Of Mouth
11. Specialty Magazines Newspaper Ads
12. Local
13. Medical Trade Journals
14. Flyers
15. Press Releases
15. Website

Mission Statement
(optional)

Our Mission is to address the following customer pain points or unmet needs and wants, which will define the opportunity for our business: _____
In order to satisfy these unmet needs and wants, we will propose the following unique solutions, which will create better value for our customers:

_____

_____

Critical Risks

Management recognizes there are several internal and external risks inherent in our business concept. Customer service quality, selection, value pricing and online convenience will be key factors in the consumers' decision to utilize our medical equipment rental services. Consumers must be willing to accept our one-stop leasing services and become repeat and referral customers in order for the company to meet its sales projections. Building a loyal and trusting relationship with our customers and referral partners is a key component to the success of _____ (company name).

Customer Service

We will take every opportunity to help the customer, regardless of what the revenue might be. We will outshine our competition by doing something "extra" and offering added-value services in a timely manner. We will take a long-term perspective and focus on the client's possible lifetime value to our business. By giving careful consideration to customer responsiveness, _____ (company name) goal will be to meet and exceed every service expectation. Quality service, and quick and informed responsiveness will be the philosophy guiding a customer-centric approach to our Medical Equipment Rental Company.

Business Plan Objectives

This business plan serves to detail the direction, vision, and planning necessary to achieve our goal of providing a superior medical equipment rental service. The purpose of this document is to provide a strategic business plan for our company and to support a request for a $ _____ ($500,000), five year bank loan to purchase medical and computer equipment, software and supplies, as part of the financing for a start-up Medical Equipment Rental Company. The plan has been adjusted to reflect the particular strengths and weaknesses of _____ (company name). Actual financial performance will be tracked closely and the business plan will be adjusted when necessary to ensure that full profit potential and loan repayment is realized on schedule. The plan will also help us to identify and quantify objectives, track and direct growth and create benchmarks for measuring success.

The Company

The business _____ (will be/was) incorporated on _____ (date) in the state of _____, as a _____ (Corporation/LLC), and intends to register for Sub-chapter 'S' status for federal tax purposes. This will effectively shield the owner(s) from personal liability and double taxation. _____ (Company Name) is a ____ (state) based corporation that will provide medical equipment rental solutions for clinics, hospitals, and related Medical facilities in its targeted market area of _____. The Company was founded in ___ (year) by _____.

Business Goals

Our business goal is to continue to develop the _____ (company name) brand name. To do so, we plan to execute on the following:
1. Offer medical equipment rental services and continuing customer support.

2. Focus on quality controls and ongoing operational excellence.
3. Recruit and train the very best ethical employees.
4. Create a marketing campaign with a consistent brand look and message content.

Location

_____ (company name) will be located in the ___ (complex name) on _____ (address) in __ (city), __ (state). The __ (purchased/leased) space is easily accessible and provides ample parking for __ (#) customers and staff. The location is attractive due to proximity to several _____ (hospitals) and _____ (medical practices).

Marketing Plan

The foundation for this plan is a combination of primary and secondary research, upon which the marketing strategies are built. Discussions and interviews were held with a variety of Medical professionals and area Medical private practice owners to develop financial and proforma detail. We consulted census data, county business patterns, and other directories to develop the market potential and competitive situation. The marketing plan will rely on an aggressive multi-media marketing campaign and a robust R&D program.

Competitive Edge

_____ (company name) will compete well in our market by offering competitive rental prices on an expanded line of medical rental equipment. Our staff will be knowledgeable and approachable, and use the latest software to match equipment to client needs. We will enable convenient online quote submissions. We will provide in-house delivery and pick up. All processing will be handled by our highly trained and certified staff provided to the customer's facility. Our custom solutions will allow the customer to acquire the equipment they need at the times they need it the most. We will provide flexibility to adjust during peak census. We will also provide biomedical services to repair equipment and service the customer's facility. Each piece of equipment will be thoroughly cleaned, maintained and inspected before being delivered to the customer.

Our TLS tracking software will generate the analytics the customer needs to see real-time statistics and monitor all of the equipment within their facility at a glance. This will reduce errors and decrease their equipment downtime. We will also produce timely and accurate reports so the customer can accurately assess their future needs. Our medical equipment rental services will provide caregivers with patient-ready equipment when and where they need it, 24/7. Furthermore, we will maintain an excellent reputation for trustworthiness and integrity with the community we serve.

Differentiation Strategy

Our customers will be able to obtain detailed, up-to-the-minute information about a breathtaking range of rental equipment over the telephone or through the Internet, without enduring the inconvenience of visiting a showroom and the often inadequate knowledge of the floor sales staff. We will operate a 24-hour-a-day, seven-day-a-week toll-free phone number for people wanting information about medical equipment and related products. When a caller expresses an interest in renting medical equipment, a company representative will ask a set of questions to narrow down the possibilities to a few good candidates. The rep and the customer will then intelligently discuss each option in detail. This approach will, in effect, allow customers to tailor the search experience to their own needs. We will also create tutorial videos that instruct customers how to achieve maximum benefit utilization of their rental equipment and to perform regular maintenance and minor problem solving tasks.

Customized Rental Packages
Our goal will be to come up with a different way to rent medical equipment. For example, we will need to rent equipment that is less feature rich for certain markets, or more rich features that they can add later. We will try to separate out additional features and benefits that people can add-on or download from the software. And instead of just being able to rent the same equipment to customers with varying need profiles, we will develop the ability to configure that equipment differently or add-on certain optional features. Software embedded in the hardware will also give us a lot more flexibility in

what kind of markets we can go into, and how we package and charge. We will work with manufacturers to be able to keep upgrading and delivering new add-on features. We will also offer different payment options, including subscription or automated recurring billing plans. Finally, customers will be able to choose from the following list of possible services: delivery, installation, training, parts replacement, 24/7 emergency servicing, and scheduled maintenance plans. We will also explore a rental pricing structure based on 'pay per use'. .

The Management Team

_____ (company name) will be lead by _____ (owner name) and _____ (co-owner name). ____ (owner name) has a _____ degree from _____ (institution name) and a _____ background within the Medical industry, having spent ____ (#) years with ____ (former employer name or type of business). During this tenure, ___ (he/she) helped grow the business from $_____ in yearly revenue to over $___. ____ (co-owner name) has a ___ background, and while employed by __ was able to increase operating profit by __ percent. These acquired recruiting skills, work experiences and educational backgrounds will play a big role in the success of our Medical Equipment Rental Company. Additionally, our president, _____ (name), has an extensive knowledge of the _____ area and has identified a niche market retail opportunity to make this venture highly successful, combining his ___ (#) years of work experience in a variety of businesses. _____ (owner name) will manage all aspects of the business and service development to ensure effective customer responsiveness while monitoring day-to-day operations. Qualified and trained clerks personally trained by _____ (owner name) in customer service skills will provide additional support services. Support staff will be added as seasonal or extended hours mandate.

Past Successful Accomplishments

____ (company name) is uniquely qualified to succeed due to the following past successes:
1. **Entrepreneurial Track Record**: The owners and

management team have helped to launch numerous successful ventures, including a _____.

2. **Key Milestones Achieved**: The founders have invested $____ to-date to staff the company, build the core technology, acquire starting inventory, test market the _____ (product/service), realize sales of $_____ and launch the website.

Start-up Funding

_____ (owner name) will financially back the new business venture with an initial investment of $_____, and will be the principal owner. Additional funding in the amount of $_____ will be sought from _____, a local commercial bank, with a SBA loan guarantee. This money will be needed to start the company. This loan will provide start-up capital, financing for a selected site lease, office remodeling, medical equipment inventory purchases, pay for permits and licensing, staff training and certification, equipment expenditures, contingent cash reserves and working capital to cover expenses during the first year of operation. This cash infusion will result in a dramatic revenue and income growth, during the 3 year planning period, and position the company to expand its recruiting services throughout the United States.

Financial Projections

We plan to open for business on ___(date). __ (company name) is forecasted to gross in excess of $____ in sales in its first year of operation, ending ___ (month/ year). Profit margins are forecasted to be at about __ percent. Second year operations will produce a net profit of $___. This will be generated from an investment of $__ in initial capital. It is expected that payback of our total invested capital will be realized in less than __ (#) months of operation. It is further forecasted that cash flow becomes positive from operations in year __ (one?). We project that our net profits will increase from $____ to over $__ over the next three years.

Financial Profile Summary

Key Indicator	2017	2018	2019

Total Revenue
_____

Expenses
_____

Gross Margin
_____

Operating Income
_____

Net Income
_____

EBITDA
_____

EBITDA = Revenue - Expenses (excluding tax, interest, depreciation and amortization)
     EBITDA is essentially net income with interest, taxes, depreciation, and   amortization added back to it, and can be used to analyze and compare   profitability between companies and industries because it eliminates the effects
     of financing and accounting decisions.
Gross Margin (%) = (Revenue - Cost of Goods Sold) / Revenue
Net Income = Total revenue - Cost of sales - Other expenses - Tax

Risk Assessment
_____ (company name) is positioned to exploit the critical shortage of capital to fund medical equipment purchases in a rapidly changing technological environment. Successful financing, strategic alliance forming, effective marketing, interactive website development and continued expansion are viewed as highly achievable.

Exit Strategy
If the business is very successful, _____ (owner name) may seek to sell the business to a third party for a significant earnings multiple. Most likely, the Company will hire a qualified business broker to sell the business on behalf of _____ (company name). Based on historical numbers, the business could generate a sales premium of up to __(#) times earnings.

Summary

Through a combination of a proven business model and a strong management team to guide the organization, _____ (company name) will be a long lasting, profitable business.

We believe our ability to create future product opportunities and growth will only be limited by our imagination and our ability to attract talented people who understand the concept of branding.

1.1.0 Tactical Objectives (select 3)

The following tactical objectives will specify quantifiable results and involve activities that can be easily tracked. They will also be realistic, tied to specific marketing strategies and serve as a good benchmark to evaluate our marketing plan success. (Select Choices)

1. Earn and maintain a rating as one of the best Medical Equipment Rental Companies in the ___ (city).
2. Establish and maintain ___ % minimum gross profit margins.
3. Achieve a profitable return on investment within _____ (one?) year.
4. Earn a ___ (15?)% internal rate of return for investors over the life of the lease.
5. Recruit a talented and motivated staff of ___ (#) people by _____ (date).
6. Offer our customers superior rental services, at an affordable price.
7. Create a company whose primary goal is to exceed customer expectations.
8. To develop a cash flow that is capable of paying all salaries, as well as grow the business, by the end of the _____ (first?) year.
9. To be an active networking participant and productive member of the community by _____ (date).
10. Create over _____ (30?) % of business revenues from repeat customers by _____ (date).

11. Achieve an overall customer satisfaction rate of ____ (98?) % by _____ (date).
12. Get a business website designed, built and operational by _____ (date), which will include an online shopping cart.
13. Achieve total sales revenues of $_____ in _____ (year).
14. Achieve net income more than ___ percent of net sales by the ____ (#) year.
15. Increase overall sales by _____ (20?) percent from prior year through superior service and word-of-mouth referrals.
16. Reduce the cost of new customer acquisition by ___ % to $ ___ by _____ (date).
17. Provide employees with continuing training, benefits and incentives to reduce the employee turnover rate to _____ %.
18. To pursue a growth rate of ____ (20?) % per year for the first ____ (#) years.
19. Enable the owner to draw a salary of $ _____ by the end of year ____ (one?).
20. To reach cash break-even by the end of year ____ (one?).
21. Increase the number of account executives by at least ____ (one?) per year.
22. Process all customer initiated proposals or quote requests within __ (#) minutes.

1.1.1 Strategic Objectives

We will seek to work toward the accomplishment of the following strategic objectives, which relate back to our Mission and Vision Statements:

1. Improve the overall quality of our medical equipment needs matching services.
2. Make the leasing experience better, faster and more client friendly.
3. Strengthen personal relationships with customers.
4. Enhance affordability, responsiveness, processing accuracy and accessibility.
5. Foster a spirit of technological innovation.

1.2.0 Mission Statement (select)

Our Mission Statement is a written statement that spells out our organization's overall goal, provides a sense of direction and acts as a guide to decision making for all levels of management. In developing the following mission statement we will encourage input from employees, volunteers, and other stakeholders, and publicize it broadly in our website and other marketing materials.

Our mission is to make medical equipment available to the medical industry with innovative, creative, responsive and flexible equipment acquisition solutions. We will conduct business under the guiding values of dedication, accessibility, accuracy, loyalty and expertise. We will guarantee exceptional customer service, speed in the completion of transactions, and appropriate follow-up. This will be achieved through a system that encourages teamwork, partnership, and respect for others. Each individual representing our company will be committed to the highest ethical standards and integrity, which will be reflected in their actions.

Our Corporate Goals:
1. To build a company whose strength is rooted in the values of service, integrity, creativity, and in our commitment to place the interests of our clients and their patients ahead of personal interests and never compromise our values.
2. To reach and maintain a reputation, which is recognized in the industry as providing true benefits to our clients and as providing medical equipment rental services that are responsive, realistic, practical, and can be implemented promptly and economically.
3. To foster and empower our clients to be innovative when creating new goals, to be strategic thinkers, and to hold fast to a philosophy of continuous improvement.
4. To guard as confidential, all information concerning the affairs of a client that is gathered during the course of a

professional assignment.
5.   To develop solutions that are resourceful, innovative, and that can be   implemented swiftly, and cost-effectively.

1.2.1   Mantra

We will create a mantra for our organization that is three or four words long. Its purpose will be to help employees truly understand why the organization exists. Our mantra will serve as a framework through which to make decisions about product and business direction. It will boil the key drivers of our company down to a sentence that defines our most important areas of focus and resemble a statement of purpose or significance.
Our Mantra is
_____

___

1.2.2   Core Values Statement

The following Core Values will help to define our organization, guide our behavior, underpin operational activity and shape the strategies we will pursue in the face of various challenges and opportunities:
       Being respectful and ethical to our customers and employees.
       Building enduring relationships with clients.
       Seeking innovation in our medical equipment industry.
       Practicing accountability to our colleagues and stakeholders.
       Pursuing continuous improvement as individuals and as a business entity.
       Performing tasks on time to satisfy the needs of our internal and external clients.
       Taking active part in the organization to meet the objectives and the   establishment of continuous and lasting relationships.

Offering professional treatment to our clients, employees, shareholders, and the community.

Continuing pursuit of new technologies for the development of the projects that add value for our clients, employees, shareholders, and the community.

Personal and professional improvement through education.

Teamwork to achieve our goals.

Honesty and integrity in all areas of our professional relationships.

Loyalty to the team and dedication to achieving our mission.

1.3 Vision Statement (select)

The following Vision Statement will communicate both the purpose and values of our organization. For employees, it will give direction about how they are expected to behave and inspires them to give their best. Shared with customers, it will shape customers' understanding of why they should work with our organization.

_____ (company name) will strive to become one of the most respected and favored Medical Equipment Rental Companies in the _____ area. To set the standard for Medical Equipment Rentals in the _____ area and beyond. It is our desire to become a landmark business in _____ (city), ____ (state), and become known not only for the quality of our Medical Equipment Rental Company Services, but also for our community and charity involvement.

_____ (company name) is dedicated to operating with a constant enthusiasm for learning about the Medical Equipment Rental business, being receptive to implementing new ideas, and maintaining a willingness to adapt to changing customer needs and wants. To be an active and vocal member of the community, and to provide continual reinvestment through participation in community activities and financial contributions. To incorporate the use of more state-of-the-art technologies to provide high-quality medical equipment rental services, and thereby improve the effectiveness, efficiency and competitiveness of the business.

1.4 Keys to Success

In broad terms, the success factors relate to providing what our clients want, and doing what is necessary to be better than our competitors. The following critical success factors are areas in which our organization must excel in order to operate successfully and achieve our objectives:

1. Personal service, attention to detail, ethical values, and an expert knowledge of the Medical Equipment Rental Company business.
2. Securing regular and ongoing client feedback
3. Depth of selection within a chosen equipment category.
4. Maintain a well trained sales force, practice good customer service and supply   quality professional support.
5. Launch a website to showcase our equipment, services and customer   testimonials, provide helpful information, and facilitate online quoting.
6. Local community involvement to form strategic business partnerships.
7. Conduct a targeted and cost-effective marketing campaign that seeks to   differentiate our one-stop medical equipment rental services from competitor   offerings.
8. Institute a pay-for-performance component to the employee compensation plan.
9. Control costs and manage budgets at all times in accordance with company goals.
10. Institute management processes and controls to insure the consistent replication of operations.
11. Recruit screened professionals with medical backgrounds and a passion for   delivering exceptional service.
12. Institute an employee training to insure the best techniques are consistently   practiced.

13. Network aggressively within the Medical community, as word of mouth will be our most powerful advertising asset.
14. Retain clients to generate repeat purchases and initiate referrals.
15. Competitive pricing in conjunction with a differentiated service business model.
16. Build our brand awareness, which will drive customers to increase their usage of our rental services and make referrals.
17. Business planning with the flexibility to make changes based on gaining new insightful perspectives as we proceed.
18. Build trust by circulating to our Code of Ethics and Service Guarantee.
19. Growing a good reputation for supplying quality Medical Professionals.
20. Good people skills and the ability to recognize a good match after interviewing prospective Medical professions.
21. Must do the necessary groundwork when it comes to background checks and police clearances.
22. A well-researched, forward-looking business plan with multiple revenue streams.
23. A cost-effective and well-directed marketing campaign directed at quickly building a valuable reputation within the local operating area.
24. Develop well-designed database software to facilitate the process of asset management.
25. Promote research and development of new service offerings and sales channels.
26. Optimize operating processes to maximize efficiency and customer satisfaction.
27. Demand for excellence in employee recruitment, retention, and customer care.
28. Must ensure references are checked, ensure that the people are qualified for the positions they seek, have the necessary experience and do not have questionable backgrounds.
29. Provide clients with the flexibility to deal with the peaks and valleys in their businesses.
30. Consider factoring accounts receivable to provide the business with the cash needed to pay employees and bills on

time. Resource: PRN Funding

31. Eliminate the red tape and make the hiring process smooth, efficient, fast and to the point.

32. Use an inexpensive and well-directed marketing campaign to quickly build a valuable reputation within the local operating region of the startup company .

33. Maintain the right mix of personal interaction with clients and the latest in IT systems and services.

34. Provide incentives for medical professionals to patronize our medical equipment rental company, such as discounted or free shipping, free delivery within our local area or volume discounts.

35. Take advantage of the cloud-computing environment to create an easier method for communication and collaboration.

36. Initially consider outsourcing back office operations to be able to focus on revenue generating activities and instead of getting absorbed with administrative concerns.

37. Persistence and relationship building are required to develop a consistent client base.

38. Responsiveness and customer service, for clients and employees, are key to retaining them.

39. Consider minimizing classroom training and maximizing hands-on field training by pairing a new hire with an experienced sales person who can act as mentor and field trainer.

40. Encourage existing customers to use social media sites, such as Facebook and Yelp, to discuss and rate their rental experiences, because when customers share positive feedback on rental equipment and sales people through social media, they are contributing free content and increasing brand awareness.

2.0 Company Summary

_____ (company name) will be a ____ (city) Medical Equipment Rental Company. _____ (company name) is a start-up _____ (Corporation/Limited Liability Company) consisting of _____ (#) principle officers with combined industry experience of _____ (#) years.

The owner of the company will be investing $ ___ of ____ (his/her) own capital into the company and will also be seeking a loan of $ __ to cover start-up costs and future growth.

_____ (company name) will be located in a _____ (purchased/rented) _____ (suite/complex) in the ____ on _____ (address) in _____ (city), __ (state). The owner, _____ , has ___ (#) years of experience in managing _____ (retail businesses?).

We will be a full-service Medical Equipment and Supply company serving _____ area. We will sell or rent medical equipment and provide service on exiting equipment. We will pride ourselves on exceptional customer service. _____ (company name) will be a clinical equipment services company that helps health care organizations increase operating efficiencies by optimizing the equipment lifecycle. We will help clients to access, manage and maintain medical equipment.

We will provide alternatives to traditional, capital-intensive methods of acquiring critical care equipment and specialize in providing customized plans that fit the individual needs of the client. Whether it's equipment financing, rental, equipment sales or services, we will offer customized solutions that work.

The company plans to use its existing contacts and customer base to generate short-term revenues. Its long-term profitability will rely on focusing on referrals, networking within community organizations and a comprehensive marketing program that includes public relations activities and a structured referral program. Sales are expected to reach $_____ within the first year and to grow at a conservative rate of ____ (20?) percent during the next two to five years.

Facilities Renovations

The necessary renovations are itemized as follows:
    Estimate
    Partition of space into functional areas.

    _____
    Build record storage areas.

    _____
    Painting and other general cosmetic repairs

    _____
    Install computer equipment

    _____
    Other _____

Total:
    _____

Hours of Operations

_____ (company name) will open for business on _____ (date) and will maintain the following office business hours:
    Monday through Thursday: _____   (7 AM

to 11 PM?)
Friday: _____
Saturday: _____
Sunday: _____

The company will invest in customer relationship management software (CRM) to track real-time sales data and collect customer information, including names, email addresses, key reminder dates and preferences. This information will be used with email, e-newsletter and direct mail campaigns to build personalized fulfillment programs, establish customer loyalty and drive revenue growth.

2.0.1 Traction (optional)

We will include this section because investors expect to see some traction, both before and after a funding event and investors tend to judge past results as a good indicator of future projections. It will also show that we can manage our operations and develop a business model capable of funding inventory purchases. Traction will be the best form of market research and present evidence of customer acceptance.

Period _____
Product/Service Focus _____
Our Sales to Date: _____
Our Number of Users to Date: _____
Number of Repeat Users _____
Number of Pending Orders: _____
Value of Pending Orders: _____
Reorder Cycle: _____
Key Reference Sites _____
Mailing List Subscriptions _____
Competitions/Awards Won _____
Notable Product Reviews _____
Actual Percent Gross Profit Margin _____
Industry Average: GPM _____

Actual B/(W) Industry Average _____

Note: Percent Gross Profit Margin equals the sales receipts less the cost of goods sold   divided by sales receipts multiplied by 100.

2.1 Company Ownership

_____ (company name) is a _____ (Sole-proprietorship /Corporation/Limited Liability Corporation (LLC)) and is registered to the principal owner, _____ (owner name). The company was formed in _____ (month) of ____ (year). It will be registered as a Subchapter S to avoid double taxation, with ownership allocated as follows: _____ (owner name) ____ % and _____ (owner name) ____ %.

The owner is a _____ (year) graduate of _____ (institution name), in _____ (city, ____ (state), with a _____ degree. He/she _____ has a second degree in _____ and certification as a _____. He/she also has ____ years of executive experience in the ____ (staffing?) industry as a _____, performing the following roles: _____.

37

His/her major accomplishments include:
_____

Ownership Breakdown:
Shareholder Name	Responsibilities	Number and Percent Class of Shares	Ownership

The remainder of the issued and outstanding common shares are retained by the Company for __ (future distribution / allocation under the Company's employee stock option plan).

Shareholder Loans
The Company currently has outstanding shareholder loans in the aggregate sum of $_____. The following table sets out the details of the shareholder loans.

Shareholder Name	Loan Amount	Loan Date	Balance Outstanding

Directors
The Company's Board of Directors, which is made up of highly qualified business and industry professionals, will be a valuable asset to the Company and be instrumental to its development. The following persons will make up the Board of Directors of the Company:

Name of Person	Educational Background	Past Industry Experience	Other Companies Served

2.2 Company Licensing & Liability Protection

We will use the services of a local attorney or Medical Equipment Rental Company consultant to help us with starting our company, as these individuals have more experience with the process, and typically have more insight into the people who will be in a position to approve or deny our application for a business license. They will also help to work through all the various legal issues that will surface, including what kind of entity to use for our business, how to best protect against liability problems, what rules apply to advertising, and so forth. We will contact an insurance agent to find out how much insurance will cost.

Our business will consider the need to acquire the following types of insurances. This will require extensive comparison shopping, through several insurance brokers, listed with our state's insurance department:

1. Workers' Compensation Insurance,
2. Business Policy: Property & Liability Insurance
3. Health insurance.
4. Commercial Auto Insurance
5. State Unemployment Insurance
6. Business Interruption Insurance (Business Income Insurance)
7. Disability Insurance
8. Life Insurance
9. Fidelity Bond Insurance
10. Professional Liability Insurance

We will provide professional liability coverage to all our healthcare professionals. We will carry business liability and property insurance and any other insurance we deem necessary after receiving counsel from our lawyer and insurance agent.

Health insurance and workers' compensation will be provided for our full-time employees as part of their benefit package. We feel that this is mandatory to ensure that they do not leave the company for one that does offer these benefits.

Workers' Compensation covers employees in case of harm attributed to the workplace.
Most states require businesses to maintain workers' compensation insurance for its employees.

The Property and Liability Insurance protects the building from theft, fire, natural disasters, and being sued by a third party. Life and Disability Insurance may be required if a bank loan is obtained.

Fidelity Insurance is insurance guaranteeing the fidelity of persons holding positions of public or private trust.
Liability Insurance includes protection in the face of day-to- day accidents, unforeseen results of normal business activities, and allegations of abuse or molestation, food poisoning, or exposure to infectious disease.
Property Insurance - Property Insurance should take care of the repairs less whatever deductible you have chosen.
Loss of Income Insurance will replace our income during the time the business is shut-down. Generally this coverage is written for a fixed amount of monthly income for a fixed number of months.

To help save on insurance cost and claims, management will do the following:
1. Stress employee safety in our employee handbook.
2. Screen employees with interview questionnaires and will institute pre- employment drug tests and comprehensive background checks.
3. Videotape our equipment and inventory for insurance purposes.
4. Create an operations manual that shares safe techniques.
5. Limit the responsibilities that we choose to accept in our contracts.
6. Consider the financial impact of assuming the exposure ourselves.
7. Establish loss prevention programs to reduce the hazards that cause losses.

8. Consider taking higher deductibles on anything but that which involves liability insurance because of third-party involvement.
9. Stop offering services that require expensive insurance coverage or require signed releases from clients using those services.
10. Improve employee training and initiate training sessions for safety.
11. Require Certificate of Insurance from all subcontractors.
12. Make staff responsible for a portion of any damages they cause.
13. We will investigate the setting-up of a partial self-insurance plan.
14. Convince underwriters that our past low claims are the result of our ongoing safety programs and there is reason to expect our claims will be lower than industry averages in the future.
15. At each renewal, we will develop a service agreement with our broker and get their commitment to our goals, such as a specific reduction in the number of incidents.
16. We will assemble a risk control team, with people from both sides of our business, and broker representatives will serve on the committee as well.
17. When an employee is involved in an accident, we will insist on getting to the root cause of the incident and do everything possible to prevent similar incidents from re-occurring.
18. At renewal, we will consult with our brokers to develop a cost-saving strategy and decide whether to bid out our coverage for competitive quotes or stick with our current carrier.
19. We will set-up a captive insurance program, as a risk management technique, where our business will form its own insurance company subsidiary to finance its retained losses in a formal structure.
20. Review named assets (autos and equipment), drivers and/or key employees identified on policies to make sure these assets and people are still with our company.
21. As a portion of our business changes, that is, closes, operations change, or outsourcing occurs, we will eliminate unnecessary coverage.
22. We will make sure our workforce is correctly classified by

our workers' compensation insurer and liability insurer because our premiums are based on the type of workers used.
23. We will become active in Trade Organizations or Professional Associations, because as a benefit of membership, our business may receive substantial insurance discounts.
24. We will adopt health specific changes to our work place, such as adopting a no smoking policy at our company and allow yoga or weight loss classes to be held in our break room.
25. We will consider a partial reimbursement of health club membership as a benefit. 26. We will find out what employee training will reduce rates and get our employees involved in these programs.

The required business insurance package will be provided by _____ (insurance carrier name). The business will open with a ____ (#) million dollar liability insurance policy, with an annual premium cost of $ _____..

The business will need to acquire the following special licenses, accreditations, certifications and permits:
1. A Sales Tax License is required through the State Department of Revenue.
2. Use Tax Registration Certificate
3. A County and/or City Occupational License.
4. Standard Business License from State Licensing Company
5. Building Code Inspections by the County Building Department.
6. Employment Company License issued by the Department of Labor (some states)
7. Medical Equipment Technician Certification

Note:
The AAMI Credentials Institute (ACI) awards certification credentials to healthcare technology professionals and entities in higher education, industry, and healthcare delivery.
Resource:
www.aami.org/professionaldevelopment/content.aspx?ItemNumber=1134
http://study.com/articles/How_to_Become_a_Medical_Equipment_

Repair_
   Technician.html

Note: In most states, you are legally required to obtain a business license, and a dba certificate. A business license is usually a flat tax assessment and a percentage of your gross income. A dba stands for Doing Business As, and it is the registration of your trade name if you have one. You will be required to register your trade name within 30 days of starting your business. Instead of registering a dba, you can simply form an LLC or Corporation and it will have the same effect, namely register your business name.

Resources:
Workers Compensation Regulations

   http://www.dol.gov/owcp/dfec/regs/compliance/wc.htm#IL
New Hire Registration and Reporting

   www.homeworksolutions.com/new-hire-reporting-information/
State Tax Obligations
   www.sba.gov/content/learn-about-your-state-and-local-tax-obligations
Resource:
www/sba.gov/content/what-state-licenses-and-permits-does-your-business-need

Note: Check with your local County Clerk and state offices or Chamber of Commerce to make sure you follow all legal protocols for setting up and running your business.

We will contact our state's public health department or medical board to find out if we need to be licensed to sell or rent the types of medical equipment we are interested in carrying. This is not required for all medical suppliers, except those specializing in specific types of equipment.

Summary of Medical Rental Business Licenses
Business Licenses

A state business license is the main document required for tax purposes and conducting other basic business functions.

Occupations and Professions
State licenses are frequently required for certain occupations. Since each state is different, check with your states licensing authorities.

Tax Registration
If the state in which you operate has a state income tax, you'll have to register and obtain an employer identification number from your state Department of Revenue or Treasury Department.

Trade Name Registration
If your business will only be operated in your local community, registering your company name with the state may be sufficient. This will not protect your name from anyone else using it. It just creates a paper trail of who is doing business under a certain name. Check with your County Clerk's office to see if you need a *rental business license*.

Employer Registrations
If you have any employees, you may be required to make unemployment insurance contributions for your rental business. For more information, contact your state Department of Revenue or Department of Labor.

Resources:

Insurance Information Institute
    www.iii.org/individuals/business/
National License Directory   www.business.gov
www.sba.gov
National Association of Surety Bond Producers   www.nasbp.org
Independent Insurance Agents & Brokers of America
    www.iiaa.org
Century Surety Group   www.centurysurety.com
B & W Insurance Agencies   www.bwinsurance.com
Find Law   http://smallbusiness.findlaw.com/starting-business/starting-business-licenses-permits/starting-business-licenses-permits-guide.html
Business Licenses   www.iabusnet.org/business-licenses
Legal Zoom   www.legalzoom.com

2.3 Start-up To-Do Checklist

1. Describe your business concept and model, with special emphasis on planned multiple revenue streams and services to be offered.
2. Create Business Plan and Opening Menu of Products and Services.
3. Determine your start up costs of Medical Equipment Rental Company business, and operating capital and capital budget needs.
4. Seek and evaluate alternative financing options, including SBA guaranteed loan, equipment leasing, social networking loan (www.prosper.com) and/or a family loan (www.virginmoney.com).
5. Do a name search: Check with County Clerk Office or Department of Revenue and Secretary of State to see if the proposed name of business is available.
6. Decide on a legal structure for business. Common legal structure options include Sole Proprietorship, Partnership, Corporation or Limited Liability Corporation (LLC).
7. Make sure you contact your State Department of Revenue, Secretary of State, and the Internal Revenue Service to secure EIN Number and file appropriate paperwork. Also consider filing for Sub-Chapter S status with the Federal government to avoid the double taxation of business profits.
8. Protect name and logo with trademarks, if plan is to go national.
9. Find a suitable location with proper zoning for a medical equipment rental company.
10. Research necessary permits and requirements your local government imposes on your type of business. (Refer to: www.business.gov & www.ttb.gov)
11. Call for initial inspections to determine what must be done to satisfy Fire Marshall, and Building Inspector requirements.
12. Adjust our budget based on build-out requirements.
13. Negotiate lease or property purchase contract.

14. Obtain a building permit.
15. Obtain Federal Employee Identification Number (FEIN).
16. Obtain State Sales Tax ID/Exempt Certificate.
17. Open a Business Checking Account.
18. Obtain Merchant Credit Card /PayPal Account.
19. Obtain City and County Business Licenses
20. Create a prioritized list for equipment, furniture and décor items.
21. Comparison shop and arrange for appropriate insurance coverage with product liability insurance, public liability insurance, commercial property insurance and worker's compensation insurance.
22. Locate and purchase all necessary equipment and furniture prior to final inspections.
23. Get contractor quotes for required alterations.
24 Manage the alterations process.
25. Obtain information and price quotes from possible supply distributors.
26. Set a tentative opening date.
27. Install 'Coming Soon' sign in front of building and begin word-of-mouth advertising campaign.
28. Document the preparation, project and payment process flows.
29. Create your accounting, purchasing, payroll, marketing, loss prevention, employee screening and other management systems.
30. Start the employee interview process based on established job descriptions and interview criteria.
31. Contact and interview the following service providers: uniform service, security service, trash service, utilities, telephone, credit card processing, bookkeeping, cleaning services, etc.
32. Schedule final inspections for premises.
33. Correct inspection problems and schedule another inspection.
34. Set a Grand Opening date after a month of regular operations to get the bugs out of the processes.
35. Make arrangements for website design.
36. Train staff.
37. Schedule a couple of practice lessons for friends and interested prospects.

38. Be accessible for direct customer feedback.
39. Distribute comment cards and surveys to solicit more constructive feedback.
40. Remain ready and willing to change your business concept and offerings to suit the needs of your actual customer base.

2.3.1 EMPLOYER RESPONSIBILITIES CHECKLIST

1. Apply for your SS-4 Federal Employer Identification Number (EIN) from the Internal Revenue Service. An EIN can be obtained via telephone, mail or online.
2. Register with the State's Department of Labor (DOL) as a new employer. State Employer Registration for Unemployment Insurance, Withholding, and Wage Reporting should be completed and sent to the address that appears on the form. This registration is required of all employers for the purpose of determining whether the applicants are subject to state unemployment insurance taxes.
3. Obtain Workers Compensation and Disability Insurance from an insurer. The insurance company will provide the required certificates that should be displayed. 4. Order Federal Tax Deposit Coupons – Form 8109 – if you didn't order these when you received your EIN. To order, call the IRS at 1-800-829-1040; you will need to give your EIN. You may want to order some blanks sent for immediate use until the pre-printed ones are complete. Also ask for the current Federal Withholding Tax Tables (Circular A) – this will explain how to withhold and remit payroll taxes, and file reports.
5. Order State Withholding Tax Payment Coupons. Also ask for the current Withholding Tax Tables.
6. Have new employees complete an I-9 Employment Eligibility Verification form. You should have all employees complete this form prior to beginning work. Do not send it to

Immigration and Naturalization Service – just keep it with other employee records in your files.
7. Have employees complete a W-4 Employees Withholding Allowance Certificate.

2.4.0 Company Location

_____ (company name) will be located in the _____ (complex name) in _____ (city), ___ (state). It is situated on a _____ (turnpike/street/avenue) just minutes from _____ (benchmark location), in the neighborhood of _____. It borders a large parking lot which is shared by all the businesses therein.
Important considerations relative to office location are competition, accessibility, community growth trends, and area demographics.

We will follow the lead of industry operators and locate nearby our core client markets, such as hospitals, nursing-care facilities, physicians and other healthcare facilities, in order to minimize transportation costs and provide fast, on-demand equipment rentals. Furthermore, we will also locate near medical device manufacturers, in order to generate a stable supply of input products.

The office location has the following advantages:
(Select Choices)
1. It is easy to locate and accessible to a number of major roadways.
2. Parking.
3. Proximity to _____ and _____ income growth areas.
4. Reasonable rent.
5. Proximity to the growing residential community of _____.
6. Low crime rate with good police and fire protection.
7. Proximity to hospitals, clinics, adult daycare centers and private practices.

2.4.1   Company Facilities

_____ (company name) signed a _____ (#) year lease for _____ (#) square foot of office space. The cost is very reasonable at $____/sq. foot. We also have the option of expanding into an additional _____ sq. ft. of space. A leasehold improvement allowance of $___ /sq. ft. would be given. Consolidated area maintenance fees would be $___/month initially. _____ (company name) has obtained a _____ (three) month option on this space effective _____ (date), the submission date of this business plan, and has deposited refundable first and last lease payments, plus a $ _____ security deposit with the leasing agent.

The facilities will incorporate the following room parameters into the office layout:

Percentage

Square Footage

1. Supplies Storage   _____

   _____

2. Reception Area   _____

   _____

3. Conference/Training Room _____

   _____

4. Admin Offices   _____

   _____

5. Utility/Computer Room   _____

   _____

6. Equipment Storage   _____

   _____

7. Maintenance Area   _____

   _____

8. Restrooms   _____

   _____

9. Vehicle Storage   _____

   _____

Totals: _____

2.4.2   Warehouse Design

We will lease a commercial warehouse that is temperature-controlled to store our inventory. Our storage facility will need to be clean and free of dust to prevent our equipment and supplies from becoming contaminated.

Our warehouses will be designed to accommodate the medical equipment inventory and material supplies to be stored, the associated handling equipment, the receiving and shipping operations and associated trucking, and the needs of the operating personnel. The design of the warehouse space will be planned to best accommodate business service requirements and the medical equipment to be stored/handled. We plan to ____ (purchase/lease) (heated/refrigerated/controlled humidity) warehouse space that provides space for bulk, rack, and bin storage, adequate aisle space, receiving and shipping space, packing and crating space, and office and toilet space.

Our warehouse will require features, common in most warehouse designs, such as higher bays, sophisticated materials-handling equipment, higher ceiling for pallet stacking, approved fire suppression system to reduce insurance costs, broadband connectivity access, and more distribution networks. Our warehouse space will also be flexible to accommodate future operations and storage needs as well as mission changes.

Our engineering system layout drawings will include specifications for the following requirements:

1. Aisles Positioning
2. Rack
3. Lighting
4. Electrical
5. Computer Wiring Systems
6. Security
7. Materials Handling Systems
8. Admin Offices

In order to be Energy-Efficient, the warehouse will possess the following features:
1. Be designed with passive solar concepts, solar geometry, and building load requirements in mind.
2. Possess light colored metal roof to reflect a large percentage of solar radiation.
3. Be planned with interior dock space in colder climates to reduce energy consumption.
4. Use ceiling mounted fans to reduce heat stratification and provide air movement.
5. Use energy-efficient fixtures, systems, and appliances with motion sensors.

To assure the Safety and Security of Personnel and Material the warehouse will possess the following features:
1. Incorporate proper signage to clearly warn of hazards or to direct personnel to take precautions.
2. Possess non-slip surface treatments on floors subject to wetting to prevent falls.
3. Have fire sprinkler systems engineered to cover the specific commodity classification in the specific storage configuration for the planned warehouse.
4. Include appropriate security systems incorporated into the warehouse design.

For the Health and Comfort of workers, the warehouse will possess the following features:
1. Provide proper ventilation under all circumstances.
2. Provide local exhaust for restrooms, kitchens, janitor's closets, copy rooms, battery-charging areas, etc.
3. Installed CO_2 sensors to provide real time monitoring of air quality.
4. Integrate daylighting with the electric lighting system.
5. Plan for natural lighting where possible and lighting controls that turn off lights when sufficient daylight exists.
6. Minimize HVAC system noise in occupied space.

7. Use furnishings, chairs, and equipment that are ergonomically designed.
8. Design equipment and furnishings reflective of healthy work practices in an effort to eliminate repetitive motions as well as prevent strains and sprains.
9. Create a 'sense of place' such that the warehouse has a unique character that engenders a sense of pride, purpose, image and dedication for workers and the community.

Resource: www.elogistics101.com/layout/sample-warehouse-layouts-Index.htm

2.5.0 Start-up Summary

The start-up costs for the Medical Equipment Rental Company will be financed through a combination of an owner investment of $ _____ and a short-term bank loan of
$ _____. The total start-up costs for this business are approximately
$ _____ and can be broken down in the following major categories:

1. Computer Equipment and Installation Expenses $ _____

2. Web Software Development $ _____

3. Office Furniture: Work Tables and Cabinets
   $ _____
4. Working Capital Requirements (12 months)
   $ _____
   For day-to-day operations, including payroll, etc.
5. Renovate Office Space $ _____

   Includes lighting update, flooring, etc.
6. Marketing/Advertising Expenses $ _____

   Includes sales brochures, direct mail, opening expenses.

7.	Utility/ (Rent?) Deposits	$
8.	Licenses and Permits	$
9.	Professional Services Expenses	$
10.	Capital Expenditures	$
12.	Medical Equipment Purchases	$
12.	Contingent Cash Reserves	$
13.	Other (Includes training, etc.)	$
Total:		$

Some Medical Equipment Rental Start-up Estimates:
Real Estate/Rent Deposit: $5000   Utility Deposits $200   Furniture Fixtures/Equip: $5000
Insurance: $2000   Training: $5000   Grand Opening $2000
Office Equipment/Supplies: $9000   Signage: $1000   Leasehold Improvements: $4000
Legal/Accounting Licenses $1000
Registering business $750
Sourced products/inventories $15,000
Promoting and networking business $1500

The company will require $_____ in initial cash reserves and additional $_____ in assets. The start-up costs are to be financed by the equity contributions of the owner in the amount of $ _____ , as well as by a ____ (#) year commercial loan in the amount of $ _____ . The funds will be repaid through earnings.

These start-up expenses and funding requirements are summarized in the tables below.

2.5.1 Inventory

| Inventory: | Supplier | Qty | Unit Cost |
Total

Equipment

Equipment Maint. Supplies

Lubricants

Cleaning Supplies

Disinfectants

Office Supplies

Computer Supplies

Marketing Materials

Stationery

Business Cards

Company Brochures

Business Forms

Contracts/Invoices

Employment Contracts

Equipment Manuals

Background Investigate Form

Employee Policy Manuals
_____

Safety Equipment
_____

Transport Materials
_____

Padding
_____

Shrink Film
_____

First Aid Kit
_____

Misc. Supplies
_____

Totals:
_____

Resources:
Sample Forms
      www.wmsupply.com/Resources/Forms.aspx
                    https://www.uhs.com/resources/

2.5.2 Supply Sourcing

Initially, _____ (company name) will purchase all of its equipment from _____ and supplies from _____, the _____ (second/third?) largest supplier in _____ (state), because of the discount given for bulk purchases. However, we will also maintain back-up relationships with two smaller suppliers, namely _____ and _____. These two suppliers have competitive prices on certain products.

2.5.4 Equipment Leasing

Equipment Leasing will be the smarter solution allowing our business to upgrade our equipment needs at the end of the term rather than being overly invested in outdated equipment through traditional bank financing and equipment purchase. We also intend to explore the following benefits of leasing some of the required equipment:

1. Frees Up Capital for other uses. 2. Tax Benefits
3. Improves Balance Sheet 4. Easy to add-on or trade-up
5. Improves Cash Flow 6. Preserves Credit Lines
7. Protects against obsolescence 8. Application Process Simpler

Our leasing strategy will also be shaped by the following factors:
1. Estimated useful life of the equipment.
2. How long our business plans to use the equipment.
3. What our business intends to do with the equipment at the end of the lease.
4. The tax situation of our business.
5. The cash flow of our business.
6. Our company's specific needs for future growth.

List Any Leases:
Leasing Company   Equipment Description   Monthly Lease   Final Payment   Period   Disposition

_____
_____
_____

Resources:
Some of the major companies offering medical equipment leases are as follows:

    GE Healthcare Financial Svcs   Agfa Finance Group

    Philips Medical Systems   Stryker Corporation

    Hill-Rom Holdings Inc.   De Lage Landen

International B.V.
    Apria Healthcare Group   Oak Leasing Ltd.
    Siemens Financial Services   Access Equipment Leasing
    Direct Capital Corp.   IBJ Leasing Company Ltd.
    National Technology Leasing Corp.   Oak Leasing Ltd.
    Prudential Leasing, Inc.   Resource Diversified Services, Inc.
    Rotech Healthcare Inc.   Stryker Corporation
    Universal Hospital Services, Inc.

LeaseQ   www.leaseq.com

An online market place that connects businesses, equipment dealers, and leasing companies to make selling and financing equipment fast and easy. The LeaseQ Platform is a free, cloud based SaaS solution with a suite of on-demand software and data solutions for the equipment leasing industry. Utilizes the Internet to provide business process optimization (BPO) and information services that streamline the purchase and financing of business equipment across a broad array of vertical industry segments.

Innovative Lease Services
    http://www.ilslease.com/equipment-leasing/

This company was founded in 1986 and is headquartered in Carlsbad, California. It is accredited by the Better Business Bureau, a long standing member of the National Equipment Finance Association and the National Association of Equipment Leasing Brokers and is the official equipment financing partner of Biocom.

2.5.4   Funding Source Matrix

Funds Source   Amount   Interest Rate   Repayment Terms   Use

2.5.5 Distribution or Licensing Agreements (if any)

Note: These are some of the key factors that investors will use to determine if we have a competitive advantage that is not easily copied.

Licensor   License Rights   License Term
    Fee or Royalty

2.5.6 Trademarks, Patents and Copyrights (if any)

Our trademark will be virtually our branding for life. Our choice of a name for our business is very important. Not only will we brand our business and services forever, but what may be worthless today will become our most valuable asset in the years to come.

A trademark search by our Lawyer will be a must, because to be told down the road that we must give up our name because we did not bother to conduct a trademark search would be a devastating blow to our business. It is also essential that the name that we choose suit the expanding product or service offerings that will be coming down the pike.

Note: These are some of the key factors that investors will use to determine if we have a competitive advantage that is not easily copied.

Resources:
Patents/Trademarks   www.uspto.gov
Copyright   www.copyright.gov

2.5.7 Innovation Strategy (optional)

____ (company name) will create an innovation strategy that is aligned with not only our firm's core mission and values, but also with our future technology, supplier, and growth strategies. The objective of our innovation strategy will be to create a sustainable competitive advantage. Our education and training systems will be designed to equip our staff with the foundations to learn and develop the broad range of skills needed for innovation in all of its forms, and with the flexibility to upgrade skills and adapt to changing market conditions. To foster an innovative workplace, we will ensure that employment policies facilitate efficient organizational change and encourage the expression of creativity, engage in mutually beneficial strategic alliances and allocate adequate funds for research and development. Our radical innovation strategies include _____ to achieve first mover status. Our incremental innovation strategies will include modifying the following _____ (products/services/processes) to give our customers added value for their money.

2.5.9 Summary of Sources and Use of Funds

Sources:
Owner's Equity Investment $ _____
Requested Bank Loans $ _____
Total: $ _____

Uses:
Capital Equipment $ _____
Beginning Inventory $ _____
Start-up Costs $ _____
Working Capital $ _____
Total: $ _____

2.5.9 Funding To Date (optional)

To date, _____'s (company name) founders have invested $_____ in _____ (company name), with which we have accomplished the following:
1. _____ (Designed/Built) the company's website
2. Developed content, in the form of __ (#) articles, for the website.
3. Hired and trained our core staff of __(#) full-time people and ___ (#) part-time   people.
4. Generated brand awareness by driving ___ (#) visitors to our website in a ___(#)   month period.
5. Successfully _____ (Developed/Test Marketed) ___ (#) new medical equipment   rental services, which compete on the basis of _____.
6. _____ (Purchased/Developed) and installed the software needed to _____   (manage _____ operations?)
7.   Purchased $ _____ worth of _____ (type of supplies)
8.   Purchased $ _____ worth of _____ equipment to make _____.

2.6 Start-up Requirements

Start-up Expenses:
Estimates
        Legal   _____
        15000
        Accountant   _____
300
        Accounting Software Package   _____
300
        State Licenses & Permits   _____

40000?
    Store Set-up   _____
25000
    Unforeseen Contingency   _____
3000
    Market Research Survey   _____
300
    Office Supplies   _____
300
    Sales Brochures   _____
300
    Direct Mailing   _____
500
    Other Marketing Materials   _____
2000
    Logo Design   _____
500
    Advertising (2 months)   _____
2000
    Consultants   _____
5000
    Insurance   _____
    Rent (2 months security)   _____
3000
    Rent Deposit   _____
1500
    Utility Deposit   _____
1000
    DSL Installation/Activation   _____
100
    Telecommunications Installation   _____
3000
    Telephone Deposit   _____
200
    Expensed Equipment   _____
1000
    Website Design/Hosting   _____
2000
    Computer System   _____

12000
    Used Office Equipment/Furniture   _____
2000
    Organization Memberships   _____
300
    Cleaning Supplies   _____
200
    Staff Training   _____
5000
    Other   _____

Total Start-up Expenses   _____ (A)

Start-up Assets:
    Cash Balance Required   _____ (T)
15000
    Start-up Equipment   _____ See schedule
    Start-up Inventory   _____ See schedule
    Other Current Assets   _____
    Long-term Assets   _____

Total Assets   _____ (B)

Total Requirements   _____ (A+B)

Start-up Funding

Start-up Expenses to Fund   _____ (A)
Start-ups Assets to Fund   _____ (B)
Total Funding Required: _____ (A+B)

Assets
Non-cash Assets from Start-up   _____
Cash Requirements from Start-up   _____ (T)
Additional Cash Raised   _____ (S)
Cash Balance on Starting Date   _____ (T+S=U)
Total Assets: _____ (B)

Liabilities and Capital

Short-term Liabilities:
Current Borrowing _____
Unpaid Expenses _____
Accounts Payable _____
Interest-free Short-term Loans _____
Other Short-term Loans _____
Total Short-term Liabilities _____ (Z)

Long-term Liabilities:
Commercial Bank Loan _____
Other Long-term Liabilities _____
Total Long-term Liabilities _____ (Y)
Total Liabilities _____ (Z+Y = C)

Capital
Planned Investment
Owner _____
Family _____
Other _____
Additional Investment Requirement _____
Total Planned Investment _____ (F)
Loss at Start-up (Start-up Expenses) (-) _____ (A)
Total Capital (=) _____
(F+A=D)
Total Capital and Liabilities _____ (C+D)
Total Funding _____ (C+F)

2.6.1 Capital Equipment List

Equipment	Cost Quantity Unit Cost	Total Cost	Model No.	New/Used	Lifespan
Computer System					

Laptop _____

Fax Machine _____

Copy Machine _____

Laser Printer _____

Land line Phone System _____

Scanner _____

Cell Phones _____

GPS System _____

Digital Camera _____

Answering Machine _____

Office Furniture _____

Accounting Software _____

Database Management Software _____

Microsoft Office Suite Software _____

Tutorial Skills Training Software _____

High Speed Internet Connection _____

Shelving Units _____

Lockers _____

Telephone headsets _____

Calculator _____

Filing & Storage Cabinets

Cabinetry

Credit Card Verification Machine

Paper Shredder

Vehicles

Forklift

Hand trucks

Equipment Maintenance Tools

Other

Total Capital Equipment

Note: Equipment costs are dependent on whether purchased new or used or leased.

All items that are assets to be used for more than one year will be considered a long-term asset and will be depreciated using the straight-line method.

Resources:
Top 40/30 Medical Device Companies
www.mddionline.com/article/top-40-medical-device-companies
www.mpo-mag.com/issues/2015-07-01/view_features/top-30-global-medical-device- companies

Estimated Formation Expenses

- Rental Deposit $ 600 – $ 4,000   - Equipment: $ 2,000 – $ 5,000

- Software: $ 500 – $ 2000   - Insurance:$ 100 – $

4,000
- Signs $ 500 – $ 1,500   - Leasehold improvements $ 0 – $ 3,000
- Legal / Accounting $ 200-3000   - Owner Salary $ 3,000 – $ 5,000
- Advertising $ 500 – $ 2000   - Telephone / Utilities $ 200 – $ 700
- Contingency Fund $1000 - $3000   - Misc $ 200 – $500

2.7.0   SBA Loan Key Requirements

In order to be considered for an SBA loan, we must meet the basic requirements:
1. Must have been turned down for a loan by a bank or other lender to qualify for most SBA Business Loan Programs. 2. Required to submit a guaranty, both personal and business, to qualify for the loans. 3. Must operate for profit; be engaged in, or propose to do business in, the United States or its possessions; 4. Have reasonable owner equity to invest; 5. Use alternative financial resources first including personal assets.

All businesses must meet eligibility criteria to be considered for financing under the SBA's 7(a) Loan Program, including: size; type of business; operating in the U.S. or its possessions; use of available of funds from other sources; use of proceeds; and repayment. The repayment term of an SBA loan is between five and 25 years, depending on the lift of the assets being financed and the cash needs of the business. Working capital loans (accounts receivable and inventory) should be repaid in five to 10 years. The SBA also has short-term loan guarantee programs with shorter repayment terms.

A Business Owner Cannot Use an SBA Loan:

To purchase real estate where the participant has issued a forward commitment to the developer or where the real estate will be held primarily for investment purposes. To finance floor plan needs. To make payments to owners or to pay delinquent withholding taxes. To pay existing debt, unless it can be shown that the refinancing will benefit the small business and that the need to refinance is not indicative of poor management.

SBA Loan Programs:
Low Doc: www.sba.gov/financing/lendinvest/lowdoc.html
SBA Express
www.sba,gov/financing/lendinvest/sbaexpress.html

Basic 7(a) Loan Guarantee Program
For businesses unable to obtain loans through standard loan programs.
Funds can be used for general business purposes, including working
 capital, leasehold improvements and debt refinancing.
www.sba.gov/financing/sbaloan/7a.html

Certified Development Company 504 Loan Program
Used for fixed asset financing such as purchase of real estate or machinery.
www. Sba.gov/gopher/Local-Information/Certified-Development-Companies/

MicroLoan 7(m) Loan Program
Provides short-term loans up to $35,000.00 for working capital or
 purchase of fixtures.
www.sba.gov/financing/sbaloan/microloans.html

2.7.1   Other Financing Options

1.   Grants:
Healthcare grants, along with education grants, represent the largest percentage of grant giving in the United States. The federal government, state, county and city   governments, as well as private and corporate foundations all award grants.

The largest percentage of grants are awarded to non-profit organizations, health care agencies, colleges and universities, local government agencies, tribal institutions, and schools. For profit organizations are generally not eligible for grants unless they are conducting research or creating jobs.

    A.   Contact your state licensing office.
    B.   Foundation Grants to Individuals: www.fdncenter.org
    C.   US Grants www.grants.gov
    D.   Foundation Center www.foundationcemter.org
    E.   The Grantsmanship Center www.tgci.com
    F.   Contact local Chamber of Commerce
    G.   The Catalog of Federal Domestic Assistance is a major provider of business grant money.
    H.   The Federal Register is a good source to keep current with the continually changing federal grants offered.
    I.   FedBizOpps is a resource, as all federal agencies must use FedBizOpps to notify the public about contract opportunities worth over $25,000.
    J.   Fundsnet Services http://www.fundsnetservices.com/
    K.   SBA Women Business Center www.sba.gov/content/womens-business-center-grant-opportunities

Local Business Grants

Check with local businesses for grant opportunities and eligibility requirements. For example, Bank of America sponsors community grants for businesses that endeavor to improve the community, protect the environment or preserve the neighborhood.

Resource: www.bankofamerica.com/foundation/index.cfm?template=fd_localgrants

Green Technology Grants

If you install green technology in the business as a way to reduce waste and make the business more energy efficient, you may be eligible for grant funding. Check your state's Economic Development Commission. This grant program was developed as part of the American Recovery and Reinvestment Act.

Resource: www.recovery.gov/Opportunities/Pages/Opportunities.aspx

2. Friends and Family Lending
www.virginmoney.com
3. National Business Incubator Association
www.nbia.org/
4. Women's Business Associations
www.nawbo.org/
5. Minority Business Development Company
www.mbda.gov/
6. Social Networking Loans
www.prosper.com
7. Peer-to-Peer Programs
www.lendingclub.com
8. Extended Credit Terms from Suppliers   30/60/90 days.
9. Community Bank
10. Prepayments from Customers
11. Seller Financing: When purchasing an existing Medical Equipment Rental Company.
12. Business Funding Directory
www.businessfinance.com
13. FinanceNet
www.financenet.gov
14. SBA Financing
www.sbaonline.sba.gov
15. Private Investor
16. Use retirement funds to open a business without taxes or penalty. First, establish a C-corporation for the new business. Next, the C-corporation establishes a new retirement plan. Then, the owner's current retirement funds are rolled over into the C-corporation's new plan. And last, the new retirement plan invests in

stock of the C-corporation. Warning: Check with your accountant or financial planner.

Resource: http://www.benetrends.com/

17. Business Plan Competition Prizes
www.nytimes.com/interactive/2009/11/11/business/smallbusiness/Competitions- table.html?ref=smallbusiness

18. Unsecured Business Cash Advance based on future credit card transactions.

19. Kick Starter
www.kickstarter.com

20. Tech Stars
www.techstars.org

21. Capital Source
www.capitalsource.com
www.msl.com/index.cfm?event=page.sba504

Participates in the SBA's 504 loan program. This program is for the purchase of fixed assets such as commercial real estate and machinery and equipment of a capital nature, which are defined as assets that have a minimum useful life of ten years. Proceeds cannot be used for working capital.

22. Commercial Loan Applications www.c-loans.com/onlineapp/

23. Sharing assets and resources with other non-competing businesses.

24. Angel Investors
www.angelcapitaleducation.org

25. The Receivables Exchange
http://receivablesxchange.com/

26. Bootstrap Methods: Personal Savings/Credit Card/Second Mortgages

27. Community-based Crowd-funding
www.profounder.com

www.peerbackers.com

A funding option designed to link small businesses and entrepreneurs with pools of prospective investors. Crowdfunding lenders are often repaid with goods or services.

28. On Deck Capital
www.ondeckcapital.com/

Created the Short Term Business Loan (up to $100,000.00) for small businesses to get quick access to capital that fits their cash flow, with convenient daily payments.

29. Royalty Lending   www.launch-capital.com/

With royalty lending, financing is granted in return for future revenue or company performance, and payback can prove exceedingly expensive if a company flourishes.

30. Stock :Loans   Southern Lending Solutions, Atlanta. GA.
    Custom Commercial Finance, Bartlesville, OK

A stock loan is based on the quality of stocks, Treasuries and other kinds of investments in a businessperson's personal portfolio. Possession of the company's stock is transferred to the lender's custodial bank during the loan period.

31. Lender Compatibility Searcher
    www.BoeFly.com
32. Strategic Investors

Strategic investing is more for a large company that identifies promising technologies, and for whatever reason, that company may not want to build up the research and development department in-house to produce that product, so they buy a percentage of the company with the existing technology.

33. Bartering
34. Small Business Investment Companies
    www.sba.gov/INV
35. Cash-Value Life Insurance
36. Employee Stock Option Plans
    www.nceo.org
37. Venture Capitalists
    www.nvca.org
38. Initial Public Offering (IPO)
39. Meet investors through online sites, including LinkedIn (group discussions), Facebook (BranchOut sorts Facebook connections by profession), and CapLinked (enables search for investment-related professionals by industry and role).
40. SBA Community Advantage Approved Lenders
    www.sba.gov/content/community-advantage-

approved-lenders

41. Small Business Lending Specialists
https://www.wellsfargo.com/biz/loans_lines/compare_lines
http://www.bankofamerica.com/small_business/business_financing/
https://online.citibank.com/US/JRS/pands/detail.do?ID=CitiBizOverview
https://www.chase.com/ccp/index.jsp?pg_name=ccpmapp/smallbusiness/home/page/bb_business_bBanking_programs

42. Startup America Partnership   www.s.co/about
Based on a simple premise: young companies that grow create jobs. Once startups apply and become a Startup America Firm, they can access and manage many types of resources through a personalized dashboard.

43. United States Economic Development Administration www.eda.gov/

44. Small Business Loans   http://www.iabusnet.org/small-business-loans

45. Tax Increment Financing (TIF)
A public financing method that is used for subsidizing redevelopment, infrastructure, and other community-improvement projects. TIF is a method to use future gains in taxes to subsidize current improvements, which are projected to create the conditions for said gains. The completion of a public project often results in an increase in the value of surrounding real estate, which generates additional tax revenue. Tax Increment Financing dedicates tax increments within a certain defined district to finance the debt that is issued to pay for the project.

46. Gust   https://gust.com/entrepreneurs
Provides the global platform for the sourcing and management of early-stage investments. Gust enables skilled entrepreneurs to collaborate with the smartest investors by virtually supporting all aspects of the investment relationship, from initial pitch to successful exit.

47. Goldman Sachs 10,000 Small Businesses
http://sites.hccs.edu/10ksb/

48.	Earnest Loans	www.meetearnest.com
49.	Biz2Credit	www.biz2credit.com
50.	Funding Circle	www.fundingcircle.com

A peer-to-peer lending service which allows savers to <u>lend</u> money directly to small and medium sized businesses

51.	Lending Club	www.lendingclub.com
52.	Equity-based Crowdfunding	www.Indiegogo.com
		www.StartEngine.com
		www.SeedInvest.com
53.	National Funding	www.nationalfunding.com

Their customers can to get working capital, merchant cash advances, credit card processing, and, equipment leasing.

54.	Quick Bridge Funding	www.quickbridgefunding.com

Offers a flexible and timely financing program to help assist small and medium sized businesses achieve their goals.

55.	Kabbage	www.kabbage.com

The industry leader in providing working capital online.

Resource: www.sba.gov/category/navigation-structure/starting-managing-business/starting-business/local-resources

http://usgovinfo.about.com/od/moneymatters/a/Finding-Business-Loans-Grants-Incentives-And-Financing.htm

3.0 Products and Services (Select)

In this section, we will not only list all of our planned products and services, but also describe how our proposed products and services will be differentiated from those of our competitors and solve a real problem or fill an unmet need in the marketplace.

We will post a **Rental Reservation Form** to our website, which will make it easier and faster for customers to submit a rental request. Example:
https://homepromedical.com/cart/index.php?main_page=rental_reservation

Medical Equipment Rental Market
Device Types:
Personal/Home Care Equipment   Electronic/Digital Equipment   Surgical Equipment
Durable Medical Equipment, Storage & Transport
End Users:
Personal/Home Care   Institutional

Equipment Rental List   (select)
Alaris 4410 Vital Signs Monitor   **Alaris** 4510 Vital Signs Monitor
Alaris 7100 Infusion Pump   **Alaris** 7130 Infusion Pump
Alaris 7200 Infusion Pump   **Alaris** 7230 Infusion Pump
Alaris 8000 PCU   **Alaris** 8015 PCU
Alaris 8100 Infusion Pump Module   **Alaris** 8110 Syringe Pump Module
Alaris 8120 PCA Pump Module   **Alaris** 8210 SpO2 Module
Alaris 8220 SpO2 Module   **Alaris** 8300 EtCO2 Module
Alaris 8660 Auto ID Scanner   **Alaris** MedSystem III 2860 Infus. Pump

Alaris MedSystem III 2865B Infus Pump
Alaris PC-4 Infusion Pump Infusion Pump
Aspect Medical Sys BIS VISTA Monitor Infusion Pump
Baxter 6201 Infusion Pump
Baxter AS50 Infusion Pump Infusion Pump
Baxter i-Pump Infusion Pump
Bird VIP Ventilator
CADD Solis 2110 Infusion Pump Vacutron Regulator
Carefusion Enve Ventilator Docking Sta. Ventilator
Corometrics 259 Infant Monitor ePump Feeding Pump
Covidien Kangaroo Joey Feeding Pump 3740 Pulse Oximeter
Diomed 15 Plus Cosmetic Laser Ventilator
Draeger Evita 4 Ventilator Delivery System
Draeger Infinity Gamma XL Monitor Infant Flow CPAP
Embla Gold Portable Sleep Monitor Sleep Monitor
Fisher Paykel MR 850 Heater Feeding Pump
Gaymar Medi-Therm II 5900 Warming Sys
Gaymar TP700 Therapy Pump Monitor
GE Dash 4000 Monitor
GE Engstrom Carestation Ventilator
Hamilton C1 Ventilator Ventilator

Alaris PC-1 Infusion Pump
Alaris PC2TX

B Braun Outlook 100

Baxter 6301 Infusion Pump
Baxter Colleague

Bird Graphics Monitor
Bird VSo2 Ventilator
Cardinal Health

Carefusion Enve

Covidien Kangaroo

Datex-Ohmeda Biox

Draeger Babylog 8000

Draeger GS Anesthesia

Electro Medical Equip

Embla X10 Portable

Flexiflo III Enteral

Gaymar Medi-Therm 6900 Warming Sys
GE Carescape V100

GE Dash 5000 Monitor
GE Mac 5000 Monitor
Hamilton C2

75

Hamilton Galileo Ventilator
Hill-Rom C2000 Incubator Infusion Pump
Hospira Plum A+ Infusion Pump Infusion Pump
Huntleigh AC600 SCD Ultrasound
Inovise Audicor Cardiography Recorder Thermometer
IVAC 2090 Thermometer
Kendall 6060 SCD
Kendall 9525 SCD
60 Feeding Pump
LifeCare 4100 PCA Pump Ventilator
Maquet SERVO-i Ventilator Monitor
Medex 2010 Syringe Pump Pump
Medex KIDS Infusion Pump Syringe Pump
Medex Trilogy Infusion Pump Syringe Pump
Medfusion 3500 128k Syringe Pump Defibrillator
Medtronic LifePak 20 Defibrillator Blood Pressure Monitor
MindRay Passport V Monitor Oximeter
Nellcor NPB-70 Capnograph Oximeter 3000 Pulse Oximeter
Nonin 4100 Monitor Monitor
Novametrix 513 Pulse Oximete Monitor
Novametrix Capnogard Monitor Monitor
Novametrix CO2SMO Plus Monitor Monitor

Hamilton T1 Ventilator
Hospira Gemstar

Hospira Plum XL

Inceptio PunctSure

IVAC 2080

Kendall 5325 SCD
Kendall 7325 SCD
Knight Medical KM-

LifeCare PLV-102

MDE Escort Prizm

Medex 2010i Syringe

Medex Medfusion 2001

Medfusion 3500

Medtronic LifePak 12

Medwave Vasotrac

Nellcor 595 Pulse

Nellcor Symphony N-

Nonin Avant 4000

Novametrix 515B

Novametrix CO2SMO

Novametrix Oxypleth

Novametrix Tidal Wave 610 Monitor
Wave 715 Monitor
Percussionaire Corp IPV-1C Ventilator
3200 Respirator
Philips PageWriter Trim III Cardiograph
PM60 Suction Device
Precision Medical PM63 Suction Device
Encore Monitor
Pulmonetics LTV 1000 Ventilator
Ventilator
Pulmonetics LTV 1200 Ventilator
Ventilator
Puritan Bennett 540 Ventilator
Ventilator
Radiometer TCM4 Monitor
Pressure Monitor
Respironics BiPap Vision Ventilator
Self-Breathing Sys
Respironics Capnostat 5 Sensor
Monitor
Respironics Esprit Ventilator
Ventilator
Respironics MisterNeb Concentrator
Monitor
Respironics Nico2 Monitor
Ventilator
Respironics STD30 Ventilator
Ventilator
Respironics V60 Ventilator
Feeding Pump
SensorMedics 3100A Ventilator
Ventilator
Sentec SDM Monitor
Sigma Spectrum Infusion Pump
Baxter Infusion Pump
Sigma Spectrum-Hospira Infusion Pump
Prizm Infusion Pump
Smiths Med Capnocheck Sleep Oximeter
ventiPac Ventilator

Novametrix Tidal

Philips CoughAssist

Precision Medical

Protocol Propaq

Pulmonetics LTV 1150

Pulmonetics LTV 950

Puritan Bennett 840

Respironics Airway

Respironics Cadence

Respironics Criterion

Respironics Focus

Respironics Nico

Respironics PLV 102

Respironics V200

Ross Patrol Enteral

SensorMedics 3100B

Sentec V-Sign Sensor
Sigma Spectrum-

Smiths Med CADD

Smiths Med Pneupnac

Smiths Med Thera-Mist Heater Nebulizer
5100C-PB Monitor
Spacelabs USCOM Monitor
Monitor
Teledyne TED-191 Monitor
Blender
Vapotherm 2000i Humidifier
Blender
Vapotherm Precision Flow Humidifier
Ventilator
Viasys Avea Ventilator
CPAP
Viasys Vela Ventilator

Somanetics INVOS

Teledyne MX300

Tri-Anim 1900

Vapotherm 2002

VersaMed iVent201

Viasys SIPAP Infant

Services

Equipment Rental Services
Equity Rental Services
Operating Lease Services
Capital Lease Services
Refurbish Equipment
Customized Solutions
Asset Management Services
Equipment Maintenance Services
Rent-to-Own Services
Clinical Engineering

3.1 Service Descriptions

In creating our service descriptions, we will provide answers to the following types of questions:
1.   What does the service do or help the customer to accomplish?
2.   Why will people decide to buy it?
3.   What makes it unique or a superior value?
4.   How expensive or difficult is it to make or copy by a

78

competitor?
5. How much will the service be sold for?

Equipment Rental Services

We will offer a variety of rental solutions, and our medical devices will be patient-ready and factory tested by certified technicians. Our customer service representatives will be available to assist customers throughout the entire process.

The following Medical Equipment Categories will be Available for Rentals:
1. Modular Systems
2. Syringe Pumps
3. Infusion Pumps
4. Patient Monitoring Systems
5. Pulse Oximeters
6. Smart Pumps
7. SCD's
8. Ventilators
9. Bi-pap Machines
10. Portable Oxygen Concentrators

We will also have a complete line of home medical equipment products and rentals including: Wheelchairs, Walkers, Hospital Beds, Oxygen / Respiratory, Power wheelchairs, Scooters, Lift Chairs, Bathroom Safety Items, Wound Care, Hot & Cold Therapy items, and Braces & Supports.
Examples:
https://www.wishingwellmedicalsupply.com/medical-equipment-rentals/

Detailed Medical Equipment Rental Listing:
WALKERS:
       standard folding walkers   standard folding walkers with wheels
       hemi-walkers   4 wheel rollator walkers with seat

79

3 wheel walkers with oxygen tote   arm supports for walkers

CANES :
standard straight canes   4 pronged canes
Canes for visually impaired

COMMODES:
standard commodes   drop-arm commodes
extra wide commodes   commode seats with wheels
portable commodes

CRUTCHES:
canadian crutches

WHEELCHAIRS:
manual wheelchairs   power wheelchairs
electric hospital beds   hoyer lifts
telescoping ramps   lightweight transport wheelchairs
scooters

Example: www.scootaround.com/mobility-rentals/wheelchair-rentals

Misc:
bedside tables   transfer bed handles
tub and shower seats   transport/companion chairs
elevated toilet seats   versa frames/bars for toilets
exercise bikes   foot peddlers
trapeze   reclining chairs
reachers   sock aids
long handled sponges   shoe horns
air mattresses (with pumps)   wheel chair cushions
iv poles   tub handles/bars
sliding boards   transfer belts

80

transfer pivot discs
vaporizers
seats
portable shower
support bars for the bathroom
support stockings
attachments
braces for ankle,wrist,knee,back,leg
support collars
urinals
blood pressure cuffs & monitors
diabetic monitoring equipment
boots
protective walking boots
trays
oxygen tank holders
impaired
medication dispensers
nebulizers
foot cradles
cushions
ostomy supples
supplies
incontinence products
equipment
motion alarms for bed, chair

cryocuffs (for icing)
portable stand assist

exercise weights
baby/room monitors
hand held shower

arm slings
bed pans
sitz baths
stethoscopes
multipodus/heel-relief

walker baskets and

phones for the visually

bandaging supplies
bathing supplies
bed positioning

oxygen tubing &

visual enhancement

Resources:
http://www.wmsupply.com/rental-equipment/

We will be an authorized rental dealer for the Alaris System and Sigma pumps. We will carry equipment from leading manufacturers such as Cardinal Health/Alaris, Smiths Medical, Medex, Baxter, Novametrix/Respironics, Sigma, GE, Kendall, Maquet, Puritan Bennett, Versamed and many others.

Equity Rental Service
Customers of our equity rental service will receive the following benefits:
1. Customer receives brand new equipment
2. Approval process normally within one hour
3. Only one month purchase order needed
4. No obligations to purchase equipment
5. 50% of each payment credited towards purchase
6. Equipment may be returned at any time.

The customer will simply issue a one-month renewable purchase order to our company, and the customer will receive brand new equipment direct from the manufacturer. The customer can rent the equipment on a month-to-month basis or, if capital budget is allocated, purchased the equipment with 50% of the rental paid going towards the purchase price. There will be no paperwork to sign, payments are made from the operating budget, and the customer may return the equipment at any time. All options will be completely customizable.

Operating Lease Service
Customers of our operating lease service will receive the following benefits:
1. Fixed term
2. Gives customer the absolute lowest possible monthly payment
3. Customer can purchase equipment at end of term at fair market value
4. Customer can return equipment at end of term with no further obligation
5. Utilizes customer's operating budget
6. Simple agreement

The customer will commit to make monthly payments based on an established term. When the term ends, the equipment can either be purchased based on its fair market value, rented for an additional 12 months, or returned to our company with no further obligation. Completing an operating lease through our company will simply be a matter of signing a proposal document and issuing a purchase order. Both the signed document and the PO will then be sent directly to our company. All options will be completely customizable.

Capital Lease Service

Customers of our capital lease service will receive the following benefits:
1. Pre-determined rental term
2. $1.00 buyout at end of term
3. Provides a budget friendly way to acquire equipment
4. Simple documentation
5. Utilizes customer's capital budget
6. Provides customer with low monthly payments

The customer will commit to a fixed term of rental payments. At the end of the lease term, the customer will own the equipment with a $1.00 buyout. There will be no option to return this equipment. The purpose of this program is simply to finance the equipment over a specified term when cash is not available for immediate purchase. Completing a capital lease through our company will be simply a matter of signing a two page proposal document and issuing a purchase order. Both the signed document and PO are then sent directly to our company. This program will be also known as Rent to Own or $1.00 Buyout Lease. All options will
be completely customizable.

Purchase Equipment and Supplies

We will also make available a list of supplies and new and refurbished equipment that will be available for sale.
Example:
http://mccannsmedical.com/used-medical-equipment-2/

Customized Solutions

We specialize in custom and innovative solutions. If a customer can't find an off-the-shelf leasing solution that works for their business, we will create one that meets their needs and allows them to acquire the equipment they need. We will provide an extremely fast response and turnaround time to customer acquisition questions and challenges.

Asset Management Services

Our Asset Management Solution will allow healthcare organizations to become more efficient and profitable through People, Processes and Technology. We will offer a variety of custom program models and will help customers assess their needs and find the perfect solution for their facility. Our creativity will allow our company to customize solutions that work best for the specific needs of the facility. We will be dedicated to saving costs, maximizing efficiency and improving patient safety.

Our menu of options will allow the customer to customize our asset management solution to best fit the needs of their facility. We will offer creative equipment acquisition through purchase, leasing or rental. Our staff will provide in-house delivery of equipment to greatly improve efficiency. Management of all of their equipment will provide increased efficiency and better infection control options. We will provide biomedical maintenance for all of their equipment as well as software analytics so they can see real-time statistics.

Equipment Maintenance Service

We will sell preventive maintenance contracts to our customers on all of their equipment, even those purchased from other vendors. We will design medical equipment service and maintenance solutions for the most complex equipment challenges while keeping cost containment in mind. We will take comprehensive medical equipment service and maintenance a step forward. We will refer to medical equipment manufacturer guidelines for preventive maintenance to ensure that medical equipment is maintained based on its unique specifications.

Rent-to-Own Services

Our "Rent-To-Own" program will provide new equipment. Rent-To-Own monthly payments will be lower than the normal rental payments We will offer free local service area delivery. After Nine (9) months the customer can own the equipment.

Examples:
http://www.goglobalmedical.com/rent-to-own-global-medical-california.htm
http://www.heartlandmedequip.com/rentals/

Clinical Engineering

We will offer this service to increase equipment uptime and ensure it is held to the highest quality standards. This service will also seek to improve equipment efficiency, reduce costs and improve compliance with codes and regulations.
Examples: www.uhs.com/medical-equipment-services/clinical-engineering/

3.1.1 Customer Leasing Benefits

1. No upfront money required, frees up critical cash
2. Customer can get the equipment right away and cash can be used for other purposes.
3. Lowest possible monthly payments
4. Operating leases with residuals allow for a very low monthly payment.
5. Flexible and delayed payment schedules
6. Financing allows the customer to receive the product today and start monthly payments at a later date.
7. Costs are moved off the balance sheet and out of capital budget
8. Frees up critical cash and improves customer credit/bond rating.
9. Hedge against technological obsolescence
10. Customer doesn't have to sell the equipment if technology improves and has flexible end of term options.
11. Fixed lease payments removes uncertainty.
12. Pre-determined schedule allows lessee to more accurately predict future equipment costs and cash needs.

13. Improved return on investment
14. Operating leases usually have a positive effect on customer's Return On Investments (ROI).
15. Only option for some start-up or over-extended businesses to acquire equipment.
16. A solution when the cash is not available.
17. Allows healthcare facilities to have state of the art technology on hand when they need it without having to continually upgrade their equipment.
18. Test new equipment before making a long-term commitment.

Source: www.newportcenterorthopedic.com/blog/medical-equipment-renting-research-predicts-steep-rise-by-2020/

3.1.2 Our Insurance Relationships

We will work with the following private and commercial insurance companies.

Aetna	Blue Cross Blue Shield
Care Centrix Network	Cigna
Humana	Homelink
Medicaid	Medicare
MultiPlan	PHCS
Tri-Care	United Health Care

ACS Affiliates

Beech Street	Health Smart
Principal Financial Group	Texas True Choice

Resource: www.acs.org/content/acs/en/membership-and-networks/insurance/health.html

3.2 Alternative Revenue Streams

1. Classified Ads in our Newsletter
2. Vending Machine Sales

3. Supply Sales. 4. Website
Banner Ads
4. Content Area Sponsorship Fees 5. Online
Survey Report Fees
6. Consulting Services 7. Facilities
Sub-leases

3.3 Production of Products and Services

We will use the following methods to locate the best suppliers for our business:

- Attend trade shows and seminars to spot upcoming trends, realize networking
 opportunities and compare prices.

- Subscribe to appropriate trade magazines, journals, newsletters and blogs.
 Medical Dealer   www.medicaldealer.com
 Medical Design

 Medical Device and Diagnostic Industry   www.mddionline.com
 An online and print resource exclusively for original equipment manufacturers of
 medical devices and in vitro diagnostic products. Its mission is to help medtech
 industry professionals develop, design, and manufacture products that comply
 with complex and demanding regulations and evolving market requirements.

 Medical Industry Equipment Publications
  www.themedica.com/publications/medical-industry-equipment.html

 Modern Healthcare   www.modernhealthcare.com
 The industry's leading source of healthcare business and policy news, research and
 information. They report on important healthcare events and trends, as they happen,
 through their weekly print magazine, websites, e-newsletters, mobile products and

events

- Join our trade association to make valuable contacts, get listed in any online directories, and secure training and marketing materials.

World Medical Device Organization   www.wmdo.org/
Medical Device Manufacturers Association
      www.medicaldevices.org
Global Harmonization Task Force for Medical Devices   www.ghtf.org/
UK Medicines and Healthcare Product Regulator
      www.mhra.gov.uk/index.htm
US Food and Drug Administration - Medical Device Regulator

www.fda.gov/MedicalDevices/default.htm

The Medical Device Manufacturers Association
A Washington DC-based national trade association, seeks to streamline policy decisions related
to the medical device sector through cooperation with the US Congress, the Food and Drug Administration (FDA) and US healthcare payer the Centers for Medicare and Medicaid (CMS).

The FDA Center for Devices and Radiological Health (US FDA/CDRH)
It is involved in the regulatory control of medical device products. This body aims to record
adverse events of medical devices on the market. One of its initiatives proposes the establishment of a database that would allow easy access to information on US FDA-
approved medical devices.

American Association for Homecare   https://www.aahomecare.org/
Works to preserve and strengthen access to care for the millions of Americans who require medical care in their homes. AAHomecare represents healthcare providers, equipment manufacturers, and other organizations in the homecare community.

ECRI Institute   www.ecri.org
A non-profit organization dedicated to bringing the discipline of applied scientific research to discover which medical procedures, devices, drugs, and processes are

best, all to enable you to improve patient care.

3.4 Competitive Comparison

The company owner is a veteran medical equipment manager and has a profound knowledge and contacts that few people possess. Furthermore, there are only ___ (#) other Medical Equipment Rental Companies in the _____ area. _____ (company name) will differentiate itself from its local competitors by offering a broader range of medical equipment rental services, maintaining a database of client preferences and transaction history patterns, offering membership club benefits to qualifying repeat clients, using a monthly newsletter to stay-in-touch with Medical Professionals and offering an array of comprehensive leasing and asset management services.

We will also place a heavy emphasis on the development of a staff training program to meet client operational demands, while also serving to control operational costs.

_____ (company name) does not have to pay for under-utilized staff. Our flexible employee scheduling procedures and use of commissioned recruiters ensure that the company is not burdened with fixed overhead. We will also adopt a pay-for-performance compensation plan, and use referral incentives to generate new business.

We will reinvest major dollars every year in professional and educational materials. We will participate in online webinars to bring clients the finest selection of domestic medical equipment rental services, and industry trend information. Our prices will be competitive with other Medical Equipment Rental Companies that offer far less in the way of service benefits, satisfaction guarantees and innovative services.

3.5 Sales Literature

____ (company name) has developed sales literature that illustrates a professional organization with vision. ____ (company name) plans to constantly refine its marketing mix through a number of different literature packets. These include the following:
- direct mail with introduction letter and product price sheet.
- product information brochures
- press releases
- new product/service information literature
- email marketing campaigns
- website content
- corporate brochures

A copy of our informational brochure is attached in the appendix of this document. This brochure will be available to provide referral sources, leave at seminars, and use for direct mail purposes.

3.6 Fulfillment

The key fulfillment and delivery of services will be provided by our director/owner, and certified company recruiters. The real core value is the medical industry expertise of the founder, and company training programs. The company will utilize job fairs, a state-of--the-art company website and a multi-media campaign to identify and satisfy customer equipment and personnel support needs.

3.7 Technology

___(company name) will employ and maintain the latest technology to enhance its office management, inventory management, payment processing, customer profiling and record keeping systems. This will speed invoice checkout while offering enhanced convenience and liability protection. We will also use a Cash Register POS system to manage our operations. Each item that gets leased will be indicated as such on our inventory list. Additionally, tracking items in our warehouse will easily be managed with handheld inventory devices that integrate with accounting system.

ARM Software www.armsoftware.com/medical-equipment-rental-software

The Automated Rental Management (ARM) Software Suite is ideal for companies specializing in Medical Equipment Rentals. Combined with powerful back office accounting features, customizable windows and screens, customizable contracts, invoices, Make Ready lists, etc., custom reporting features and advanced lookup capabilities, ARM makes managing the inventory of your medical equipment rental business as seamless as possible. Various features are available such as the ability to copy contract details from history into new contracts, automatic rebilling for long term contracts, lump sum billing, and the ability to track unit details like number of times rented, revenue, costs and maintenance history. ARM mitigates risk and uncertainty with seamless integration between financials, contracts, reservations, inventory and customer information.

Point of Rental Software
www.point-of-rental.com/campaigns/medical-equipment-rental-management-software/

Directory of Rental Software www.capterra.com/rental-software/

RMI Software
www.rmiusa.com/Industries/medical.htm

Sertifi
www.sertifi.com.

The company has worked closely with health care agencies to provide a viable electronic signature solution that could reduce paperwork and speed signature processes. Sertifi is the industry's most trusted e-sign provider and has processed millions of electronic signature documents.

Mobile Phone Credit Card Reader https://squareup.com/

Square, Inc. is a financial services, merchant services aggregator and mobile payments company based in San Francisco, California. The company markets several software and hardware products and services, including Square Register and Square Order. Square Register allows individuals and merchants in the United States, Canada, and Japan to accept offline debit and credit cards on their iOS or Android smartphone or tablet computer. The app supports manually entering the card details or swiping the card through the Square Reader, a small plastic device which plugs into the audio jack of a supported smartphone or tablet and reads the magnetic stripe. On the iPad version of the Square Register app, the interface resembles a traditional cash register.

Google Wallet https://www.google.com/wallet/
A mobile payment system developed by Google that allows its users to store debit cards,
credit cards, loyalty cards, and gift cards among other things, as well as redeeming sales promotions on their mobile phone. Google Wallet can be used near field communication
(NFC) to make secure payments fast and convenient by simply tapping the phone on any
PayPass-enabled terminal at checkout.

Apple Pay http://www.apple.com/apple-pay/
A mobile payment and digital wallet service by Apple Inc. that lets users make payments using the iPhone 6, iPhone 6 Plus, Apple Watch-compatible devices (iPhone 5and later models), iPad Air 2, and iPad Mini 3. Apple Pay does not require Apple-specific contactless payment terminals and will work with Visa's PayWave, MasterCard's PayPass, and American
Express's ExpressPay terminals. The service has begun initially only for use in the US, with international roll-out planned for the future.
Resource: www.wired.com/2017/01/shadow-apple-pay-google-wallet-expands-online-reach/

WePay https://www.wepay.com/
An online payment service provider in the United States. WePay's

payment API focuses exclusively on platform businesses such as crowdfunding sites, marketplaces andsmall business software. Through this API, WePay allows these platforms to access its payments capabilities and process credit cards for the platform's users.

Chirpify
Connects a user's PayPal account with their Twitter account in order to enable payments through tweeting.

Article: www.prnewswire.com/news-releases/tips-to-leverage-mobile-payments-in-your-marketing-strategy-300155855.html

3.8 Future Products and Services

_____ (company name) will continually expand our offering of services based on industry trends and changing client needs. We will not only solicit feedback via
surveys and comments cards from clients on what they need in the future, but will also
work to develop strong relationships with all of our clients and vendors. We also plan to
open ____ (#) additional locations in the _____ area starting in _____ (year).

Home Medical Equipment Rentals
We plan to enter the home medical equipment rental business because in the coming years, the Home Medical Equipment Rentals industry will benefit from more people with private insurance and an aging population. Demand will pick up, as healthcare reform provides insurance for a greater number of people who could not afford equipment previously. Nevertheless, increased Medicare and Medicaid regulations may hamper industry operations in the next five years.

The Home Medical Equipment Rentals industry exhibits a medium level of capital intensity. Using wages as a proxy for labor and depreciation as a proxy for capital, IBISWorld estimates that for every dollar spent on labor in 2012, $0.14 will be spent on capital. Firms in this industry must invest substantially in distribution and storage centers and inventory management equipment. While the level of these investments vary among firms in the industry, the most successful players use large networks of distribution and storage centers to reach a broad base of customers, giving them significant economies of scale. To achieve this, firms must invest in a labor force. Employees manage complex inventory management systems and pack and deliver orders.

We will stock the following types of Home Equipment:

Scooter Rentals (ECVs)

Wheelchair Rentals

Electric Wheelchairs

Patient Lifts

Hospital Beds

Oxygen and Respiratory

Bath & Commode Rentals

Reclining Lift Chairs

Nebulizers

Transformers

Enteral Feeding Pumps

Equipment Repair Services

We will start our equipment repair service by becoming experts in the repair of wheelchairs and scooters. We will become ATP RESNA certified, which is now required by Medicare and other insurance companies in order to provide certain Complex Rehab wheelchairs. With our RESNA certified Assistive Technology Professionals, and factory trained service technicians, our repair services will be differentiated in the marketplace.

Equipment Management Program

We plan to offer a customizable, site-based program that manages, maintains and deploys medical equipment and support personnel within a health care facility. The program will deliver patient-ready equipment when and where it's needed, allowing caregivers to focus on patient care.

Online Ordering & Equipment Management
Our clients will be able to keep their fingers on the pulse of outsourced UHS medical equipment with our convenient online tool. Through this secure portal, clients will be able to order and track equipment, manage inventory, manage patient usage, view invoices, and generate reports for immediate access.

Equipment Training Programs
We will develop equipment training programs that will enable our clients to maximize
the productivity returns on their rental investments and to make certain that equipment is running at peak performance levels. Clients will also be instructed on how to safely use all equipment and to keep it clean between service calls.

Clinical Engineering Services
This service will not only include our preventive maintenance services to prevent costly breakdowns, but we all offer to configure equipment to create complete systems that will improve productivity and lower rental costs.

Surgical Support Services
We will provide our clients will worry-free access to cutting-edge surgical and laser technology, and expert technical support that keeps it all working. This will help to ensure our clients get the most out of their mobile surgical laser procedures.

Used Equipment Sales

We will offer our used rental equipment for sale after a certain point in its lifecycle. Each piece of equipment will be cleaned and repaired, if necessary, by our certified biomed technicians, and will be inspected and made ready to ship to our customers from our distribution center.

Buy and Sell Used Equipment
We will buy and sell refurbished medical equipment. We will maintain a list of the equipment that our customers are interested in purchasing, and advise them when have

located such an item. We will also refurbish these acquired items before reselling them

for a profit. We will offer buy and sell used ultrasound machines, MRI equipment, x-ray

and imaging devices, mobility scooters and mammography devices.
Examples:
Med Standard   www.medstandard.org

Medical Equipment Recycling Program
This program will provide refurbished medical equipment to people in our service area who lack the insurance coverage or means to buy new medical equipment. In addition, the program will educate individuals and their family members about other community-based resources that can address specific needs. This program will create both corporate tax and goodwill benefits to our medical equipment rental company.

Wholesale Rental Program
We will target mom-and-pop Pharmacies and small Home Healthcare Companies. We will seek to open these businesses as wholesale medical equipment rental accounts. They will basically take rental orders, on a commission basis, using our retail rental catalog and we will then manage all aspects of the rental process, including delivery, pickup, maintenance and payment processing. We will also seek to make available to companies with a limited inventory of medical rental equipment, our more extensive inventory, on a temporary fill-in basis.

Resources:

IMCO   www.imcoinc.com

Its mission is to strengthen the Independent Medical Distribution Channels by providing access to products, contract negotiations, marketing and business services through our relationships and programs with their vendor partners.

Example:
https://www.hudsonpharmacyandsurgical.com/Rental-Equipment-

Online Rental Platform
We will research the development of an ecommerce platform to rent our medical
equipment to professionals and end users.

Example:
Henry Schein Medical carries over 190,000 wholesale medical supplies and products including national and Henry Schein private-brand specialty medical and surgical supplies, equipment and instruments, pharmaceuticals and vaccine supplies.
For more than 78 years Henry Schein has been providing medical supplies and equipment to healthcare practitioners, hospital physicians and doctors in private practice in more than 190 countries. They are the largest online distributor of medical supplies in all of North America and Europe combined. Henry Schein helps healthcare professionals to maximize efficiency and profitability. In most cases they can ship products the same day with free freight and a 99% fill rate.
Source: www.henryschein.com/medical-supplies.aspx
Resource: www.shopify.com

Medical Equipment Repairs
We will partner with manufacturers to meet some or all of their service needs. offering
both stand-alone and hybrid service programs that provide targeted, scalable solutions
to our clients. We will provide quick repair turnaround time and warranty our workmanship.
We will also offer service maintenance contracts.

Examples:
http://meraserv.com/

Resource:
www.bls.gov/ooh/installation-maintenance-and-repair/medical-equipment-repairers.htm

New Equipment Installations
We will specialize in the technical installation of medical and research equipment.

Examples:
http://www.merco.biz/

Product Sales of Natural Remedies
We plan to also specialize in organic herbs, natural remedies, herbal teas, dietary supplements and natural cosmetics from around the world.

4.0 Market Analysis Summary

Our Market Analysis will serve to accomplish the following

goals:
1.   Define the characteristics, and needs and wants of the target market.
2.   Serve as a basis for developing sales, marketing and promotional strategies.
3.   Influence the e-commerce website design.

There are a variety of reasons why businesses may need ___'s (company name) services:
- Spikes in work load
- Business expands into an area that in-house capabilities do not yet match
- Special health fair events
- Limited capital funding reserves.
- Rapidly changing technology.

The company approaches businesses primarily through networking and cold calls. Our intention is to utilize a PR company for more coverage as soon as possible. _____ (company name) is a member of the area Chamber of Commerce and actively participates in as many goodwill activities as possible. The proprietor is a member of the Women's Business Network, and the Professional Women's Organization and we are in the process of connecting with several local medical trade associations.

Prior to start-up, _____ (company name) also surveyed several area Medical practices about their use of equipment rentals. The company will use its website and other marketing materials that describe what medical equipment rental services we provide and explain how simple it is to work with us. _____ (company name) will also advertise in local papers and Medical trade journals when necessary.

Prior to the company start-up, the company started recruiting by administering ____ (#) medical practice surveys and advertising locally to create a sense of local demand for medical equipment rentals.

Forces and trends in the market environment will affect _____ (company name), like all businesses. These include economic, competitive, legal/political, technology, and recordkeeping issues.

- **Economic Environment**—It is believed that the Medical Equipment Rental Company business is basically recession proof because of the aging population and the limited availability of financial resources.
- **Legal/Political Environment**—Town of _____ supports the opening of this needed business venture and has issued and approved building permits and business licenses to support use of the chosen property.
- **Technology and Recordkeeping Environment**—Use of computerized databases and web-based software programs will capture and generate accounting and personnel detail. Computer programs will greatly simplify asset management, and financial recordkeeping and the tax preparation functions, with which all businesses must comply. We will outsource the accounting tax functions, but will maintain the daily financial records in-house.

_____ (company name) has a defined target market of Medical organizations that will be the basis of this business. Effective marketing combined with an optimal rental service offering mix is critical to our success. The owner possesses solid information about the medical industry and knows a great deal about the common attributes of those that are expected to be loyal clients. This information will be leveraged to better understand who we will serve, their specific needs, and how to better communicate with them. The owner strongly believes that as more and more products become commodities that require highly competitive pricing, it will be increasingly important to focus on the development of innovative services, that can be structured and professionally managed.

4.1 Secondary Market Research

We will research demographic information for the following reasons:

1. To determine which segments of the population, such as Hispanics and the elderly, have been growing and may now be

underserved.
2. To determine if there is a sufficient population base in the designated service area to realize the company's business objectives.
3. To consider what products and services to add in the future, given the changing demographic profile and needs of our service area.

We will pay special attention to the following general demographic trends:
1. Population growth has reached a plateau and market share will most likely be increased through innovation and excellent customer service.
2. Because incomes are not growing and unemployment is high, process efficiencies and sourcing advantages must be developed to keep prices competitive.
3. The rise of non-traditional households, such as single working mothers, means developing more innovative and personalized programs.
4. As the population shifts toward more young to middle aged adults, ages 30 to 44, and the elderly, aged 65 and older, there will be a greater need for child-rearing and geriatric mobile support services.
5. Because of the aging population and high unemployment, new ways of dealing with the resulting stress levels will need to be developed.

We will collect the demographic statistics for the following zip code(s):

_____

_____
We will use the following sources: www.census.gov, www.zipskinny.com, www.city-data.com, www.demographicsnow.com and www.claritas.com/claritas/demographics.jsp. This information will be used to decide upon which targeted programs to offer and to make business growth projections.
Resource: www.sbdcnet.org/index.php/demographics.html

Snapshots of consumer data by zip code are also available online:
http://factfinder.census.gov/home/saff/main.html?_lang=en
http://www.esri.com/data/esri_data/tapestry.html
http://www.claritas.com/MyBestSegments/Default.jsp?ID=20

1. **Total Population** _____
2. **Number of Households** _____
3. **Population by Race:** White ____% Black ___%
   Asian Pacific Islander ___%
   Other ____%
4. **Population by Gender** Male ____% Female ____%
5. **Income Figures:** Median Household Income $_____

   Household Income Under $50K ____%

   Household Income $50K-$100K ____%

   Household Income Over $100K ____%
6. **Housing Figures** Average Home Value - $_____

   Average Rent $_____
7. **Homeownership:** Homeowners ____%

   Renters ____%

8. **Education Achievement** High School Diploma % _____

   College Degree % _____

   Graduate Degree % _____
9. **Stability/Newcomers** Longer than 5 years % _____
10. **Marital Status** ___% Married ___% Divorced ___% Single

102

___% Never Married ___% Widowed ___% Separated

**11.	Occupations**	___%Service ___% Sales ___% Management

___% Construction ___% Production

___% Unemployed ___% Below Poverty Level

**12.	Number of Children**	_____

**13.	Children Age Distribution**	___%Under 5 years ___ %5-9 yrs ___ %10-12 yrs

___% 13-17 yrs ___ %18- years

___% 20-29 ___ % 30-39 ___% 40-49 ___% 50-59

___% 60-69 ___% 70-79 ___% 80+ years

**14.	Prior Growth Rate**	_____% from _____ (year)

**15.	Projected Population Growth Rate**	_____%

**16.	Employment Trend**	_____

**17.	Business Failure Rate**	_____

**18.	Number of Hospitals**	_____

Secondary Market Research Conclusions:
This area will be demographically good for our business for the following reasons:
_____
_____
_____

Resources:
www.allbusiness.com/marketing/segmentation-targeting/848-1.html
http://www.sbdcnet.org/industry-links/demographics-links
http://factfinder2.census.gov/faces/nav/jsf/pages/index.xhtml

4.1.1 Primary Market Research

We plan to develop a survey for primary research purposes and mail it to a list of local business magazine subscribers, purchased from the publishers by zip code. We will also post a copy of the survey on our website and encourage visitors to take the survey. We will use the following survey questions to develop an Ideal Customer Profile of our potential client base, so that we can better target our marketing communications. To improve the response rate, we will include an attention-grabbing _____ (discount coupon/ dollar?) as a thank you for taking the time to return the questionnaire.

1. What is your business zip-code?
2. What is your annual sales volume?
3. How many employees do you have?
4. What is your business specialty focus?
5. What is your educational level?
6. What is your profession?
7. What are your favorite trade magazines?
8. What is your favorite local newspaper?
9. What is your favorite radio station?
10. What organizations are you a member of? _____
11. Does our community have an adequate number of Medical Equipment Rental Companies?
12. Does your practice currently patronize a local Medical Equipment Rental Company?
13. Are you satisfied with your current Medical Equipment Rental Co.? Yes/ No
14. How many times on average per year do you use a Medical Equipment Rental Company?
15. What services do you typically purchase? _____
16. On average, how much do you spend on Medical Equipment Rental Company services per year? __
17. What is the name of your currently patronized Medical Equipment Rental Company?
18. What are their strengths as service providers?
19. What are their weaknesses or shortcomings?

20. What would it take for us to earn your Medical Equipment Rental Company   business?

21. What is the best way for us to market our Medical Equipment Rental Company?

22. Do you live in _____ community?

23. Do you work or study in _____ community?

24. What are your perceived future medical equipment rental needs?

25. Would you be interested in joining our Company Club that would offer special
    Membership benefits?

26. Describe your experience with other Medical Equipment Rental Companies.

27. Please rank (1 to 14) the importance of the following factors when choosing
    an Medical Equipment Rental Company:

　　___ Quality of Services　　　　　　___ Service Selection
　　___ Reputation　　　　　　　　　　___ Speed of Service
　　___ Flexibility　　　　　　　　　　___ Inspection Process
　　___ Convenient location　　　　　　___ Competitive Pricing
　　___ Referral/References　　　　　　___ Complaint Handling
　　___ Access to Hire Talent　　　　　___ Personnel Availability
　　___ Service Guarantees　　　　　　___ Understand Business Needs
　　___ Other _____

28. What thought processes are undertaken when considering leasing arrangements?

29. What information would you like to see in a company newsletter?

30. Which online social groups have you joined? Choose the ones you access.

　　___ Facebook　　　　　　___ MySpace
　　___ Twitter　　　　　　　___ LinkedIn
　　___ Ryze　　　　　　　　___ Ning

31. What types of Medical Equipment Rental Company services would most interest   you?
32. What is your general need for an Medical Equipment Rental Company?
    Circle Months: J F M A M J J A S O N D (All)
    Circle Days: S M T W T F S (All)
    Indicate Hours: _____ or (24 hours)
33. What are your suggestions for realizing a better Medical Equipment Rental   Company experience?
34. Are you on our mailing list? Yes/No   If No, can we add you? Yes / No
35. Would you be interested in attending a free seminar on Medical equipment   technological and leasing trends?
36. Can you supply the name and contact info of person who might be interested in our medical equipment rental services?

Please note any comments or concerns about medical equipment rental services in general.

We very much appreciate your participation in this survey. If you provide your name, address and email address, we will sign you up for our e-newsletter, inform you of our survey results, advise you of any new Medical Equipment Rental Company opening in your community, and enter you into our monthly drawing for a free _____.

Name   Address
Email   Phone

4.1.2   Voice of the Customer

To develop a better understanding of the needs and wants of our Medical Equipment Rental Company clients, we will institute the following ongoing listening practices:
1.   Focus Groups
     Small groups of customers (6 to 8) will be invited to meet with a facilitator to   answer open-ended questions about priority of

needs and wants, and our company, its products or other given issues. These focus groups will provide useful insight into the decisions and the decision making process of target consumers.

2. Individual Interviews

We will conduct face-to-face personal interviews to understand customer thought processes and preferences.

3. Customer Panels

A small number of customers will be invited to answer open-ended questions on a regular basis.

4. Customer Tours

We will invite customers to visit our facilities to discuss how our processes can better serve them.

5. Visit Customers

We will observe customers as they actually use our products to uncover the pains and problems they are experiencing during usage.

6. Trade Show Meetings

Our trade show booth will be used to hear the concerns of our customers.

7. Toll-free Numbers

We will attach our phone number to all products and sales literature to encourage the customer to call with problems or positive feedback.

8. Customer Surveys

We will use surveys to obtain opinions on closed-ended questions, testimonials, constructive feedback, and improvement suggestions.

9. Mystery Shoppers

We will use mystery shoppers to report on how our employees treat our customers.

10. Salesperson Debriefing

We will ask our salespeople to report on their customer experiences to obtain insights into what the customer faces, what they want and why they failed to make a sale.

11. Customer Contact Logs

We will ask our sales personnel to record interesting customer revelations.

12. Customer Serviceperson's Hotline

We will use this dedicated phone line for service people to

report problems.
13. Discussions with competitors.
14. Installation of suggestion boxes to encourage constructive feedback. The suggestion card will have several statements customers are asked to rate in terms of a given scale. There are also several open ended questions that allow the customer to freely offer constructive criticism or praise. We will work hard to implement reasonable suggestions in order to improve our service offerings as well as show our commitment to the customer that their suggestions are valued.

4.2   Market Segmentation

Market segmentation is a technique that recognizes that the potential universe of
users may be divided into definable sub-groups with different characteristics.
Segmentation enables organizations to target messages to the needs and concerns of these
subgroups. We will segment the market based on the needs and wants of select customer groups. We will develop a composite customer profile and a value proposition for each of these segments. The purpose for segmenting the market is to allow our marketing/sales program to focus on the subset of prospects that are "most likely" to purchase our medical equipment rental services. If done properly this will help to insure the highest return for our marketing/sales expenditures.

The global medical equipment rental market has been segmented based on device category, end-users and geography. The device category has been further segmented into personal/home care equipment, electronic/digital equipment, surgical equipment, durable medical equipment, and storage and transport. The durable medical equipment segment accounted for the largest share of over 40% of the medical equipment rental market in terms of revenue in 2013. The segment is expected to lead the market during the forecast period from 2014 to 2020, expanding at a CAGR of over 5%. High cost and increased demand has led to the growth of the durable equipment rental segment. The trend is likely to continue due to the increasing geriatric population across the world.

Based on end-users, the medical equipment rental market has been segmented into personal/home care medical equipment rental and institutional medical equipment rental. The chronic and geriatric patients sub-segment accounted for the largest share of over 50.0% of the personal/home care medical equipment rental segment in 2013. It is expected to lead the market during the forecast period. The chronic and geriatric patients segment is expected to rise with the increase in the number of patients suffering from chronic illnesses and the increasing geriatric population.

We will be serving several Medical segments: hospitals, nursing homes; private practices, home Medical centers, ambulatory care centers and laboratory services.

The total potential market in units is shown in the following table and chart.
    There are approximately ___ (#) Medical-based businesses in ___ (city) that could potentially be our customers for our Rental Services.
    There are ___ (#) residents in ___ (city), according to the 200? U.S. Census, with __ (5) % projected growth over the next ten years.
    There are ___ (#) seniors in the city of _____, requiring home Medical services.

Target Markets:
    Hospitals   Outpatient Clinics.
    Private Practices   Adult Day Care Centers
    Nursing Homes   Government Agencies
    Schools   Social Service Organizations
    Home Healthcare Cos.   Assisted Living Facilities

Composite Customer Profile:
By assembling this composite customer profile we will know what

needs and wants to focus on and how best to reach our target market. We will use the information gathered from our customer research survey to assemble the following composite customer profile:

Ideal

Customer Profile
Who are they?
Location of business headquarters (city)

_____

Type of Business

_____

Number of employees

_____

Approximate annual revenues

_____

Years in business

_____

Company growth stage

_____

Publications subscribed to

_____

Trade associations the company belongs to?

_____

What is the total sq/ft. of the facility?

_____

Where are they located (zip codes)?

_____

Trend Preferences?   Trendsetter/Trend follower/Other _____
How often do they buy?

_____

What are most important purchase factors? Price/Brand Name/Quality/Terms/Service/

      Convenience/Green/Other_____
What is their key buying motivator?

_____

How do they buy it?
      Cash/Credit/Terms/Other_____

Where do they buy it from (locations)?
_____

What problem do they want to solve?
_____

What are the key frustrations/pains that these customers have when buying?
_____

What info search methods do they use?
_____

What is preferred problem solution?
_____

Table: Market Analysis

Potential Customers	Growth	2017	2018	Number of Potential Customers 2019
Hospitals	10%			
Clinics	10%			
Private Practices	10%			

Adult Daycare Centers	10%
Nursing Homes	10%
Government Agencies	10%
Home Healthcare Providers	10%
Hospice Care Providers	10%
Other	10%
Totals:	10%

4.3 Target Market Segment Strategy

Our target marketing strategy will involve identifying a group of customers to which to direct our medical equipment rental services. Our strategy will be the result of intently listening to and understanding customer needs, representing customers' needs to those responsible for service delivery, and giving them what they want. In developing our targeted customer messages we will strive to understand things like: where they party and play, where they shop and go to school, how they spend their leisure time, what trade organizations they belong to, and where they volunteer their time. We will use research, surveys and observation to uncover this wealth of information to get our product details and brand name in front of our clients when they are most receptive to receiving our messaging.

Target Market Worksheet
        (optional)
Note: Use this worksheet to explore potential target markets for your products and   services.
Product Benefits: Actual factor (cost effectiveness, design, performance, etc.) or   perceived factor

112

(image, popularity, reputation, etc.) that satisfies what a customer needs or wants. An advantage or value that the product will offer its buyer.

Products Features: One of the distinguishing characteristics of a product or service that helps boost its appeal to potential buyers. A characteristic of a product that describes its appearance, its components, and its capabilities. Typical features include size and color.

Product or Service	Product/ Potential Service Target Markets Benefits	Product/ Service Features

We will focus on the following well-defined target market segments and emphasize our extensive inspection and equipment matching practices, reliability, breadth of service selections, satisfaction guarantees and exceptional customer service. Target markets will include: hospitals, clinics, medical offices, hospices care providers, nursing homes, home health care providers, assisted living facilities, handicap schools, social service and nonprofit organizations and government-run health care programs. We will contact hospital directors, administrative directors, human resource managers, medical office managers, business owners and nonprofit organization leaders in our target markets to advertise our leasing services and to determine their medical equipment rental needs in our area.

We will target physicians, managed care organizations, hospitals, medical groups, home health agencies, and case managers.

Target Managed Care Organizations
The Managed Care Organization Directory includes all Health

Maintenance Organizations, Prepaid Health Services Plans, Special Needs Plans, and Primary Care and Partial Capitation Providers. Includes listings for HMOs and PPOs, Medicare and Medicaid Managed Care Plans.
Resources:
National Directory of Managed Care Organizations Online Database

    www.themcic.com/mcic_db.html

    www.hin.com/store/dmc6.html

Target Hospitals
The continued growth in the elderly population and continued increase in heart disease, disease, Alzheimer's, and associated disease states will force an older and sicker resident population into institutional settings due to the intensity of care required to manage these disease states. We will target hospitals because we understand the challenges hospitals and healthcare facilities face today. Whether it's a frozen capital budget, reluctance to commit long-term, or needing equipment and forced into traditional rental, we will have the knowledge and resources to help them overcome these challenges from a vendor or hospital perspective.

We will utilize the following Hospital Directories:

American Hospital Directory
www.ahd.com/freesearch.php3
Listings of hospital through the USA as well as statistical information.
US News & World Report
http://health.usnews.com/best-hospitals
Profiles of each of the more than 6,000 hospitals are presented here in snapshot form.

Medilexicon
www.medilexicon.com/hospitalsdirectory.php
Search through database of worldwide hospitals (currently 12,000 entries). Search by
combination of country, alphabetical letter or keyword.

Hospital Link
www.hospitallink.com/
Use the HospitalLink.com® web site directory to locate more than 6,000 hospitals
and 1,700 web sites by city, state, hospital name and/or zip code.

American Hospital Association
www.ahd.com/
Comprehensive reference book of U.S. hospitals includes service line offerings and detailed profile information such as facility ownership, C-suite contact names, admissions, beds, outpatient visits, and more.

Target Case Managers
Case managers are advocates who help patients understand their current health status, what they can do about it and why those treatments are important. In this way, case managers are catalysts by guiding patients and providing cohesion to other professionals in the health care delivery team, enabling their clients to achieve goals more effectively and efficiently.
Resource:
Case Management Society of America
www.cmsa.org/Individual/Networking/CMSAMembershipDirectory/tabid/211/Default.
	aspx

Target Geriatric Patients
The chronic and geriatric patients sub-segment accounted for the largest share of over 50.0% of the personal/home care medical equipment rental segment in 2013. It is expected to lead the market during the forecast period. The chronic and geriatric patients segment is expected to rise with the increase in the number of patients suffering from chronic illnesses and the increasing geriatric population.
Source:
www.transparencymarketresearch.com/medical-equipment-rental.html

Target Nursing Homes

We will target nursing homes because they regularly use leasing arrangements to temporarily fill equipment needs and scheduling gaps.

Target Assisted Living Facilities
These facilities assist their tenants to renting medical equipment. We will train commissioned field sales reps to penetrate this market.

Target Home Health Care Providers
The Homecare markets will continue to grow due to continued growth in the elderly population (65+), which is projected by the Census Bureau to grow from 34.7 million in 2000 to 53.2 million by 2020, a total increase of 53%. We will join their trade association and present seminars at their networking events. We will work to educate these healthcare providers to maximize the benefits derived from our rental equipment.

Target Hospice Care Providers
Our goal is to become the most patient-focused, comprehensive and responsive home medical equipment company in the hospice service industry. We will be dedicated to improving the lives of hospice patients and their families. Our fully-trained Patient Service Associates will deliver and set up a wide variety of durable medical equipment. We will also have a full staff of knowledgeable Patient Service Representatives on hand to answer questions and take orders Monday through Friday from 9:00 am to 5:00 pm. We will also have on-call staff available to handle any after-hours emergencies.

The following are just a few examples of the durable medical equipment we will carry:
1. Beds & Accessories
2. Bedside Commodes, Shower Chairs, Bath Transfer Benches and other specialized products.
3. Wheelchairs, Geri-Chairs, and Walkers, Rollators and Group 3 Wheelchairs.
4. Respiratory equipment including Concentrators, Liquid Oxygen, both CPAP and BiPAP machines, Cough Assists for ALS and other individuals, Trach Equipment, and Oxygen for patients requiring up to 15 LPM.

5.	For enteral feeding needs we will carry Pumps, Bags, and IV Poles.
6.	Bariatric Beds, Wheelchairs, Walkers, Bedside Commodes, Shower Chairs and Geri Chairs.
7.	Pediatric Wheelchairs, Walkers, Oxygen Masks and Cannulas.

Target Clinics and Private Practices

Clinics and private practices are always looking for temporary solutions to fill equipment downtime voids, take up the slack during equipment shortages and cover unexpected peaks in admissions. We will join the trade associations of certain Medical practices and exhibit our medical equipment rental services at their trade show events. We will also place ads in their Medical journals.

Target Health and Wellness Centers

We will target these centers because they may have an interest in acting as a sub-contractor, and helping to place some types of specialty rental equipment with their patients. It may also be an opportunity to seek a mutual referral relationship.

Target Pharmaceutical Companies

We will target drug companies conducting clinical trials. We will be able to provide any medical equipment for Clinical Trials, offering no minimum hire period, no deposits, full service-back up and worldwide delivery and collection.
Example:
www.woodleyequipment.com

Target Adult Day Care Centers

Adult day care centers are providing caregiver roles for the assistance of disabled and elderly in their regular activities. With new adult day care centers coming up every day, these centers are in great need of flexible leasing arrangements.

Target Federal or State Government Agencies

We will apply for a GSA Schedule and actively pursue federal contracts. Government officials utilize GSA Schedules as a means of procuring goods and services, knowing that companies on these schedules have been qualified and thoroughly vetted by the General Services Administration (GSA). Getting our company on a GSA schedule will expand our reach not only to the federal level, but also to numerous state and county agencies throughout the region as they will be able to take advantage of our home care products at set government pricing. We will also target Federal and State Agencies, such as CMS, NCHS, and State Medicaid Departments. We will respond to government bid requests and use independent sales reps to pursue these accounts.

Resources:
Directory of Home Health Care Agencies
https://www.caring.com/local/home-health-agencies
http://www.nahcagencylocator.com/
https://data.medicare.gov/Home-Health-Compare/Home-Health-Care-Agencies/6jpm- sxkc/data

Target Professional Organizations
We will target Professional Organizations such as AHIMA, CPC, AHA, and AMA and seek to establish mutual referral relationships.

Target Medical Associations
We will sponsor medical conventions or health fairs, and send news releases to local medical associations and professional groups.

Resources:
Directory of Medical Associations
    www.omnimedicalsearch.com/associations.html
    https://en.wikipedia.org/wiki/Category:Medical_associations_based_
    in_the_United_States

Target Local Ethnic Groups
Ongoing demographic trends suggest that, in the coming decades, programs will be serving a population of people which is increasingly diverse in economic resources, racial and ethnic background, and family structure. Our plan is to reach out to professionals of various ethnic backgrounds, especially Hispanics, who comprise nearly 13 percent of the country's total population. In

addition to embarking on an aggressive media campaign of advertising with ethnic newspapers and radio stations, we will set up programs to actively recruit bilingual employees and make our company more accessible via signage printed in various languages based on the store's community. We will accurately translate our marketing materials into other languages. We will enlist the support of our bilingual employees to assist in reaching the ethnic people in our surrounding area through a referral program. We will join the nearest _____ (predominate ethnic group) Chamber of Commerce and partner with _____ (Hispanic/Chinese/Other?) Advocacy Agencies. We will also develop programs that reflect cultural influences and brand preferences.

Helpful Resources:
U.S. census Bureau Statistics
    www.census.gov
U.S. Dept. of Labor/Bureau of Labor Statistics
    www.bls.gov/data/home.htm
National Hispanic Medical Association

4.3.1   Market Needs

Home medical equipment market is expected to grow tremendously in the coming years, as the delivery of healthcare services will see an evident shift from clinical settings (such as hospitals and private nursing care) to the home. The overall home medical equipment rental market influenced by several market drivers such as more people with private insurance, aging population across the world, increased life expectancy, consistent rise in geriatric population, escalating national healthcare spending and increased incidence of chronic disorders across the globe. Over the time frame of 2015-2021, health spending is expected to grow at the rate of 6.2% annually. It reflects the net result of the aging of the population, Affordable Care Act, and generally improving socio-economic conditions.

Source: http://www.digitaljournal.com/pr/3352118

Demographic trends pointing to a greater need for Medical Equipment Rental Company Services:
- The life expectancy in the U.S. continues to rise. Women live an average of 80 years, while men can expect to live to about 74 years of age.
- The number of Americans over 65 years of age will double to 70 million in the next thirty years.
- 75% of baby boomers are nearing retirement in the next decade.

Lifestyle trends pointing to a greater need for Medical Equipment Rental Company services:
- Most adults age 60+ live in their own homes and have enough income to live comfortably.
- About 80% of the elderly prefer to remain in their own homes, where comfort, independence and quality of life are enhanced.
- As many as 12.8 million Americans of all ages need assistance from others to carry out everyday activities.

4.4 Buying Patterns

A Buying Pattern is the typical manner in which /buyers consumers purchase goods or services or firms place their purchase orders in terms of amount, frequency, timing, etc. In determining buying patterns, we will need to understand the following:
- Why consumers make the purchases that they make?
- What factors influence consumer purchases?
- The changing factors in our society.

The global medical device industry is likely to continue going from strength to strength, with the US keeping its top spot for the foreseeable future. The US remains a leader thanks to cutting edge technological innovation and demand from growing markets such as

India and China. The industry as a whole is growing largely because of an ageing global population and climbing societal risk factors. In particular, diet-related chronic diseases, such as cardiovascular disease and diabetes, continue to create demand for medical healthcare services.

Equally, the need for medical devices continues to climb, with life expectancy jumping nearly 20 years over the past 50 years. In fact, worldwide demographics are increasingly shifting towards older populations: between 2000 and 2050, populations in developed regions will see those aged over 60 grow from less than 20% to 34%, while the proportion of children aged under 15 is set to decline by 2% from 18%. According to a United Nations report on ageing, by the 2050s, life expectancy at birth will reach 80 years for almost 60% of the global female population. This ageing population, combined with lifestyle-related disease, is the medical device industry's assurance of increasing market demand.

4.5   Market Growth

We will assess the following general factors that affect market growth:

Current Assessment

1. Interest Rates
   _____

2. Government Regulations
   _____

3. Perceived Environment Impact
   _____

4. Consumer Confidence Level
   _____

5. Population Growth Rate
   _____

6. Unemployment Rate
   _____

7. Political Stability

8. Currency Exchange Rate

9. Innovation Rate

10. Home Sales

11. Gasoline Prices

12. Overall Economic Health

The healthcare industry worldwide is growing, fuelled by demographic factors such as increased life-expectancy, aging population, rising incidence of chronic diseases, escalating national healthcare spending and expansion of private healthcare. Public and private healthcare organizations are under constant pressure to keep pace with the advancements in medical technology, and offer patients optimum treatment and care despite budget cutbacks. New equipment purchase involves high upfront costs, while rapid technology developments shorten the technology life-cycle (TLC) requiring frequent and expensive upgrades. With the productive life cycle of medical equipment becoming lesser than its operational life, medical equipment rental and leasing services provide strong financial benefits. Market acceptance of these services is additionally supported by the escalating costs of new sophisticated medical equipment.

Limited budgets of hospitals, healthcare practitioners, physicians, clinics, nursing facilities, diagnostics laboratories and blood banks, is also providing opportunities for growth in the market. Economic constraints and insufficient funding have the potential to affect the quality of healthcare services rendered. Also, with growing competition redefining the healthcare system, hospitals are under constant pressure to provide best in-class services at low costs. Medical equipment leasing, in this regard, enables healthcare facilities to access new technologies in times of need for a fee thereby reducing the pressure on capital funds. Leasing and rental services allow healthcare providers to closely match monthly payments with monthly patient throughput rates, thus optimizing profits and strengthening corporate bottom lines.

Leasing services are witnessing rapid growth largely because "leases" are easier to secure than loans, and offer a host of taxation and pecuniary benefits. Small healthcare facilities, homecare and hospice are forecast to emerge into robust end-users of leasing services.

The 2007-2009 economic recession, and the weak recovery witnessed in the following years have catalyzed opportunities for equipment leasing, among both large and small healthcare facilities. Rising debts, budget deficits, and fiscal consolidation needs are compelling developed economies to reform their healthcare systems and reduce healthcare expenditures. Limited budgets are creating the need for alternate financing options for healthcare devices and equipment among public and private medical institutions. In developing countries like China, India, Turkey and Russia, governments are undertaking ambitious goals to cost effectively overhaul and develop national healthcare infrastructure. All of these factors are expected to fuel growth in the medical equipment leasing market.

Rising health care expenditure and increasing demand for novel medical equipment have led to a surge in the medical equipment manufacturing industry. However, product pricing is affected by the demand-supply gap or increased raw material costs. In either case, procuring new equipment is seen as an expensive proposition for several medical institutions, especially those with funding restraints. Renting/leasing medical equipment has emerged as a boon or an alternative to equipment purchasing to these medical institutions, benefiting the end-users or patients indirectly.

Home care products have seen a similar pattern with a majority of products being quite expensive for acute care patients, as the duration of the product requirement is too small to avail any benefits in the long run. The rental market, therefore, has seen a surge in recent times, with preference of the personal/home care patients for smaller devices and of medical institutions for larger equipment. The multi-billion dollar medical equipment rental market is expected to rise by a little less than half by the end of the decade and would remain dynamic for the next few years.

Additionally, the home medical equipment market is expected to grow tremendously in the coming years, as the delivery of healthcare services will see an evident shift from clinical settings, such as hospitals and private nursing care, to the home. The overall home medical equipment rental market is influenced by several market drivers, such as more people with private insurance, aging population across the world, increased life expectancy, consistent rise in geriatric population, escalating national healthcare spending and increased incidence of chronic disorders across the globe. External factors, like diligent insurance reimbursement policies, also make healthcare providers more consistently focused on lowering costs of healthcare. This has been accomplished in part by shifting limited resources to acute cases, and relying on patients and their families to take on a more active role in their own health care. However, it also presents unique challenges and issues like potential safety checklists to both, patients and caregivers, operating environment and skills, supplying equipment, regulatory restrains and industry standards.

Source:
www.prweb.com/releases/medical_equipment/rental_and_leasing/prweb10619128.htm
www.digitaljournal.com/pr/3352118
www.prnewswire.com/news-releases/global-medical-equipment-rental-personalhome-care-equipment-electronicdigital-equipment-surgical-equipment-durable-medical-equipment-storage--transport-market---trends-and-forecast-2014---2020-289831651.html

American Demographics projects the number of U.S. households will grow by 15% to 115 million by the year 2014. These busy households will require a greater range of medical support products and services.

We believe there is a market for our Medical equipment rental services in ___ (city) and that the market has potential for growth.

_____ County's population in the year 2000 was _____ and is expected to grow at a rate of ___ (5)% over the next ten years. _____ (city) is dedicated to remaining a travel destination "hot spot" without losing its "small town" feel. Because of its unique appeal it is likely to attract many vacationers and settlers for years to come. Our business will grow as customers become familiar with our unrivaled Medical equipment rental services and maintenance options.

The general industry analysis shows that _____ (city) is expected to experience _____ (double digit?) population, housing and commercial business growth. This suggests that as more families continue to move into the _____ area, there will be an increasing demand for quality medical equipment services, and this makes it a prime location for a Medical Equipment Rental Company that is willing to think outside-of-the-box.

4.6.0   Service Business Analysis

Healthcare facilities have found that renting medical equipment is not only a wise decision, but a cost effective one as well. A market report published in 2015 by Transparency Market Research based on the global medical equipment rental market forecasted that this industry is expected to reach US$49, 112.8 million by 2020, which is an expansion at CAGR of 5.8%.

Budget Restraints
Renting medical equipment gives hospitals and other medical facilities an opportunity to offer the most accurate treatment possible without going over budget. Renting instead of buying medical equipment is quickly becoming a popular option with many hospitals and healthcare facility administrators around the globe.

Convenience
Renting medical equipment allows healthcare facilities to have state of the art technology on hand when they need it without having to continually upgrade their equipment. If a machine breaks down or

needs to be calibrated or adjusted, they do not have to worry about making repairs. Rented equipment is a setup that needs regular maintenance by the owners, so the healthcare facilities don't have to worry about scheduling appointments or paying for visits from a repair tech.

Newest Technologies
With today's innovative technologies, new machines are often obsolete after six months or a year. Renting equipment allows a facility to have the most advanced sets of medical equipment in hand at all times, enabling them to provide the highest quality of care possible. Equipment is regularly updated to make sure the equipment is set to the latest technological standards.

Financial Benefits
The financial benefits of renting medical equipment are many. The healthcare facility does not have to worry about the cost of upgrades, repairs or regular maintenance. In addition, if the machine is needed only for a short period of time, the facility does not have to purchase it outright and have the hassle of trying to sell it once it is no longer needed.

As with most industries, the medical device sector was not untouched by the economic crisis, though it has not deterred the industry's overall growth. Smaller firms, unable to pick up the slack of product development costs previously covered by venture capital investors - now made more cautious by the economic slump - were obliged to curb their activity. Some other small firms, however, chose to merge with larger firms, thereby continuing technological advances without bearing the full burden of the cost. Domestic and international acquisitions and mergers allow a cross-border sharing of resources and knowledge, facilitating continued medical technology innovation despite the tough economic climate.

4.7 Barriers to Entry

_____ (company name) will benefit from the following

combination of barriers to entry, which cumulatively present a moderate degree of entry difficulty or obstacles in the path of other Medical Equipment Rental Companies wanting to enter our market.

1. Business Experience.
2. Community Networking
3. Referral Program
4. People Skills
5. Marketing Skills
6. Personnel Management
7. Operations Management
8. Cash Flow Management
9. Website Design
10. Capital Investment
11. Computer Skills
12. Maintenance Knowledge
13. Medical Industry Contacts

4.7.1 Porter's Five Forces Analysis

We will use Porter's five forces analysis as a framework for the industry analysis and business strategy development. It will be used to derive the five forces which determine the competitive intensity and therefore attractiveness of our market. Attractiveness in this context refers to the overall industry profitability.

Competitors The degree of rivalry is high in this segment, but less when compared to _____ the overall category. There are ____ (#) major competitors in the _____ area and they include: _____

Threat of Substitutes
Substitutes are moderate for this industry. These include other medical _____ equipment rental companies, medical supply companies, manufacturers _____ direct lease options, etc.

Bargaining Power of Buyers

127

Buyer power is moderate in the business. Buyers are sensitive to quality and pricing as the segment attempts to capitalize on the pricing and quality advantage.

Bargaining Power of Suppliers
Supplier power is moderate in the industry. Inventory can be obtained from a number of manufacturers and distributors. A high level of operational efficiency for managing supplies can be achieved.

Threat of New Entrants
Relatively high in this segment. The business model can be easily copied.

Conclusions: _____ (company name) is in a competitive field and has to move fast to retain its competitive advantage. The key success factors are to develop operational efficiencies, innovative programs, cost-effective marketing and customer service excellence.

4.8 Competitive Analysis

Competitor analysis in marketing and strategic management is an assessment of the strengths and weaknesses of current and potential competitors. This analysis will provide both an offensive and defensive strategic context through which to identify our business opportunities and threats. We will carry out continual competitive analysis to ensure our market is not being eroded by developments in other firms. This analysis will be matched with the target segment needs to ensure that our products and services continue to provide better value than the competitors. The competitive analysis will show very clearly why our medical supply products and leasing services are preferred in some market segments to other offerings and to be able to offer reasonable proof of that assertion.

We will conduct good market intelligence for the following reasons:
1. To forecast competitors' strategies.
2. To predict competitor likely reactions to our own strategies.
3. To consider how competitors' behavior can be influenced in our own favor.

Overall competition in the area is _____ (weak/moderate/strong).

Competitive analysis conducted by the company owners has shown that there are
__ (# or no other?) Medical Equipment Rental Companies currently offering the same combination of services in the __ (city) area. However, the existing competitors offer only a limited range of traditional services. In fact, of these, __ (# or none) of the competitors offered a range of services comparable with what _____ (company name) plans to offer to its clients.

Competitor Can Do Can't	What We Can Do and They Can't	What They and We Can't
_____	_____	_____
_____		

Self-assessment
Competitive Rating Assessment: 1 = Weak ……………………5 = Strong

	Our Company	Prime Competitor Compare
Our Location	_____	_____
Our Facilities	_____	_____
Our Services and Amenities	_____	_____

Our Management Skills   _____   _____

Our Training Programs   _____   _____

Our Research & Development   _____   _____

Our Company Culture   _____   _____

Our Business Model   _____   _____

Overall Rating   _____   _____

Rationale:
_____
___

The following Medical Equipment Rental Companies are considered direct competitors in _____ (city):
Competitor Address Market   Primary   Secondary
Strengths   Weaknesses
                     Share   Focus   Services

_____
_____
_____

Indirect Competitors include the following (General Employment Agencies):
_____
_____
_____

Alternative Competitive Matrix
Competitor Name: Us   _____

Location: _____

Location Distance (miles)   _____

130

Comparison Items:

Sales Revenue _____

Service Focus _____

Membership Programs _____

Profitability _____

Market Share _____

Brand Name _____

Specialty _____

Other Services _____

Capitalization _____

Target Markets _____

Service Area _____

Operating Hours _____

Operating Policies _____

Payment Options _____

Other Financing _____

Pricing Strategy _____

Price Level L/M/H _____

Discounts _____

Yrs in Business _____

Reputation _____

Reliability _____

Quality _____

Marketing Strategy _____

Methods of Promotion _____

Alliances _____

Brochure/Catalog _____

Website _____

Sales Revenues _____

No. of Staff _____

Competitive Advantage _____

Credit Cards Accepted Y/N _____

Prescreening Methods _____

Guarantees _____

Comments _____

Competitor Profile Matrix

	Our	Competitor 1	Competitor 2	Competitor 3
Critical Success Factors	Score	Rating Score	Rating Score	Rating Score

Advertisement _____

Product Quality _____

Price Competition _____

Management _____

Financial Position _____

Customer Loyalty _____

Brand Identity _____

Market Share _____

Total _____

We will use the following sources of competition analysis information:
1. Competitor company websites.
2. Mystery shopper visits.
3. Annual Reports (www.annual reports.com)
4. Thomas Net (www.thomasnet.com)
5. Trade Journals
6. Trade Associations
7. Sales representative interviews
8. Research & Development may come across new patents.
9. Market research can give feedback on the customer's perspective
10. Monitoring services will track a company or industry you select for news.
    Resources: www.portfolionews.com www.Office.com
11. Hoover's www.hoovers.com
12. www.zapdata.com (Dun and Bradstreet) You can buy

one-off lists here.

13. www.infousa.com (The largest, and they resell to many other vendors)

14. www.onesource.com (By subscription, they pull information from many sources)

15. www.capitaliq.com (Standard and Poors).

16. Obtain industry specific information from First Research (www.firstresearch.com) or IBISWorld, although both are by subscription only, although you may be able to buy just one report.

17. Get industry financial ratios and industry norms from RMA (www.rmahq.com) or by using ProfitCents.com software.

18. Company newsletters

19. Industry Consultants

20. Suppliers

21. Customer interviews regarding competitors.

22. Analyze competitors' ads for their target audience, market position, product features, benefits, prices, etc.

23. Attend speeches or presentations made by representatives of your competitors.

24. View competitor's trade show display from a potential customer's point of view. 25. Search computer databases (available at many public libraries).

26. Review competitor Yellow Book Ads.

27. www.bls.gov/cex/ (site provides information on consumer expenditures nationally, regionally, and by selected metropolitan areas).

28. www.sizeup.com

29. Business Statistics and Financial Ratios www.bizstats.com

4.9 Market Revenue Projection

For each of our chosen target markets, we will estimate our market share in number of customers, and based on consumer behavior, how often do they buy per year? What is the average dollar amount of each purchase? We will then multiply these three numbers to project sales volume for each target market.

Target Market Dollar Total Amount per Purchase	Number of Customers Sales Volume	No. of Purchases per Year	Average
A x		B x	C
= D			

_____
_____
_____

Using the target market number identified in this section, and the local demographics, we have made the following assessments regarding market opportunity and revenue potential in our area:

Potential Revenue Opportunity =

　　　　　_____ Local No. of Medical Organizations
(x)　　_____ Expected ___% Market Share
(=)　　_____ Number of likely local clients
(x) $ _____ Average annual recruiting fee dollar amount
(=) $ _____ Annual Revenue Opportunity.

Or

　　　　　　　　No. of Clients　(x)　Avg. Sale　(=) Daily Income
　　　　　　　　Per Week

Services　　　_____　　　_____

Other　　　　_____　　　_____
　　　　_____
Total:
　　　　_____
Annualized:　　　　　　　　　　　　　　　　(x)
50
Annual Revenue Potential:

Recap:

Month   Jan Feb Mar Apr May Jun Jul Aug Sep Oct
Nov Dec   Total
Products

_____

Services

_____

Gross Sales:

_____

(-) Returns

_____

Net Sales

_____

Revenue Assumptions:
1.   The sources of information for our revenue projection are:

_____

2.   If the total market demand for our product/service = 100%, our projected sales   volume represents ____% of this total market.
3.   The following factors might lower our revenue projections:

_____

5.0   Industry Analysis

The Medical Equipment, Supplies & Distribution industry consists of companies engaged in the manufacturing and distribution of basic medical equipment and supplies. The industry includes forceps, surgical knives and gloves, bandages and dressings, syringes, stethoscopes, medical laboratory equipment, x-ray films, dental drills, veterinarian instruments and other related supplies. The

Medical Equipment, Supplies & Distribution industry excludes retail sales of drugs and medical supplies, and manufacturing and distribution of high-tech medical equipment

Although the $3.4-billion Medical Equipment Rental Manufacturing industry was slowed down by the recession, it is forecast to continue growing in the coming years. Over the five years to 2013, IBISWorld expects revenue to fall at an average annual rate of 1.6%, which actually includes an anticipated 0.7% increase from 2012 to 2013. According to IBISWorld industry analyst Nima Samadi, "After recession-related downturns, demand for medical equipment rentals has grown as a result of increased public and private health spending and new product introductions."

The Medical Equipment Rental industry provides healthcare institutions with an alternative to purchasing medical equipment. Over the past five years, the number of sophisticated diagnostic tests that require technologically advanced equipment at hospitals and medical centers has kept demand steady for leased equipment rather than outright purchases. "Medical devices and machinery have high purchase costs and become obsolete quickly, two factors that encourage hospitals and medical centers to rent," says Samadi. "Moreover, a lease can be put together much quicker than a loan for equipment purchase"

These trends are projected to continue during the five years to 2019. Demographic shifts and increases in healthcare funding will help demand for medical equipment rentals grow. The aging US population is a major factor driving demand because the occurrence of health issues that require the use of medical equipment is higher in the elderly population. This demographic is forecast to expand as a percentage of the total population during the five years to 2019, which will help maintain industry growth. Furthermore, IBISWorld estimates that federal spending on Medicare and Medicaid will increase over the period. The rise in spending will continue to support demand for medical equipment rentals.

The Medical Equipment Rental industry has a low degree of market share concentration, with the majority of its companies operating a single location. According to the US Census, 86.6% of industry operators have just one location, while only four companies have more than 25 locations. Over the past five years, only Universal Hospital Services increased its market share through merger and acquisition activity. In 2011, the company acquired Emergent Group, a leading provider of laser and mobile surgical equipment services, and the equipment rental divisions of two regional medical equipment manufacturers. Other major players include Kinetic Concepts and Hill-Rom.

Source:
www.prweb.com/releases/2013/2/prweb10475553.htm

IBISWorld Inc.
www.ibisworld.com
Recognized as the nation's most trusted independent source of industry and market research, IBISWorld offers a comprehensive database of unique information and analysis on every US industry. With an extensive online portfolio, valued for its depth and scope, the company equips clients with the insight necessary to make better business decisions. Headquartered in Los Angeles, IBISWorld serves a range of business, professional service and government organizations through more than 10 locations worldwide.

5.1 Key Industry Statistics

Global market for Medical Equipment Rental and Leasing is projected to reach US$56.8 billion by 2019, driven by rapid technological obsolesce, need for frequent and expensive upgrades, limited budgets and growing pressure to reduce healthcare expenditure.

5.2 Industry Trends

We will determine the trends that are impacting our consumers and indicate ways in which our customers' needs are changing and any relevant social, technical or other changes that will impact our target market. Keeping up with trends and reports will help management to carve a niche for our business, stay ahead of the competition and deliver products that our customers need and want.

The worldwide healthcare market is influenced by a number of demographic trends, including the following:

Growing and Aging Population: The U.S. Census Bureau predicts that the majority of the U.S. "baby boom" population (28% of the total U.S. population) will begin to turn 65 between 2010 and 2020

Consumer expectations for improved healthcare are increasing in both developed and developing countries

Reimbursement and coverage of medical expenses by insurances companies and employers are on the decline—customers/patients have to contribute more money

Technology is giving rise to new clinical therapies, which in turn are addressing more and more medical ailments and aiding in earlier diagnosis and prevention of diseases.

Healthcare spending per capita has grown significantly across the world. In the U.S., it has increased from $144 per capita in 1960 to almost $4,400 by 1999. The U.S. per capita spending is projected to grow to $7,500 by 2008. Equipment suppliers understand that in order to be successful in the medical market they have to be focused and successful in the U.S.
2013 Frost & Sullivan outlook study identified the following top 5 technology trends in the medical devices market:

1. Interoperability
The rise of new technologies capable of integrating medical devices into a connected platform enhances the functionality of devices, reduces man power burden, and minimizes errors.

2. Multi-functional
Due to price sensitivity and availability of floor space, highly-

specialized pieces of equipment are losing out in purchase decision making to versatile systems capable of addressing multiple needs.

3.   Big Data
The amount of health care data being captured due to recent IT infrastructure upgrades is expected to greatly enhance 'smart' and AI functionality for diagnostic and treatment devices.

4.   Low-cost Alternates
Cost-containment initiatives are spurring new types of innovation in medical technologies that provide comparable diagnostic and therapeutic utility at fractions of the cost.

5.   Nano-technology
Nanotechnology provides the benefits of biocompatibility and functionality at an unparalleled scale, allowing it to be better able to influence diseases happening at a cellular level.

5.3   Industry Key Terms

We will use the following term definitions to help our company to understand and speak the common language of our industry, and aid efficient communication.

Capped Rental
Applies to more expensive equipment (e.g., semi-electric hospital beds, wheelchairs and patient lifts). Capped rental is Medicare's version of a "rent to own" program. To qualify for coverage, the equipment must be rented and installed through a Medicare provider/dealer. Medicare pays 80% of the monthly rental fee for up to 13 continuous months of use. You pay the remaining 20% of the monthly rental amount. At 10 months, you may decide to buy or return the equipment. If you decide to purchase, after 13 months, Medicare will discontinue rental payments and, as the owner, you will pay the remaining installments to the supplier. Home oxygen equipment has special guidelines and may be rented for up to 36

months.

Durable Medical Equipment
Any reusable medical equipment. A doctor or other healthcare provider must prescribe DME for your use in the home. Includes wheelchairs, bathroom safety solutions, home care beds, patient lifts and walking aids as well as other health care products for the home.

Resources:
Medical Equipment Glossaries
    http://www.medequipdict.com/
    http://pubs.rsna.org/doi/full/10.1148/rg.231025136
    https://homestore.allinahealth.org/Resource-Center/Medical-Glossary.aspx

5.4 Industry Leaders

We plan to study the best practices of industry leaders and adapt certain selected practices to our business model concept. Best practices are those methods or techniques resulting in increased customer satisfaction when incorporated into the operation.

Resources:
http://internetmedicine.com/top-40-medical-device-companies/

The global medical equipment rental market is highly fragmented, with only a few large players dominating it. The key players in this market are Agfa Finance Corp., Access Equipment Leasing, De Lage Landen International B.V., Apria Healthcare Group (USA), Hill-Rom Holdings, Inc., GE Healthcare Financial Services, Siemens Financial Services, National Technology Leasing Corp., Prudential Leasing, Inc., Oak Leasing Ltd, Rotech Healthcare Inc., and Stryker Corporation. They offer equipment in multiple device categories and cater to varied end-user segments. Their presence in developed and emerging regions along with flexible offerings has made them attractive providers in the global market. Other companies include Centric Health Corporation, Hill-Rom Holdings, Inc., Nunn's Home

Medical Equipment, Port Huron Hospital Medical Equipment, US Med-Equip, Inc., Universal Hospital Services, Inc., Woodley Equipment Company Ltd., The key players in this market are Agfa Finance Corp., Access Equipment Leasing, De Lage Landen International B.V., GE Healthcare Financial Services, National Technology Leasing Corp., Prudential Leasing, Inc., Oak Leasing Ltd, Rotech Healthcare Inc., Walgreen Co., and Westside Medical Supply, Inc.

Centric Health Corporation www.centrichealth.ca/
A Canada-based provider of healthcare services. The Company's segments include Specialty Pharmacy, and Surgical and Medical Centres. The Specialty Pharmacy segment includes dispensing, compliance packaging and auxiliary products and services for retirement homes and long-term care residents. The Specialty Pharmacy segment also offers dispensing services in Ontario and British Columbia for employees insured by corporate health plans. The Surgical & Medical Centres segment includes a range of services, including primary care, executive medical, urgent care and diagnostic services, including computerized tomography (CT) and magnetic resonance imaging (MRI) scan capabilities. The Surgical & Medical Centres segment also offers surgical specialties, including plastic, reconstructive, cosmetic, orthopedic, gynecology, urology, neurosurgery, bariatric, endoscopic and otolaryngology. It operates across approximately 500 locations across the country.

Apria Healthcare Group Inc
www.apria.com.
Provides home healthcare products and services in the United States. The company offers home respiratory therapy, home medical equipment, and home infusion therapy services. Its home respiratory therapy products and services include oxygen systems, ventilators, respiratory assist devices, continuous positive airway pressure and bi-level devices, infant apnea monitors, nebulizers, home-delivered respiratory medications, and related services, which are used to treat chronic obstructive pulmonary diseases, respiratory conditions associated with nervous system disorders or injuries, congestive heart failures, and lung cancer. The company's home medical equipment comprises manual wheelchairs and ambulatory

equipment, such as canes, crutches, and walkers; hospital room equipment consisting of hospital beds and bedside commodes; bathroom equipment, such as bath and shower benches, elevated toilet seats and toilet, tub, or wall grab bars; phototherapy systems, such as blankets, wraps, or treatment beds for babies with jaundice; and support surfaces, such as pressure pads and mattresses for patients at risk for developing pressure sores or decubitus ulcers. Its home infusion therapy is used to administer drugs and other therapeutic agents directly into the body through various catheters or tubing to treat patients with cancer, infectious and gastrointestinal diseases, chronic or acute pain syndromes, immune deficiencies, cardiovascular disease, or chronic genetic diseases, as well as to patients, who require therapies associated with bone marrow or solid organ transplantation. The company markets its products and services through its field sales force primarily to physicians, managed care organizations, hospitals, medical groups, home health agencies, and case managers. The company was founded in 1924 and is headquartered in Lake Forest, California. Apria Healthcare Group Inc. is a subsidiary of Sky Acquisition LLC.

Hill-Rom, Inc. www.hill-rom.com

Manufactures medical technologies and provides related services to the healthcare industry. The company offers hospital beds and long term care beds, wound therapy systems, support surfaces and mattresses, patient handling/support systems, architectural products, stretchers, furniture, respiratory care products, clinical workflow solutions, surgical equipment, safe mobility and handling solutions, non-invasive therapeutic products for various acute and chronic medical conditions, and information technology solutions. It also offers design, equipment, capital, medical equipment rental, technology implementation, and home care buy and rental services.

Universal Hospital Services, Inc. www.uhs.com

UHS is a leading provider of medical equipment management and service solutions to the health care industry. UHS manages more than 585,000 pieces of medical equipment for over 8,675 clients in all 50 states. For more than 70 years, UHS has delivered management and service solutions that help clients reduce costs, increase operating efficiencies, improve caregiver satisfaction and support optimal patient outcomes.

Med One Capital
www.medonecapital.com

Provides medical equipment financing, rental, sale, and service for acute care hospitals and health care institutions in the United States. It sells and rents equipment, such as pre-owned equipment, modular systems, syringe and infusion pumps, patient monitoring systems, pulse oximeters, smart pumps, SCDs, ventilators, and bi-pap machines. The company also offers funding solutions to medical equipment manufacturers for products they sell; and biomedical solutions, including repair and services for infusion, oximetry, monitoring, imaging, and respiratory equipment. It provides various lease solutions, such as capital lease, operating lease, and renewable options. Med One Capital, Inc. was formerly known as Med One Financial Group. The company was founded in 1991 and is based in Sandy, Utah.

US Med-Equip   www.usmedequip.com

Houston-based US Med-Equip is an innovative healthcare company specializing in the rental, sales and service of movable biomedical equipment for high acuity medical systems. The company has received ISO 9001:2008 certification for its medical equipment management processing system and is widely known for its 24/7 personalized attention to customer needs. Ranked in 2011 and 2012 by Inc. Magazine as one of the nation's fastest growing companies, US Med-Equip offers flexible options for managing biomedical equipment rentals and purchases, maintaining equipment and providing hospitals equipment tracking technology for enhanced asset management. It offers customers MY SMARTS, a proprietary, web-based software that provides instant access to critical management reports such as equipment on rent, pick-up confirmations and preventative maintenance prompts. Customers also have the ability to order and request equipment pickups online. The company's STAR Trax RFID-enabled asset management system enables hospitals to dramatically increase equipment utilization rates while equipping them with the tools to solve inventory and purchasing challenges. Dedication to patient care and to promoting the healing process is at the core of the US Med-Equip culture and drives daily operations focused on quality healthcare solutions. The company serves eight states from its 13 locations.

Home Health Depot   www.hhdepot.com
One of the largest home medical equipment companies in the Midwest. Headquartered in Indianapolis, Indiana, Home Health Depot has served the needs of thousands of patients for over 14 years. With locations in Indiana and Georgia, their talented team of caring and knowledgeable professionals is dedicated to helping patients stay healthier at home longer.

Walgreen's
Walgreens Boots Alliance, Inc., incorporated on October 2, 2014, is a holding company. The Company is a pharmacy-led health and wellbeing company. The Company operates through three segments: Retail Pharmacy USA, Retail Pharmacy International and Pharmaceutical Wholesale. The Retail Pharmacy USA segment consists of the Walgreen Co. (Walgreens) business, which includes the operation of retail drugstores and convenient care clinics, in addition to providing specialty pharmacy services. The Retail Pharmacy International segment consists primarily of the Alliance Boots pharmacy-led health and beauty stores, optical practices and related contract manufacturing operations. The Pharmaceutical Wholesale segment consists of the Alliance Boots pharmaceutical wholesaling and distribution businesses. The Company's portfolio of retail and business brands includes Walgreens, Duane Reade, Boots and Alliance Healthcare, as well as global health and beauty product brands, including No7, Botanics, Liz Earle and Soap & Glory. www.walgreens.com/store/c/home-medical-supplies-and-equipment/ID=359443-tier1

Kwipped   www.kwipped.com/rentals/medical/15
The KWIPPED rental marketplace captures rental demand for specific privately owned equipment, at the time it is underutilized and with the renter criteria specified by the equipment owners. Their proprietary technology matches the owner's medical equipment to the right application, qualifies the renters, offers the first layer of

customer service and takes the hassle out of the rental business.

Integrated Rental Services, Inc.
This company is a subsidiary of Avante Health Solutions (www.avantehs.com). Founded in 1997, Integrated Rental specializes in medical equipment rental for hospitals, surgery centers, clinics, research labs, and medical facilities across the United States.

Rentus.com
Provides a platform to reach more and more committed rental customers. Rentus.com invests large amounts of money and has a dedicated team of Internet marketing professionals driving traffic to the listings on the website. Listing is free even for companies. Rentus.com's Software as a service (SaaS) backend system allows rental companies to manage bookings, sales and inventory all in one convenient dashboard. At Rentus.com users are able to rent just about anything from tools and equipment, to party supplies, photo and video gear, medical equipment and sporting gear. Rentus.com offers "Boost Packages" for companies to get more exposure and more leads. The Rentus.com mobile app is available for iOS on the iTunes store.

RentItToday.com
A resource platform for everything rent related. Their goal is to make the renting experience easy for individuals looking for items, while making it affordable for companies to market their rentals. Rent It Today's philosophy is to brand their company name by educating the world that renting no longer just means tuxedos and cars. They plan on eventually marketing all that is available for rent. Example: www.rentittoday.com/medical-equipment-rentals/Jacksonville-Medical-Equipment-   Rentals---Wheelchairs-For-Rent---Florida-Medical-Supplies-818

6.0 Strategy and Implementation Summary

_____ (company name) intends to develop a referral network from doctors, surgeons, hospitals, and post operative clinics within the target market. Since the Company is marketing directly to medical professionals and establishments, the costs associated with advertising are minimal. The Company will also use traditional forms of marketing that are targeted towards medical professionals in the target market community, such as trade association newsletters. Management intends to market directly within locally based Medical Journals. In regards to larger clients, like hospitals and outpatient facilities, _____ (company name) will directly contact these businesses with our team of sales reps to establish ongoing business relationships. We will rapidly establish these relationships so that the business can immediately generate revenue from these sources. Finally, _____ (company name) will develop its own website that will feature information about our medical equipment rental business, contact information, and the benefits of various leasing options.

Our sales strategy is based on serving our niche markets better than the competition and leveraging our competitive advantages. These advantages include superior attention to understanding and satisfying customer needs and wants, creating a one-stop rental solution, and value pricing.

The objectives of our marketing strategy will be to recruit new clients and retain existing customers, get good customers to spend more and return more frequently to satisfy their medical equipment rental needs. Establishing a loyal customer base is very important because such core customers will not only generate the most lifetime sales, but also provide valuable referrals.

We will generate word-of-mouth buzz through direct-mail campaigns, exceeding customer expectations, developing a Web site, getting involved in community events with local businesses, and donating our services at charity functions in exchange for press release coverage. Our sales strategy will seek to convert potential and first-time customers into long-term relationships and referral agents. The combination of our competitive advantages, targeted marketing campaign and networking activities will enable _____ (company name) to continue increasing our market share.

6.1.0   Promotion Strategy

Given the importance of word-of-mouth/referrals among the area's medical practices, we shall strive to efficiently service all our customers to gain their rental business regularly, which is the recipe for our long-term success. We shall focus on direct marketing, publicity, informational seminars, and advertising as proposed. Our promotion strategy will focus on generating referrals from existing clients and professionals, community involvement and direct mail campaigns.

Our promotional strategies will also make use of the following tools:
- **Advertising**
    - Yearly anniversary parties to celebrate the success of each year.
    - Yellow Pages ads in the book and online.
    - Flyers promoting special promotional events and new equipment introductions.

- **Local Marketing / Public Relations**
    - Client raffle for gift certificates or discount coupons
    - Participation in local civic groups and medical trade associations.
    - Press release coverage of our sponsoring of health fair events at the local community center for families and residents.
    - Article submissions to magazines describing medical technology advancements and the financial benefits of leasing.
    - Sales Brochure to convey the details of our leasing programs.
    - Seminar presentations to local civic groups, explaining

the importance of having rapid access to state-of-the-art medical equipment.
- 0 Giveaway of free informational booklets with our company contact information and a listing of the equipment categories we offer for rental.

- **Local Media**
    - o Direct Mail - We will send quarterly postcards and annual direct mailings to private practices and clinics with a ___ (20?) mile radius of our company. It will contain an explanation of the benefits of our responsive medical equipment rental services.
    - o Radio Campaign - We will make "live on the air" presentations of our trial coupons to the disk jockeys, hoping to get the promotions broadcasted to the listening audience. We will also make our medical equipment expertise available for talk radio programs.
    - o Newspaper Campaign - Placing several ads in local community newspapers to launch our initial campaign. We will include a trial coupon for a free consultation.
    - o Website – We will collect email addresses for a monthly newsletter.
    - o Cable TV advertising on local community-based shows focused on health and wellness issues.

6.1.1 Grand Opening

Our Grand Opening celebration will be a very important promotion opportunity to create word-of-mouth advertising results. We will advertise the date of our grand opening in local newspapers, trade newsletters and on the local radio.

We will do the following things to make the open house a successful event:

1. Enlist local business support to contribute a large number of door prizes.

2. Use a sign-in sheet to create an email/mailing list.
3. Sponsor a competition or trivia contest.
4. Schedule appearance by local celebrities.
5. Create a festive atmosphere with balloons, beverages and music.
6. Get the local radio station to broadcast live from the event and handout fun gifts.
7. Offer an application fee waiver.
8. Giveaway our logo imprinted T-shirts as a contest prize.
9. Allow potential customers to view your facility and ask questions.
10. Print promotional flyers and pay a few kids to distribute them locally.
11. Arrange for beverages and snacks for everyone.
12. Arrange for local politician to do the official opening ceremony so all the local   newspapers came to take pictures and do a feature story.
13. Arrange that people can tour our facility on the open day in order to see our   facilities, collect sales brochures and find out more about our medical equipment   rental services.
14. Allocate staff members to perform specific duties, handout business cards and   sales brochures and instruct them to deal with any questions or queries.
16. Organize a drawing with everyone writing their name and phone numbers on the   back of business cards and give a voucher as a prize to start a marketing list.

Ex: _____ **(company name) Opens** _____ **(city) Branch**
_____ (company name), a provider of quality medical equipment rental solutions based in _____ (city), ____ (state) announced today that the company opened its newest office in _____ (city), _____ (state). _____ (Executive Name), who brings extensive medical equipment experience to the position, will manage the _____ (city) location.

_____ (company name) is an industry leader in placing medical equipment into short- and long-term leasing arrangements. Solely focused on the needs of healthcare practices and clinics, _____ (company name) can match medical equipment to customer needs within 24 hours.

6.1.2 Value Proposition

Our value proposition will summarize why a Medical organization should use our medical equipment rental services. We will enable quick access to our broad line of innovative services, out of our conveniently located company offices in the _____ (city) area. Our value proposition will convince prospects that our medical equipment rental services will add more value and better solve their need for a convenient, one-stop rental services company. We will add value to our clients by having the continual ability to provide state-of-the art equipment and guarantee adherence to strict quality assurance standards.

We will use this value proposition statement to target customers who will benefit most from using our services. These are hospitals and home healthcare businesses that are looking for just-in-time servicing with no major capital tie-up. Our value proposition will be concise and appeal to the customer's strongest decision-making drivers, which are one-stop convenience, competitive pricing, remote online database access, a satisfaction guarantee, thoroughness of the equipment inspection and maintenance processes, and quality of personal relationships.

Recap of Our Value Proposition:

Trust – We are known as a trusted business partner with strong customer and vendor endorsements. We have earned a reputation for quality, integrity, and delivery of cost effective medical equipment rental solutions.

Quality – We offer medical equipment rental experience and extensive professional backgrounds in _____ at competitive rates.

Experience – Our ability to bring people with years of healthcare management experience with deep technical knowledge of _____ is at the core of our success.

True Vendor Partnerships – Our true vendor partnerships enable us to offer the resources of much larger organizations with greater flexibility.

Customer Satisfaction and Commitment to Success – Through partnering with our customers and delivering quality solutions, we have been able to achieve an impressive degree of repeat and referral business. Since ____ (year), more than ____% of our business activity is generated by existing customers. Our philosophy is that "our clients' success is our success." Our success is measured in terms of our clients' success through the solutions we provide to them.

6.1.3 Positioning Statement

Our positioning strategy will be the result of conducting in-depth consumer market research to find out what benefits consumers want and how our medical equipment rental services can meet those needs. Many service-oriented professions are leaning toward differentiating themselves on the basis of convenience. This is also what we intend to do. For instance, we plan to have extended, 24/7 "people" hours, 7 days of the week.

We also plan to develop specialized medical equipment rental services that will enable us to pursue a niche focus on specific interest based programs, such as skills development services and consulting services. These objectives will position us at the _____ (mid-level/high-end) of the market and will allow the company to realize a healthy profit margin in relation to its low-end, discount rivals and achieve long-term growth.

Market Positioning Recap
Price: The strategy is to offer competitive prices that are lower that the market leader, yet set to indicate value and worth. .
Quality: The medical equipment quality will have to be very good as the finished rental service results will be showcased in highly visible situations.
Service: Highly individualized and customized service will be the key to success in this type of business. Personal attention to the

customers will result in higher sales and word of mouth advertising.

6.1.4 Unique Selling Proposition (USP)

Our unique selling proposition will answer the question why a customer should choose to do business with our company versus any and every other option available to them in the marketplace. Our USP will be a description of a unique important benefit that our Medical Equipment Rental Company offers to customers, so that price is no longer the key to our sales.

Our USP will include the following:
Who our target audience is:
_____

What we will do for them:
_____

What qualities, skills, talents, traits do we possess that others do not:
_____

What are the benefits we provide that no one else offers:
_____

Why that is different from what others are offering:
_____

Why that solution matters to our target audience:
_____

6.1.4 Distribution Strategy

Customers can contact the _____ (company name) by telephone, fax, internet and by dropping in. Our nearest competitors' are ___ (#) miles away in either direction.

Our customers will have the following access points:
1. **Order by Phone**
    Customers can contact us 24 hours a day, 7days a week at _____.

153

Our Customer Service Representatives will be available to assist customers Monday through Friday from ___ a.m. to ___ p.m. EST.
2. **Order by Fax**
Customers may fax their orders to _____ anytime.
They must provide: Account number, Billing and shipping address, Purchase order number, if applicable, Name and telephone number, Product number/description, Unit of measure and quantity ordered and Applicable sales promotion source codes.
3. **Order Online**
Customers can order online at www._____.com. Once the account is activated, customers will be able to place orders, browse the catalog, check stock availability and pricing, check order status and view both order and transaction history.
4. **In-person**
All customers can be serviced in person at our facilities Monday through Friday from ___ a.m. to ___ p.m. EST.
5. **Sales Reps**

We plan to pursue the following distribution channels: (select)

Chosen	Sales Costs	Number	Reason
1.	Our own retail outlets		
2.	Independent distributors		
3.	Independent commissioned sales reps		
4.	In-house sales reps		
5.	Direct mail using own catalog or flyers		
6.	In-house telemarketing		
7.	Contracted telemarketing call center		
8.	Cybermarketing via own website		

9. TV and Cable Direct Marketing

6.1.6 Sales Rep Plan

We will develop detailed training programs for our sales because healthcare organizations and individuals expect sales reps to provide information that will help them solve critical business/practice issues.
Source: www.spisales.com/5-best-practices-sales-success-in-todays-healthcare-market/

The following parameters will help to define our sales rep plan:
1. In-house or Independent

2. Salaried or Commissioned

3. Salary or Commission Rate

4. Salary Plus Commission Rate

5. Special Performance Incentives

6. Negotiating Parameters   Price Breaks/Added Services/

7. Performance Evaluation Criteria   No. of New Customers/Sales Volume/

8. Number of Reps

9. Sales Territory Determinants

Geography/Demographics/

10. Sales Territories Covered

11. Training Program Overview

12. Training Program Cost

13. Sales Kit Contents

14. Primary Target Market
Hospitals/_____
15. Secondary Target Market

Rep Name   Compensation Plan   Assigned Territory

We will locate sales reps using the following techniques:
1. Place classified ads in trade magazines that serve medical practices.
2. Seek other company owner recommendations.
3. Ask the managers of medical practices the names of reps showing products to them.
4. Attend medical trade shows where the reps are showing their product lines.

Resource:
www.medreps.com/medical-sales-careers/8-of-the-best-blogs-for-successful-medical- sales-reps/

6.2.0 Competitive Advantages

A **competitive advantage** is the thing that differentiates a business from its competitors. It is what separates our business from everyone else. It answers the questions: "Why do customers buy from us versus a competitor?", and "What do we offer customers that is unique?". We will incorporate our key competitive advantages into all of our marketing materials. We will use the following competitive advantages to set us apart from our competitors. The distinctive competitive advantages which _____ (company name) brings to the marketplace are as follows: (Note: Select only those you can support)

_____ (company name) will compete well in our market by offering competitive rental prices on an expanded line of medical rental equipment. Our staff will be knowledgeable and approachable, and use the latest software to match equipment to client needs. We will enable convenient online quote submissions. We will provide in-house delivery and pick up. All processing will be handled by our highly trained and certified staff provided to the customer's facility. Our custom solutions will allow the customer to acquire the equipment they need at the times they need it the most. We will provide flexibility to adjust during peak process times. We will also provide biomedical services to repair equipment and service the customer's facility. Each piece of equipment will be thoroughly cleaned, maintained and inspected before being delivered to the customer. Our TLS tracking software will generate the analytics the customer needs to see real-time statistics and monitor all of the equipment within their facility at a glance. This will reduce errors and decrease their equipment downtime. We will also produce timely and accurate reports so the customer can accurately assess their future needs.

Other competitive advantages include:
1. Around-the Clock Accessibility, with Equipment Consultants

available 24-hours a day, 7 days a week to provide the most efficient service possible.

2. Maintenance of stringent screening processes to ensure that the equipment we send exceeds our client's expectations in performance and value.

3. Development of a thorough pre-employment screening process, which includes competency tests and a thorough background check for all our employees.

4. We are able to recruit and maintain a staff of qualified Medical professionals, enabling us to fill a variety of requests in a time efficient manner.

5. We have earned a glowing reputation of being a leader in medical equipment leasing.

6. Our business revolves around motivated practitioners performing quality work.

7. We offer competitive salaries, insurance coverage, completion bonuses, and more to our staff.

8. Our clients have access to the largest inventory of inspected Medical Equipment in the country.

9. By having owners of the company being the principle managers of the company we will reduce employee costs and will ensure the honesty and reliability of our staff.

10. Our involvement with the community and our presence and availability on a regular basis will give our customers the opportunity to give direct feedback.

11. We will enable our customers to have online access to our total inventory of medical equipment.

12. We will train our staff to answer most customers questions, so that their time is valued.

13. We constantly are search of the latest technology to update our operations and reinforce the image in customer minds that we are among the most progressive medical equipment providers in the area.

14. We will utilize a software package that provides document management services and advanced management tools, such as basic and intermediate reporting functions, cost-benefit analysis, inventory management and audit functionality, in addition to electronic records storage and retrieval.

15. We will offer discounts and other incentives for referrals.

16. We have the technological and professional rental capabilities to provide our customers with the highest possible level of personalized service.
17. We have an ethnically diverse and multilingual staff, which is critical for a service-oriented business.
18. We have formed alliances that enable us to provide one-stop shopping or an array of leasing services through a single access point.
19. We developed a specialized training program for the staff so they will be proficient at administering our leasing programs.
20. Our superior customer service, delivered through our trained staff, sets us apart and provides our competitive advantage
21. We regularly conduct focus groups to understand changing customer expectations.
22. We hire and train our employees to be responsive and empathetic to customer needs.
23. We do not service any other field except for the Medical Industry.
24. Our Proprietary Marketing Systems enable us to have more than twice as much traffic as any publicly traded Medical Equipment Firm.
25. We provide customized solutions that meet the unique financial, clinical and operational goals of the customer's facility.

____ (company name) has developed one of the largest and most comprehensive quality assurance programs in the equipment rental industry, the success of which is evident in our endorsements by several state hospital associations, and by the large clinical services team who supports our Medical professionals and client facilities.

6.2.1 Branding Strategy

Our branding strategy involves what we do to shape what the customer immediately thinks our business offers and stands for. The purpose of our branding strategy is to reduce customer perceived purchase risk and improve our profit margins by allowing use to charge a premium for our Medical Equipment Rental Company services.

We will invest $____ every year in maintaining our brand name image, which will differentiate our medical equipment rental business from other companies. The amount of money spent on creating and maintaining a brand name will not convey any specific information about our products, but it will convey, indirectly, that we are in this market for the long haul, that we have a reputation to protect, and that we will interact repeatedly with our customers. In this sense, the amount of money spent on maintaining our brand name will signal to consumers that we will provide products and services of consistent quality.

We will use the following ways to build trust and establish our personal brand:
1. Build a consistently published blog and e-newsletter with informational content.
2. Create comprehensive social media profiles.
3. Contribute articles to related online publications.
4. Earn Career Certifications

Resources:
https://www.abetterlemonadestand.com/branding-guide/

Our key to marketing success will be to effectively manage the building of our brand platform in the marketplace, which will consist of the following elements:

Brand Vision - our envisioned future of the brand is to be the local source for medical equipment rental needs to manage the complications of state-of-the-art equipment availability and maintenance.

Brand Attributes - Partners, problem solvers, responsive, comprehensive, reliable, flexible, technical experts and easy to work with.

Brand Essence - the shared soul of the brand, the spark of which is present in every experience a customer has with our products, will be "Problem Solving" and "Responsive" This will be the core of our organization, driving the type of people we hire and the type of behavior we expect.

Brand Image - the outside world's overall perception of our organization will be that we are the 'medical equipment rental' pros who are alleviating the complications of having access to the right piece of functional equipment at the right time.

Brand Promise - our concise statement of what we do, why we do it, and why customers should do business with us will be, "To save money and improve the level of healthcare service with the help of our knowledgeable staff"

We will use the following methodologies to implement our branding strategy:

1. Develop processes, systems and quality assurance procedures to assure the consistent adherence to our quality standards and mission statement objectives.
2. Develop business processes to consistently deliver upon our value proposition.
3. Develop training programs to assure the consistent professionalism and responsiveness of our employees.
4. Develop marketing communications with consistent, reinforcing message content.
5. Incorporate testimonials into our marketing materials that support our promises.
6. Develop marketing communications with a consistent presentation style.
   (Logo design, company colors, slogan, labels, packaging, stationery, etc.)
7. Exceed our brand promises to achieve consistent customer loyalty.
8. Use surveys, focus groups and interviews to consistently monitor what our brand means to our customers.
9. Consistently match our brand values or performance benchmarks to our customer requirements.
10. Focus on the maintenance of a consistent number of key brand values that are tied to our company strengths.
11. Continuously research industry trends in our markets to stay relevant to customer needs and wants.

12. Attach a logo-imprinted product label and business card to all products, marketing communications and invoices.
13. Develop a memorable and meaningful tagline that captures the essence of our brand.
14. Prepare a one page company overview and make it a key component of our sales presentation folder.
15. Hire and train employees to put the interests of customers first.
16. Develop a professional website that is updated with fresh content on a regular basis.
17. Use our blog to circulate content that establishes our niche expertise and opens a two-way dialogue with our customers.

The communications strategy we will use to build our brand platform will include the following items:

- Website - featuring product line information, database searches, research, testimonials, cost benefit analysis, frequently asked questions, and policy information. This website will be used as a tool for both our sales team and our customers.
- Presentations, brochures and mailers geared to the purchasing agent, explaining the benefits of our medical equipment rental services as part of a comprehensive inventory access and maintenance plan.
- Presentations and brochures geared to the corporate decision maker explaining the benefits of our programs in terms of positive outcomes, reduced costs from equipment downtime and capital tie-up, and reduced risk of lawsuits or negative survey events.
- A presentation and recruiting brochure geared to prospective sales people that emphasizes the benefits of joining our organization.
- Training materials that help every employee deliver our brand message in a consistent manner.

6.2.2 Brand Positioning Statement

We will use the following brand positioning statement to summarize what our brand means to our targeted market:

To _____
(target market)
_____ (company name) is the brand of
_____ (product/service frame of reference) that enables the customer to _____ (primary performance benefit) because ____ (company name) _____ (products/services)
_____ (are made with/offer/provide) the best
_____ (key attributes)

6.3   Business SWOT Analysis

Definition: SWOT Analysis is a powerful technique for understanding our Strengths   and Weaknesses, and for looking at the Opportunities and Threats faced.
Strategy: We will use this SWOT Analysis to uncover exploitable opportunities and   carve a sustainable niche in our market. And by understanding the   weaknesses of our business, we can manage and eliminate threats that   would otherwise catch us by surprise. By using the SWOT framework, we   will be able to craft a strategy that distinguishes our business from our   competitors, so that we can compete successfully in the market.

Strengths   (select)
What Medical Equipment Rental Company services are we best at providing?
What unique resources can we draw upon?
1.   Company led by a strong management team

2.   The facility has been established as a computer center for ___ years.
3.   The nearest competition is __ miles and has a minimal medical equipment   inventory.

163

4. Our offices have been extensively renovated, with many upgrades.
5. Seasoned executive management professionals, sophisticated in business knowledge, experienced in the Medical Equipment Rental Company business.
7. Strong networking relationships with many different organizations, including _____.
8. Excellent staff are experienced, highly trained and customer attentive.
9. Wide diversity of Medical equipment rental service offerings.
10. High customer loyalty.
11. The proven ability to establish excellent personalized client service.
12. Strong relationships with suppliers that offer flexibility and respond to special customer requirements.
13. Good referral relationships.
14. Client loyalty developed through a solid reputation with repeat clients.
15. Our company has a focused target market of _____ (hospitals?).
16. Sales staff with heath care education credentials.
17. Our relationships with decision makers at homecare chains.
18. Our ability to effectively build a strong national clinical sales team.
19. Our ability to build a comprehensive long-range marketing strategy. 20. Our ability to generate a steady cash flow from equipment maintenance contracts.
21.

_____

Weaknesses
In what areas could we improve?
Where do we have fewer resources than others?

1. Lack of developmental capital to complete Phase I start-up.
2. New comer to the area.
3. Lack of marketing experience.
4. The struggle to build brand equity.
5. A limited marketing budget to develop brand awareness.
6. Finding dependable and people oriented staff.
7. We need to develop the information systems that will improve our productivity and inventory management.
8. Don't know the needs and wants of the local population.
9. The owner must deal with the logistics experience learning curve.
10. Challenges caused by the technology changing nature of the business.
11. Management expertise gaps.
12. Inadequate monitoring of competitor strategies and responses.
13. _____

Opportunities

What opportunities are there for new and/or improved services?

What trends could we take advantage of?

1. Inadequate equipment inventory levels maintained by our competitors.
2. Could take market share away from existing competitors.
3. Greater need for mobile home services by time starved dual income families and immobile seniors.
4. Growing market with a significant percentage of the target market still not aware that _____ (company name) exists.
5. The ability to develop many long-term customer relationships.

6. Expanding the range of product/service packaged offerings.
7. Greater use of direct advertising to promote our services.
8. Establish referral relationships with local businesses serving the same target market segment.
9. Networking with non-profit organizations.
10. The aging population will need and expect a greater range of ___ services.
11. Increased public awareness of the importance of 'green' matters.
12. Strategic alliances offering sources for referrals and joint marketing activities to extend our reach.
13. _____ (supplier name) is offering co-op advertising.
14. A competitor has overextended itself financially and is facing bankruptcy.
15. _____

___

Threats

What trends or competitor actions could hurt us?
What threats do our weaknesses expose us to?

1. Another Medical Equipment Rental Company could move into this area.
2. Further declines in the economic forecast.
3. Inflation affecting operations for gas, labor, and other operating costs.
4. Keeping trained efficient staff and key personnel from moving on or starting their own business venture.
5. Imitation competition from similar indirect service providers.
6. Price differentiation is a significant competition factor.
7. The government could enact legislation that could affect licensing and certification

166

practices.

8. The government also plays a role in determining if medical technology companies can get paid for their devices and therapies.

9. Medicare is a major factor when it comes to how Americans pay for their healthcare, and if the government pulls back on how much it's willing to pay for various therapies or devices, that can have a major impact on the sector.

10. We need to do a better job of assessing the strengths and weaknesses of all of our competitors.

11. Sales or rentals of customized devices by mass discounters..

12.

_____

———

Recap:

We will use the following strengths to capitalize on recognized opportunities:

1.

_____

—

2.

_____

—

We will take the following actions to turn our weaknesses into strengths and prepare to defend against known threats.

1.

_____

———

2.

_____

———

6.4.0 Marketing Strategy

Marketing Objectives

1. Establish relationships with hospitals, outpatient facilities, assisted living facilities, and physician offices.

2. Implement a local campaign with the Company's targeted market via the use of flyers, local newspaper advertisements, and word of mouth advertising among consumers.

3. Develop an online presence by developing a website and placing the Company's name and contact information with online directories.

Overview:
We will make appointments with local Medical facilities to talk with the heads of purchasing departments and office managers. We will introduce our company and its medical equipment rental services through these meetings and hand out sales brochures highlighting the availability of our staff and the medical equipment specialties we cover. We will set up a phone line to handle the requests for equipment rentals on a 24-hour basis and utilize software that is specifically designed for Medical Equipment Rental tracking purposes. We will create a website where customers can request equipment rental quotes and ask questions.

Our Marketing strategy will focus on the following:
1. Developing a reputation for a broad selection Medical equipment rental services, competitive prices, reliability and exceptional customer service.
2. Keeping the staff focused, satisfied and motivated in their roles, to help keep our productivity and customer service at the highest obtainable levels.

3. Maintaining the visibility of our offices through regular advertising to our target community.
4. Reaching out to potential hospitals, clinics, private practices and community organizations, with commissioned independent sales reps.
5. Doing activities that can stimulate additional business: seminars, publishing helpful articles about Medical equipment maintenance techniques, sharing interesting and educational training knowledge, publishing a newsletter, offering customer service through a website, and automatic reminder notices based on historical patterns.
7. Extending our market penetration beyond the physical boundaries of the office location through outside sales reps and a website.

In phase one of our marketing plan, we will gain exposure to our target markets through the use of discounts and grand opening promotional tactics. We will be taking a very aggressive marketing stance in the first year of business in hopes of gaining customer loyalty. In our subsequent years, we will focus less resources on advertising as a whole, but, we do plan to budget for advertising promotions on a continual and season specific basis.

We will start our business with our known personal referral contacts and then continue our campaign to develop recognition among other Medical professional groups and organizations. We will develop and maintain a database of our contacts in the field. We will work to maintain and exploit our existing relationships throughout the start-up process and then use our marketing tools to communicate with other potential referral sources.

The marketing strategy will create awareness, interest and appeal from our target market. Its ultimate purpose is to encourage repeat purchases and get customers to refer friends and professional contacts. To get referrals we will provide incentives and excellent service, and build relationships with clients by caring about what the client needs and wants to improve human resource utilization and productivity.

Our marketing strategy will revolve around two different types of media, flyers and a website. These two tools will be used to make clients aware of our broad range of medical equipment rental services. One focus of our marketing strategy will be to drive customers to our website for information about our leasing programs and equipment database search options.

A combination of local media and event marketing will be utilized. _____ (company name) will create an identity oriented marketing strategy with executions particularly in the local media. Our marketing strategy will utilize trade journal print ads, press releases, yellow page ads, flyers, and newsletter distribution. We will make effective use of direct response advertising, and include coupons for free consultations and equipment audits in all print ads.

We will use comment cards, newsletter sign-up forms and surveys to collect customer email addresses and feed our client relationship management (CRM) software system. This system will automatically send out, on a predetermined schedule, follow-up materials, such as article reprints, seminar invitations, email messages, surveys and e-newsletters. We will offset some of our advertising costs by asking our alliance partners to place ads in our newsletter.

Marketing Budget

Our marketing budget will be a flexible $_____ per quarter. The marketing budget can be allocated in any way that best suits the time of year.

Marketing budget per quarter:

Newspaper Ads	$_____	Radio advertisement	$_____	
Web Page	$_____	Customer raffle	$_____	
Direct Mail	$_____	Sales Brochure	$_____	
Home Shows	$_____	Seminars	$_____	

170

Superpages	$ _____	Google Adwords	$ _____
Giveaways	$ _____	Vehicle Signs	$ _____
Business Cards	$ _____	Flyers	$ _____
Labels/Stickers	$ _____	Videos/DVDs	$ _____
Samples	$ _____	Newsletter	$ _____
Bench Signs	$ _____	Email Campaigns	$ _____
Sales Reps Comm.	$ _____	Other	

Total: $ _____

Our objective in setting a marketing budget has been to keep it between ____ (5?) and ____ (7?) percent of our estimated annual gross sales.

Video Marketing

We will link to our website a series of YouTube.com based video clips that talk about our range of medical equipment rental services, and demonstrate our expertise with certain medical practice needs. We will create business marketing videos that are both entertaining and informational, and improve our search engine rankings.

The video will include:
- **Client testimonials** - We will let our best customers become our instant sales force because people will believe what others say about us more readily than what we say about ourselves.
- **Product Demonstrations** - Train and pre-sell our potential clients on our most popular services by talking about and showing them. Often, our potential clients don't know the full range and depth of our services because we haven't taken the adequate time to show and tell them.
- **Include Business Website Address**
- **Owner Interview:** Explanation of company mission statement

and unique selling proposition.
- **Record Frequently Asked Questions Sessions** - We will answer questions that we often get, and anticipate objections we might get and give great reasons to convince potential clients that we are the best Medical Equipment Rental Company in the area.
- **Include a Call to Action** - We have the experience and the know-how to supply your practice with equipment needed on a temporary or permanent basis. So call us, right now, and let's get started.
- **Seminar** - Include a portion of a seminar on how to evaluate medical equipment rental companies.
- **Comment on industry trends and product news** - We will appear more in-tune and knowledgeable in our market if we can talk about what's happening in our medical equipment industry and local marketplace.

Resources: www.businessvideomarketing.tv
www.hotpluto.com
www.hubspot.com/video-marketing-kit
www.youtube.com/user/mybusinessstory

Analytics Report
http://support.google.com/youtube/bin/static.py?hl=en&topic=1728599&guide=1   714169&page=guide.cs

Note: Refer to Video Marketing Tips in rear marketing worksheets section.

Examples:
https://www.youtube.com/channel/UCI7NNHleqSRJUQpadBt3p5g
http://www.youtube.com/watch?v=PLpre76mSmM

Top 12 places where we will share our marketing videos online:
YouTube
www.youtube.com
This very popular website allows you to log-in and leave comments and ratings on the videos. You can also save your favorite videos and allows you to tag posted videos. This makes it easier for your videos to come up in search engines.
Google Video

http://video.google.com/

A video hosting site. Google Video is not just focused on sharing videos online, but this is also a market place where you can buy the videos you find on this site using Google search engine.

Yahoo! Video

http://video.yahoo.com/

Uploading and sharing videos is possible with Yahoo Video!. You can find several types of videos on their site and you can also post comments and ratings for the videos.

Revver

http://www.revver.com/

This website lets you earn money through ads on your videos and you will have a 50/50 profit split with the website. Another great deal with Revver is that your fans who posted your videos on their site can also earn money.

Blip.tv   http://blip.tv/

Allows viewers to stream and download the videos posted on their website. You can also use Creative Commons licenses on your videos posted on the website. This allows you to decide if your videos should be attributed, restricted for commercial use and be used under specific terms.

Vimeo

http://www.vimeo.com/

This website is family safe and focuses on sharing private videos. The interface of the website is similar to some social networking sites that allow you to customize your profile page with photos from Flickr and embeddable player. This site allows users to socialize through their videos.

Metacafe

http://www.metacafe.com/

This video sharing site is community based. You can upload short-form videos and share it to the other users of the website. Metacafe has its own system called VideoRank that ranks videos according to the viewer reactions and features the most popular among the viewers.

ClipShack

http://www.clipshack.com/

Like most video sharing websites you can post comments on the videos and even tag some as your favorite. You can also share the

videos on other websites through the html code from ClipShack and even sending it through your email.
Veoh
> http://www.veoh.com/

You can rent or sell your videos and keep the 70% of the sales price. You can upload a range of different video formats on Veoh and there is no limit on the size and length of the file. However when your video is over 45 minutes it has to be downloaded before the viewer can watch it.

Jumpcut http://download.cnet.com/JumpCut/3000-18515_4-10546353.html

Jumpcut allows its users to upload videos using their mobile phones. You will have to attach the video captured from your mobile phone to an email. It has its own movie making wizard that helps you familiarize with the interface of the site.

DailyMotion
> www.dailymotion.com

As one of the leading sites for sharing videos, Dailymotion attracts over 114 million unique monthly visitors (source: comScore, May 2014) 1.2 billion videos views worldwide (source: internal). Offers the best content from users, independent content creators and premium partners. Using the most advanced technology for both users and content creators, provides high-quality and HD video in a fast, easy-to-use online service that also automatically filters infringing material as notified by content owners.

Offering 32 localized versions, their mission is to provide the best possible entertainment experience for users and the best marketing opportunities for advertisers, while respecting content protection.

CitySquares

A leader in video marketing and advertising solutions for local businesses working to expand their online exposure and generate new prospective customers. Building innovative video applications that deliver the best ways for local businesses to connect with customers. Their full-service video marketing platform makes it easy and affordable for any small or medium sized business to utilize video to grow their online brand. Services include Video Creation and Online Distribution, YouTube In-Stream Advertising, Facebook Advertising and Lead Capturing, and CitySquares Local Business Directory, which is fast becoming the largest video business directory on the web.

Business Cards
Our business card will include our company logo, complete contact information, name, photo and title, association logos, slogan or markets serviced, licenses and certifications. The center of our bi-fold card will contain a listing of the medical equipment rental services we offer. We will give out multiple business cards to friends, family members, business associates and to each customer, upon the completion of the sales presentation or rental service. We will also distribute business cards in the following ways:
1.   Attached to invoices, surveys, flyers and sales brochures.
2.   Included in seminar handout packages.
3.   We will leave a stack of business cards in a Lucite holder with the local Chamber   of Commerce and any medical businesses offering free counter placement.

We will use fold-over cards because they will enable us to list all of our services and complete contact instructions on the inside of the card. We will also give magnetic business cards to new clients for ease of posting.

We will place the following referral discount message on the back of our business cards:
         - Our business is very dependent upon referrals. If you have associates who could   benefit from our quality services, please write your name at the bottom of this card and give it to them. When your friend presents this card upon their first visit, he or she will be entitled to 10% off discount. And, on your next   invoice, you will also get a 10% discount as a thank you for your referral.
Resource: www.vistaprint.com

Direct Mail Package
To build name recognition and to announce the opening of our Medical Equipment Rental Company, we will offer a mail package consisting of a tri-fold brochure containing a medical equipment audit coupon to welcome our new customers. We plan to make a mailing to local subscribers of Medical Practice Journals. From those identified local customers, we shall ask them to complete a survey

and describe their perception of our services, and any leasing arrangements or maintenance services they would like to see added. Those customers returning completed surveys would receive a premium (giveaway) gift.

Trade Shows

We will exhibit at as many local trade shows per year as possible. These include Professional Association Trade Shows, health fairs and business spot-lights with our local Chamber of Commerce, and more. The objective is to get our company name and service availability out to as many people as possible. We will do our homework and ask other medical equipment companies where they exhibit their services. When exhibiting at a trade show, we will put our best foot forward and represent ourselves as professionals. We will be open, enthusiastic, informative and courteous. We will exhibit our medical equipment rental services with sales brochures, logo-imprinted giveaways, a photo book for people to browse through and a computer to run our video presentation through. We will use a 'free drawing' for a gift basket prize and a sign-in sheet to collect names and email addresses. We will also develop a questionnaire or survey that helps us to assemble an ideal customer profile and qualify the leads we receive. We will train our booth attendants to answer all type of questions and to handle objections. We will also seek to present educational seminars on hiring trends at the show to gain increased publicity, and name and expertise recognition. Most importantly, we will develop and implement a follow-up program to stay-in-touch with prospects.

Resources: www.tsnn.com   www.expocentral.com
             www.acshomeshow.com/
         www.EventsInAmerica.com
             www.Biztradeshows.com

Our Proposed Trade Show Schedule
MedAssets Healthcare Business Summit
Location: Las Vegas, Nevada   Web site: www.medassets.com

Clinical Laboratory Management Association ThinkLab'11 (CLMA)
Location: Baltimore, Maryland   Web site:www.clma.org

Event: Health Connect Partners Hospital O.R. and Surgery Conference
Location: Miami, Florida   Web site: www.hlthcp.com/

Event: Academy of Medical-Surgical Nurses (AMSN)
Location: Boston, Massachusetts   Web site: www.amsn.org

Event: Emergency Nurses Association (ENA)
Location: Tampa, Florida   Web site: www.ena.org

Event: Health Connect Partners Fall Pharmacy Conference
Location: Phoenix, Arizona   Web site: www.hlthcp.com/

Event: National Conference on Correctional Healthcare (NCCHC)
Location: Baltimore, Maryland   Web site: www.ncchc.org

Event: American Academy of Physician Assistants Annual PA Conference
Location: Las Vegas, Nevada   Website: www.aapa.org

Event: National Society for Histotechnology
Location: Cincinnati, OH   Website: www.nsh.org/content/registration

Event: Society of Diagnostic Medical Sonographers
Location: Atlanta, GA   Website: www.sdms.org/meetings/default.asp

Bench Ads
These ads will provide us with an affordable way to improve our visibility.
Resource: www.BenchAds.net

Networking
Networking will be a key to success because referrals and alliances formed can help to improve our community image and keep our company growing. We will strive to build long-term mutually beneficial relationships with our networking contacts and join the following types of organizations:
1.   We will form a LeTip Chapter to exchange business leads.

2. We will join the local BNI.com referral exchange group.
3. We will join the Chamber of Commerce to further corporate relationships.
4. We will join the Rotary Club, Lions Club, Kiwanis Club, Church Groups, etc.
5. We will do volunteer work for American Heart Assoc. and Habitat for Humanity.
6. We will become an affiliated member of the local board of Realtors and the Women's Council of Realtors.
7. We will visit local chapters of Medical associations or groups, such as the American Academy of Family Practice.

We will use our metropolitan _____ (city) Chamber of Commerce to target prospective medical practice contacts. We will mail letters to each prospect describing our medical equipment rental services. We will follow-up with phone calls.

We will hold a Chamber business mixer in our facility. This popular networking event will offer the following two benefits:
1. Many business colleagues will visit our new facility.
2. Some attendees may want to rent/purchase items.
Resource: http://www.uschamber.com/chambers/directory/default

Examples:
http://poplarbluffchamber.org/t-o-s-home-medical-equipment

Newsletter

We will develop a one-page newsletter to be handed out to customers to take with them as they attend our seminars or visit our facilities or trade show booths. The monthly newsletter will be used to build our brand and update clients on equipment acquisitions and special promotions. The newsletter will be produced in-house and for the cost of paper and computer time. We will include the following types of information:
1. Our involvement with charitable events.
2. New Rental Equipment Introductions
3. Featured employee/customer of the month.
4. New medical equipment industry technologies and trends.

5. Customer endorsements/testimonials.
6. Classified ads from local sponsors and suppliers.
7. Announcements / Upcoming seminar events.

Resources: Microsoft Publisher   www.getresponse.com

We will adhere to the following newsletter writing guidelines:
1. We will provide content that is of real value to our subscribers.
2. We will provide solutions to our subscriber's problems or questions.
3. We will communicate regularly on a weekly basis.
4. We will create HTML Messages that look professional and allow us to track how many people click on our links and/or open our emails.
5. We will not pitch our business opportunity in our Ezine very often.
6. We will focus our marketing dollars on building our Ezine subscriber list.
7. We will focus on relationship building and not the conveying of a sales message.
8. We will vary our message format with videos, articles, checklists, quotes, pictures and charts.
9. We will recommend occasionally affiliate products in some of our messages to help cover our marketing costs.
10. We will consistently follow the above steps to build a database of qualified prospects and customers.

Resources:
www.constantcontact.com
www.mailchimp.com
http://lmssuccess.com/10-reasons-online-business-send-regular-newsletter-customers/
www.smallbusinessmiracles.com/how/newsletters/
www.fuelingnewbusiness.com/2010/06/01/combine-email-marketing-and-social-media- for-ad-agency-new-business/

Vehicle Signs

We will place magnetic and vinyl signs on our vehicles and include our company name, phone number, company slogan and website address, if possible. We will create a cost-effective moving billboard with high-quality, high-resolution vehicle wraps. We will wrap a portion of the vehicle or van to deliver excellent marketing exposure. Resource: http://www.fastsigns.com/

Design Tips:
1. Avoid mixing letter styles and too many different letter sizes.
2. Use the easiest to recognize form of your logo.
3. The standard background is white.
4. Do not use a background color that is the same as or close to your vehicle color.
5. Choose colors that complement your logo colors.
6. Avoid the use too many colors.
7. Use dark letter colors on a light background or the reverse.
8. Use easy to read block letters in caps and lower case.
9. Limit content to your business name, slogan, logo, phone number and website- address.
10. Include your license number if required by law.
11. Magnetic signs are ideal for door panels (material comes on 24" wide rolls).
12. Graphic vehicle window wraps allow the driver to still see out.
13. Keep your message short so people driving by can read it at a glance.
14. Do not use all capital letters.
15. Be sure to include your business name, phone number, slogan and web address.

Vehicle Wraps

Vehicle wrapping will be one of our preferred marketing methods. According to company research, wrapped vehicles have more impact than billboards, create a positive image for the company and prompt the public to remember the words and images featured in the company's branding. Vehicle wrapping is also an inexpensive marketing strategy. A typical truck wrap costs about $2,500, and is a one-time payment for an ad that spans the life of a truck's lease.

Advertising Wearables

We will give all preferred club members an eye-catching T-shirt or sweatshirt with our company name and logo printed across the garment to wear about town. We will also give them away as a thank you for customer referral activities. We will ask all employees to wear our logo-imprinted shirts.

Stage Events

We will stage events to become known in our community. This is essential to attracting referrals. We will schedule regular events, such as medical conventions, seminar talks, health fairs, demonstrations, catered open house events and fundraisers. We will offer seminars through trade organizations to promote the benefits of our medical equipment rental services. We will use event registration forms, our website and an event sign-in sheet to collect the names and email addresses of all attendees. This database will be used to feed our automatic customer relationship follow-up program and newsletter service.

Resources:
www.eventbrite.com

Sales Brochures

The sales brochure will enable us to make a solid first impression when pursing business from commercial accounts and private practice clients. Our sales brochure will include the following contents and become a key part of our sales presentation folder and direct mail package:

- Contact Information
- Business Description
- Customer Testimonials
- List of Services/Benefits
- Competitive Advantages
- Owner Resume/Bio
- Coupon
- Map of office location.
- Business Hours
- Industry Trends

Examples:
https://www.uhs.com/wp-content/uploads/Rental_Brochure_FINAL-1.pdf

Sales Brochure Design
1. Speak in Terms of Our Prospects Wants and Interests.
2. Focus on all the Benefits, not Just Features.
3. Put the company logo and Unique Selling Proposition together to reinforce the fact that your company is different and better than the competition.
4. Include a special offer, such as a discount, a free report, a sample, or a free trial to increase the chances that the brochure will generate sales.

We will incorporate the following Brochure Design Guidelines:
1. Design the brochure to achieve a focused set of objectives (marketing of programs) with a target market segment (residential vs. commercial).
2. Tie the brochure design to our other marketing materials with colors, logo, fonts and formatting.
3. List capabilities and how they benefit clients.
4. Demonstrate what we do and how we do it differently.
5. Define the value proposition of our engineering installing services
6. Use a design template that reflects your market positioning strategy.
7. Identify your key message (unique selling proposition)
8. List our competitive advantages.
9. Express our understanding of client needs and wants.
10. Use easy to read (scan) headlines, subheadings, bullet points, pictures, etc.
11. Use a logo to create a visual branded identity.
12. The most common and accepted format for a brochure is a folded A3 (= 2 x A4), which gives 4 pages of information.
13. Use a quality of paper that reflects the image we want to project.
14. Consistently stick to the colors of our corporate style.

15. Consider that colors have associations, such as green colors are associated with the environment and enhance an environmental image.

16. Illustrations will be appropriate and of top quality and directly visualize the product assortment, product application and production facility.

17. The front page will contain the company name, logo, the main application of your product or service and positioning message or Unique Selling Proposition.

18. The back page will be used for testimonials or references, and contact details.

Sales Presentation Folder Contents

1.	Resumes	2.	Staff Photos
3.	Contract/Application	4.	Frequently Asked Questions
5.	Sales Brochure	6.	Business Cards
7.	Testimonials/References	8.	Program Descriptions
9.	Informative Articles	10.	Referral Program
11.	Company Overview	12.	Operating Policies
13.	Order Forms		

Coupons

Research indicates that coupons generate more than a third of online searches. We will use coupons with limited time expirations to get prospects to try our leasing programs. We will also accept the coupons of our competitors to help establish new client relationships. We will run ads directing people to our Web site for a $___ coupon certificate or a free equipment audit consultation. Research indicates that we can use our coupons to spark online searches of our website and drive sales. This will help to draw in new clients and collect e-mail addresses for the distribution of a monthly newsletter. We will include a coupon with each sale, or send them by mail to our mailing list.

Examples:
https://www.retailmenot.com/view/discountmedicalsupplies.com
http://www.goodsearch.com/medical-equipment-category/coupons
http://www.northsideoxygen.com/coupons.htm

We will use coupons selectively to accomplish the following:
1. To introduce a new product or service.
2. To attract loyal customers away from the competition
3. To prevent customer defection to a new competitor.
4. To help celebrate a special event.
5. To thank customers for a large order and ensure a repeat order within a certain limited time frame.

Types of Coupons:
1. Courtesy Coupons   Rewards for repeat business
2. Cross-Marketing Coupons Incentive to try other products/services.
3. Companion Coupon   Bring a friend incentive.

Resources: http://www.google.com/offers/business/how-it-works.html

Websites like Groupon.com, LivingSocial, Eversave, and BuyWithMe sell discount vouchers for services ranging from custom _____ to _____ consultations. Best known is Chicago-based Groupon. To consumers, discount vouchers promise substantial savings — often 50% or more. To merchants, discount vouchers offer possible opportunities for price discrimination, exposure to new customers, online marketing, and "buzz." Vouchers are more likely to be profitable for merchants with low marginal costs, who can better accommodate a large discount and for patient merchants, who place higher value on consumers' possible future return visits.
Examples:
https://www.groupon.com/coupons/stores/discountmedicalsupplies.com

Cross-Promotions
We will develop and maintain partnerships with local businesses that

cater to the needs of our customers, such as insurance companies, laboratories, and adult daycare centers, and conduct cross-promotional marketing campaigns. These cross-promotions will require the exchanging of customer mailing lists and endorsements.

Premium Giveaways
We will distribute logo-imprinted promotional products at events, also known as giveaway premiums, to foster top-of-mind awareness (www.promoideas.org). These items include logo-imprinted T-shirts, business cards with magnetic backs, mugs with contact phone number, drink recipe booklets and calendars that feature important celebration date reminders.

Local Newspaper Ads
We will use these ads to announce the opening of our company and get our name established. We will adhere to the rule that frequency and consistency of message are essential. We will include a list of the positions we are looking to fill, and our top specialty medical equipment rental services and benefits. We will include a coupon to track the response in zoned editions of Community Newsletters and Newspapers. We will also submit public relations and informative articles to improve our visibility and establish our rental expertise and trustworthiness. These publications include the following:
1. Neighborhood Newsletters
2. Local Chamber of Commerce Newsletter
3. Realtor Magazines

Resource: Hometown News
  www.hometownnews.com
  Pennysaver
  www.pennysaverusa.com

Publication Type   Ad Size   Timing   Circulation Section   Fee

Article Submissions

We will pitch articles to medical and hospital trade journals, local newspapers, business magazines and internet articles directories to help establish our specialized expertise and improve our visibility. Hyperlinks will be placed within written articles and can be clicked on to take the customer to another webpage within our website or to a totally different website. These clickable links or hyperlinks will be keywords or relevant words that have meaning to our medical equipment rental business. We will create keyword-rich article titles that match the most commonly searched keywords for our topic. In fact, we will create a position whose primary function is to link our company with opportunities to be published in local publications.

Publishing requires an understanding of the following publisher needs:
1. Review of good work.
2. Editor story needs.
3. Article submission process rules
4. Quality photo portfolio
5. Exclusivity requirements.
6. Target market interests

Our Article Submission Package will include the following:
1. Well-written materials
2. Good Drawings
3. High-quality Photographs
4. Well-organized outline.

Examples of General Publishing Opportunities:
1. Document a new solution to old problem
2. Publish a research study
3. Addiction prevention advice
4. Present a different viewpoint
5. Introduce a local angle on a hot topic.
6. Reveal a new trend.
7. Share specialty niche expertise.
8. Share health benefits

Examples of Specific Article Titles:

1. Everything You Ever Wanted to Know About the Medical Equipment Leasing   Options
2. How to Evaluate and Compare Medical Equipment Rental Companies
3. Hospital Equipment Rentals and Quality of Care.
4. Trends in medical equipment technologies
5. A Study of Medical Equipment Practice Problems
6. The Role of Medical Equipment in Improving Healthcare Quality.
7. The Advantages Of Working With A Medical Equipment Rental Company
8. What You Need to Know When Choosing a Medical Equipment Rental Company
9. Medical Equipment Rental Company–Business Due Diligence Tips
10. The ROI of Medical Equipment Rentals
11. Unlocking the Secrets to Successful Medical Equipment Planning
      Ex: www.ecri.org/events/Pages/Medical-Equipment-Planning.aspx
12. How to Make the Renting vs Buying Medical Equipment Decision
      www.healthblurbs.com/renting-vs-buying-medical-equipment/

Write Articles With a Closing Author Resource Box or Byline
1. Author Name with credential titles.
2. Explanation of area of expertise.
3. Mention of a special offer.
4. A specific call to action
5. A Call to Action Motivator
6. All possible contact information
7. Helpful Links
8. Link to Company Website.

Article Objectives:
   Article Topic   Target Audience
   Target Date

Article Tracking Form

Subject	Publication Target Date	Target Audience	Business Development	Resources Needed

Possible Magazines to submit articles on healthcare rental include:

1. The Wall Street Journal
2. The New York Times
3. HealthLeaders Media
4. Modern Healthcare
5. Medical Economics
6. New England Journal of Medicine
7. Columbia News Service
8. Managed Care Weekly

Medical Equipment Locator
www.melocator.com

A monthly magazine that provides a comprehensive information on new, used and reconditioned medical equipment used in hospitals. This is a US based magazine, which is especially designed to serve the needs of more than 32,000 qualified industry professionals, end users and marketing specialists involved in medical industry. The magazine is an informational source for U.S. hospitals, medical groups, medical clinics, veterinarian hospitals, medical laboratories, surgery centers, medical equipment dealers, re manufacturers, and repairers.

Surgical Products Magazine
http://www.surgprodmag.com/scripts/default.asp

A leading magazine, published and printed twelve times in a year by Advantage Business Media. It is a US based magazine, which has a circulation of 71,000. This magazine is highly useful for surgeons, anesthesiologists and department heads of emergency or operating rooms. It provides news about medical or surgical equipment, supplies and services. Every month, it publishes information about latest products, technology solutions, and industry insights pertaining to surgical/healthcare field.

International Medical Devices Magazine
http://www.imdmagazine.com/
An international magazine that features information on developments and trends in medical devices design, engineering, manufacturing, materials & processes around the world.

Resources: Writer's Market
               www.writersmarket.com
                       Directory of Trade Magazines
               www.techexpo.com/tech_mag.html

Internet article directories include:
http://ezinearticles.com/
        http://www.mommyshelpercommunity.com
http://www.wahm-articles.com
        http://www.ladypens.com/
http://www.articlecity.com
        http://www.amazines.com
http://www.articledashboard.com
        http://www.submityourarticle.com/articles
http://www.webarticles.com
        http://www.articlecube.com
http://www.article-buzz.com   http://www.free-articles-zone.com
www.articletogo.com   http://www.content-articles.com
http://article-niche.com
        http://superpublisher.com
www.internethomebusinessarticles.com   http://www.site-reference.com
http://www.articlenexus.com   www.articlebin.com
http://www.articlefinders.com

189

www.articlesfactory.com
http://www.articlewarehouse.com
http://www.easyarticles.com
http://ideamarketers.com/
//groups.yahoo.com/group/article_announce
http://clearviewpublications.com/articles.com
http://www.goarticles.com/
www.authorconnection.com/
http://www.webmasterslibrary.com/
www.businesstoolchest.com
http://www.connectionteam.com
women.com/submitarticle.htm
http://www.MarketingArticleLibrary.com
http://www.dime-co.com
http://www.allwomencentral.com
seek.com
http://www.reprintarticles.com
http://www.articlestreet.com
http://www.articlepeak.com
http://www.simplysearch4it.com
http://www.zongoo.com
http://www.mainstreetmom.com
http://www.valuablecontent.com
http://www.article99.com
professionals.com

www.buzzle.com
www.isnare.com

www.ebusiness-articles.com

www.digital-
www.searchwarp.com
www.articleshaven.com
www.marketing-

www.articles411.com
www.articleshelf.com
www.articlesbase.com
www.articlealley.com
www.selfgrowth.com
www.LinkGeneral.com
www.articleavenue.com
www.virtual-

Classified Ad Placement Opportunities

The following free classified ad sites, will enable our Medical Equipment Rental Company to thoroughly describe the benefits of our using our services:

1.	**Craigslist.org**	2.	Ebay Classifieds
3.	Classifieds.myspace.com	4.	KIJIJI.com
5.	//Lycos.oodle.com Webclassifieds.us	6.	
7.	USFreeAds.com	8.	www.oodle.com
9.	Backpage.com stumblehere.com	10.	

11.	Classifiedads.com	12.	gumtree.com
13.	Inetgiant.com	14.	www.sell.com
15.	Freeadvertisingforum.com Classifiedsforfree.com	16.	
17.	www.olx.com	18.	www.isell.com
19.	Base.google.com	20.	www.epage.com
21.	Chooseyouritem.com www.adpost.com	22.	
23.	Adjingo.com	24.	Kugli.com
25.	global-free-classified-ads.com free4uclassifieds.com	26.	
27.	Salespider.com www.adsonmap.com	28.	
29.	www.usnetads.com Sawitonline.com	30.	
31.	www.freeclassifieds.com www.openclassifiedsads.com	32.	
33.	www.jwiz.com www.ClassifiedsGiant.com	34.	
35.	http://klondajk.us http://www.dotmed.com/	36.	

Sample Craigslist Classified Ad:
Medical Equipment Rental Company
WE RENT ALL TYPES OF MEDICAL EQUIPEMENT
IF THEY MAKE IT, WE WILL TRACK IT DOWN, AND RENT IT
DAILY, WEEKLY, MONTHLY RENTAL ARRANGEMENTS
ALSO RENT TO OWN
OUR INVENTORY INCLUDES: BEDS, LIFTS, LIFT CHAIRS, SCOOTERS, WHEELCHAIRS ALL SIZES, POWER WHEELCHAIRS, OXYGEN, PORTABLE OXYGEN, WALKERS, CPAP, TRANSPORT CHAIRS, BED ALARMS, HOT AND COLD THERAPY, KNEE WALKERS, PATIENT LIFTS, NEBULIZERS.
24/7 SERVICE WE DELIVER .....FEE DEPENDENT ON

DISTANCE.
Satisfaction Guaranteed.
Office Location: _____

Contact us: _____ Email us: _____
_____
Visit us online: _____

Two-Step Direct Response Classified Advertising
We will use 'two-step direct response advertising' to motivate readers to take a step or action that signals that we have their permission to begin marketing to them in step two.
Our objective is to build a trusting relationship with our prospects by offering a free unbiased, educational report in exchange for permission to continue the marketing process. This method of advertising has the following benefits:
1. Shorter sales cycle.   2. Eliminates need for cold calling.
3. Establishes expert reputation.   4. Better qualifies prospects
5. Process is very trackable.   6. Able to run smaller ads.

Sample Two Step Lead Generating Classified Ad:
FREE Report Reveals "Top 10 Mistakes to Avoid When Leasing Medical Equipment"
Or….. "Effective Medical Equipment Inspection Tips".
Call 24 hour recorded message and leave your name and address. Your report will be sent out immediately.
Note: The respondent has shown they have an interest in our Medical Equipment Rental Company services. We will also include a section in the report on our medical equipment rental services and our complete contact information, along with a time limited coupon and sales brochure.

Yellow Page Ads
Research indicates that the use of the traditional Yellow Page Book is declining, but that new residents or people who don't have many personal acquaintances will look to the Yellow Pages to establish a

list of potential businesses to call upon. Even a small 2" x 2" boxed ad can create awareness and attract the desired target client, above and beyond the ability of a simple listing. We will use the following design concepts:

1. We will use a headline to sell people on what is unique about our rental services.
2. We will include a service guarantee to improve our credibility.
3. We will include a coupon offer and a tracking code to monitor the response rate and decide whether to increase or decrease our ad size in subsequent years.
4. We will choose an ad size equal to that of our competitors, and evaluate the response rate for future insertion commitments.
5. We will include our hours of operation, motto or slogan and logo.
6. We will include our key competitive advantages.
7. We will list under the same categories as our competitors.
8. We will use some bold lettering to make our ad standout.
9. We will utilize yellow books that also offer an online dimension.

Resource: www.superpages.com   www.yellowpages.com
Ex: http://www.yellowpages.com/miami-fl/medical-equipment-supplies

Ad Information:
Book Title: _____ Coverage Area: _____
Yearly Fee: $_____
Ad Size: _____ page   Renewal date: _____
Contact: _____

Cable Television Advertising

Cable television will offer us more ability to target certain market niches or demographics with specialty programming. We will use our marketing research survey to determine which cable TV channels our customers are watching. It is expected that many watch Medical themed programs. Our plan is to choose the audience we want, and to hit them often enough to entice them to take action. We will also take advantage of the fact that we will be able to pick the

specific upper income areas we want our commercial to air. Ad pricing will be dependent upon the number of households the network reaches, the ratings the particular show has earned, contract length and the supply and demand for a particular network.
Resource:
Spot Runner   www.spotrunner.com
Television Advertising
          http://televisionadvertising.com/faq.htm

Ad Information:
          Length of ad "spot": ___ seconds   Development costs: $____ (onetime fee)
          Length of campaign: __ (#) mos.   Runs per month: Three times per day
          Cost per month.: $_____   Total campaign cost: $_____.

Radio Advertising

We will use non-event based radio advertising. This style of campaign is best suited for non-promotional sales driven retail businesses, such as our medical equipment rental company. We will utilize a much smaller schedule of ads on a consistent long-range basis (48 to 52 weeks a year) with the We will use non-event based radio advertising. This style of campaign is best suited for non-sales driven retail businesses, such as our company. We will utilize a much smaller schedule of ads on a consistent long-range basis (48 to 52 weeks a year) with the objective of continuously maintaining top-of-mind-awareness. This will mean maintaining a sufficient level of awareness to be either the number one or number two choice when a triggering-event, such as an _____, moves the customer into the market for rental services and forces "a consumer choice" about which company in the consumer's perception might help them the most. This consistent approach will utilize only one ad each week day (260 days per year) and allow our company to cost-effectively keep our message in front of consumers once every week day. The ad copy for this non-event campaign, called a positioning message, will not be time-sensitive. It will define and differentiate our business' "unique market position", and will be repeated for a year.

Note: On the average, listeners spend over 3.5 hours per day with radio.

Radio will give us the ability to target our audience, based on radio formats, such as news-talk, classic rock and the oldies. Radio will also be a good way to get repetition into our message, as listeners tend to be loyal to stations and parts of the day.

1. We will use radio advertising to direct prospects to our Web site, advertise a limited time promotion or call for an informational brochure on staffing.
2. We will try to barter our services for radio ad spots.
3. We will use a limited-time offer to entice first-time customers to use our rental services.
4. We will explore the use of on-air community bulletin boards to play our public announcements about community sponsored events.
5. We will also make the radio station aware of our expertise in the Medical rentalfield and our availability for interviews.
6. Our choice of stations will be driven by the market research information we collect via our surveys.
7. We will capitalize on the fact that many stations now stream their programming on the internet and reach additional local and even national audiences, and if online listeners like what they hear in our streaming radio spot, they can click over to our website.
8. Our radio ads will use humor, sounds, compelling music or unusual voices to grab attention.
9. Our spots will tell stories or present situations that our target audience can relate to, such as the growing demand for temporary Medical staffing,
10. We will make our call to action, a website address or vanity phone number, easy to remember and tie it in with our company name or message.
11. We will approach radio stations about buying their unsold advertising space for deep discounts. (Commonly known at radio stations' as "Run of Station")

On radio, this might mean very early in the morning or late at night. We will talk to our advertising representatives and see what discounts they can offer when   one of those empty spaces comes open.

Resources: Radio Advertising Bureau   www.RAB.com
                  Radio Locator   www.radio-locator.com
                  Radio Directory
          www.radiodirectory.com

Ad Information:
          Length of ad "spot": ___ seconds   Development costs: $____ (onetime fee)
          Length of campaign: __ (#) mos.   Runs per month: Three times per day
          Cost per month.: $_____   Total campaign cost: $_____.

Blog Talk Radio

National Public Radio (www.NPR.org) plays host to a radio program called _____. The program features _____ (type of experts) who talk and blog about medical equipment usage tips. This will help to establish our _____ expertise and build the trust factor with potential clients. Even if we can't get our own nationally syndicated talk show, we will try to make guest appearances and try our hand with podcasting by using apps like Spreaker or joining podcasting communities like BlogTalkRadio.

Resources:
National Public Radio   www.npr.org
Spreaker   http://www.spreaker.com/
Blog Talk Radio   http://www.blogtalkradio.com/

With BlogTalkRadio, people can either host their own live talk radio show with any phone and a computer or listen to thousands of new shows created daily.

Press Release Overview:

We will use market research surveys to determine the media outlets that our demographic customers read and then target them with press releases. We will draft a cover letter for our media kit that explains that we would like to have the newspaper print a story about the start-up of our new medical equipment rental business or a milestone that we have accomplished. And, because news releases may be delivered by feeds or on news services and various websites, we will create links from our news releases to content on our website. These links which will point to more information or a special offer, will drive our clients into the sales process. They will also increase search engine ranking on our site. We will follow-up each faxed package to the media outlet with a phone call to the lifestyle and employment section editors.

Media Kit
We will compile a media kit with the following items:
1. A pitch letter introducing our company and relevant impact newsworthiness for their readership.
2. A press release with helpful newsworthy story facts.
3. Biographical fact sheet or sketches of key personnel.
4. Listing of product and service features and benefits to customers.
5. Photos and digital logo graphics
6. Copies of media coverage already received.
7. Frequently Asked Questions (FAQ)
8. Customer testimonials
9. Sales brochure
10. Media contact information
11. URL links to these online documents instead of email attachments.
12. Our blog URL address.

Press Releases
We will use well-written press releases to not only catch a reader's attention, but also to clearly and concisely communicate our business' mission, goals and capabilities.
The following represents a partial list of some of the reasons we will issue a free press release on a regular basis:
1. Announce Grand Opening Event and the availability of leasing services.
2. Planned Open House Event
3 Addition of new product releases or service introduction.

4.   Support for a Non-profit Cause or other local event, such as a Blood Drive.
5.   Presentation of a free seminar or workshop on how to improve profitability with   medical equipment leasing arrangements.
6.   Report Market Research Survey Results
7.   Publication of an article or book on medical equipment technology trends.
8.   Receiving a Medical Equipment Association Award.
9.   Additional training/certification/licensing received.

Examples:
www.uhs.com/universal-hospital-services-to-hold-2017-second-quarter-earnings-call-on-   august-9/

We will use the following techniques to get our press releases into print:
1.   Find the right contact editor at a publication, that is, the editor who specializes in   healthcare issues.
2.   Understand the target publication's format, flavor and style and learn to think like   its readers to better tailor our pitch.
3.   Ask up front if the journalist is on deadline.
4.   Request a copy of the editorial calendar--a listing of targeted articles or subjects   broken down by month or issue date, to determine the issue best suited for the   content of our news release or article.
5.   Make certain the press release appeals to a large audience by reading a couple of   back issues of the publication we are targeting to familiarize ourselves with its   various sections and departments.
6.   Customize the PR story to meet the magazine's particular style.
7.   Avoid creating releases that look like advertising or self-promotion.
8.   Make certain the release contains all the pertinent and accurate information the   journalist will need to write the article and accurately answer the questions "who,   what, when, why and where".
9.   Include a contact name and telephone number for the reporter

to call for more information.

PR Distribution Checklist
We will send copies of our press releases to the following entities:
1. Send it to clients to show accomplishments.
2. Send to prospects to help prospects better know who you are and what you do.
3. Send it to vendors to strengthen the relationship and to influence referrals.
4. Send it to strategic partners to strengthen and enhance the commitment and support to our firm.
5. Send it to employees to keep them in the loop.
6. Send it to Employees' contacts to increase the firm's visibility exponentially.
7. Send it to elected officials who often provide direction for their constituents.
8. Send it to trade associations for maximum exposure.
9. Put copies in the lobby and waiting areas.
10. Put it on our Web site, to enable visitors to find out who we are and what our firm is doing, with the appropriate links to more detailed information.
11. Register the Web page with search engines to increase search engine optimization.
12. Put it in our press kit to provide members of the media background information about our firm.
13. Include it in our newsletter to enable easy access to details about company activities.
14. Include it in our brochure to provide information that compels the reader to contact our firm when in need of legal counsel.
15. Hand it out at trade shows and job fairs to share news with attendees and establish credibility.

Media List

Journalist	Interests	Organization	Contact Info

Distribution: www.1888PressRelease.com
www.ecomwire.com
www.prweb.com
www.WiredPRnews.com
www.PR.com
www.eReleases.com
www.24-7PressRelease.com
www.NewsWireToday.com
www.PRnewswire.com
www.onlinePRnews.com
www.digitaljournal.com
www.PRLog.org
www.businesswire.com
www.marketwire.com
www.primezone.com
www.primewswire.com
www.xpresspress.com/
www.ereleases.com/index.html
www.Mediapost.com

Journalist Lists: www.mastheads.org
www.easymedialist.com
www.helpareporter.com

Media Directories
Bacon's – www.bacons.com/   AScribe – www.ascribe.org/
Newspapers – www.newspapers.com/   Gebbie Press – www.gebbieinc.com/

Support Services
PR Web -   http://www.prweb.com
Yahoo News –   http://news.yahoo.com/
Google News –   http://news.google.com/

Resource:

HARO ("Help A Reporter Out")
www.helpareporter.com/

An online platform that provides journalists with a robust database of sources for upcoming stories. It also provides business owners and marketers with opportunities to serve as sources and secure valuable media coverage.

Direct Mail Campaign

A direct mail package consisting of a tri-fold brochure, letter of introduction, and reply card will be sent to a list of new businesses in _____ County. This list can be obtained from International Business Lists, Inc. (Chicago, IL) and is compiled from Secretary of State incorporation registrations, business license applications, announcements from newspaper clippings, and tax records. The letter will introduce _____ (company name), and describe our competitive advantages. The package will also include a promotional offer—the opportunity to try our Medical Equipment Rental Company services at a limited-time special reduced rate. Approximately ten days after the mailing, a telephone follow-up will be conducted to make sure the brochure was received, whether the client has any questions, or would like to schedule an appointment.

Our direct mail program will feature the following key components:

1. A call to action.
2. Test marketing using a limited 100-piece mailing.
3. A defined set of target markets.
4. A follow up phone call.
5. A personalized cover letter.
7. A special trial offer with an expiration date.

Resource:
www.directmailquotes.com/rfq/quote1.cfm?affiliate=14

Postcards

1. We will use a monthly, personalized, newsletter styled postcard, that includes medical equipment rental news to stay-in-touch with customers.
2. Postcards will offer cheaper mailing rates, staying power and attention grabbing graphics, but require repetition, like most other advertising methods.
3. We will develop an in-house list of potential clients for routine communications from open house events, seminar registrations, direct response ads, etc.

4. We will use postcards to encourage users to visit our website, and take advantage of a special offer or engage in online Medical profile matching.
5. We will grab attention and communicate a single-focus message in just a few words.
6. The visual elements of our postcard (color, picture, symbol) will be strong to help get attention and be directly supportive of the message.
7. We will facilitate a call to immediate action by prominently displaying our phone number and website address.
8. We will include a clear deadline, expiration date, limited quantity, or consequence of inaction that is connected to the offer to communicate immediacy and increase response.

Resources:
www.Postcardmania.com
www.purepostcards.com/

Flyers

1. We will seek permission to post flyers on the bulletin boards in local businesses, community centers, clinics, hospitals, job centers and colleges.
2. We will also insert flyers into our direct mailings.
3. We will use our flyers as part of a handout package at open house events and seminars.
4. The flyers will feature an introductory coupon to track return on investment.
5. The flyers will contain a listing of our service categories along with the benefits of temporary medical equipment rental services.

Resource:
www.stocklayouts.com

Referral Program

We understand the importance of setting up a formal referral network through contacts with the following characteristics:
1. We will give a premium reward based simply on people giving referral names on the registration form or customer

satisfaction survey.
2. Send an endorsed testimonial letter from a loyal customer to the referred prospect.
3. Include a separate referral form as a direct response device.
4. Provide a space on the response form for leaving positive comments that can be used to build a testimonial letter, that will be sent to each referral.
5. We will clearly state our incentive rewards, and terms and conditions.
6. We will distribute a newsletter to stay in touch with our clients and include articles about our referral program success stories.
7. We will encourage our staff at weekly meetings to seek referrals from their personal contacts.

Methods:
1. Always have ready a 30-second elevator speech that describes what you do and who you do it for.
2. Use a newsletter to keep our name in front of referrals sources.
3. Repeatedly demonstrate to referral sources that we are also thinking about their practice or business.
4. Regularly send referrals sources articles on unique yet important topics that might affect their businesses.
5. Use Microsoft Outlook to flag our contacts to remind us it is time to give them some form of personal attention.
6. Ask referral sources for referrals.
7. Get more work from a referral source by sending them work.
8. Immediately thank a referral source, even for the mere act of giving his name to a third party for consideration.
9. Remember referral sources with generous gift baskets and gift certificates.
10. Schedule regular lunches with former school classmates and new contacts.

We will offer an additional donation of $ _____ to any organization whose member use a referral coupon to become a client. The coupon will be paid for and printed in the organization's newsletter.

Referral Tracking Form

Referral Source Name	Actions to be Taken	Presently Target Referring Date Yes/No	No. of Clients Referred	Anticipated Revenue

Sample Referral Program

We want to show our appreciation to established customers and business network partners for their kind referrals to our business. ____ (company name) wants to reward our valued and loyal customers who support our Leasing Programs by implementing a new referral program. Ask any of our team members for referral cards to share with your family and friends to begin saving towards your next rental purchase. We will credit your account $___ (?) for each new customer you refer to us as well as give them 10% off their first visit. When they come for their first visit, they should present the card upon arrival. We will automatically set you up a referral account.

The Referral Details Are As Follows:

1. You will receive a $__ (?) credit for every customer that you refer for _____ (products/services). Credit will be applied to your referral account on their initial visit.
2. We will keep track of your accumulated reward dollars and at any time we can let you know the amount you have available for use in your reward account.
3. Each time you visit ____ (company name), you can use your referral dollars to pay up to 50% of your total charge that day
4. Referral dollars are not applicable towards the purchase of _____ products.
5. All referral rewards are for __products and cannot be used towards ___ services.

Referral Coupon Template

Company Name:
_____

Address:
_____
_____

Phone: _____ Website: _____

Print and present this coupon with your first order and the existing customer who referred you will receive a credit for $_____ .

Current customer	**Referred customer**
Name: _____	Name: _____
Address: _____	Address: _____
Phone: _____	Phone: _____
Email: _____	Email: _____

Date referred: _____

Office use only
Credit memo number:_____
Credit issued date: _____   Credit applied by: _____

Invite-A-Friend

We will setup an aggressive invite-a-friend referral program. We will encourage new members or newsletter subscribers, during their initial registration process, to upload and send an invitation to multiple contacts in their email address books. We will encourage them by providing an added incentive, such as a free _____.

Customer Reward/Loyalty Program

As a means of building business by word-of-mouth, customers will be encouraged and rewarded as repeat customers with rebates or special 24/7 service privileges.

Example:
ScooterPoints are the currency of our ENGAGE loyalty program.

Earn points every time you rent from us. Then redeem your points for great rewards like discounts, free rentals, and even a brand new mobility scooter!
Source: http://www.scootaround.com/loyalty-programs/engage-members

E-mail Marketing

We will use the following email marketing tips to build our mailing list database, improve communications, boost customer loyalty and attract new and repeat business.

1. Define our objectives as the most effective email strategies are those that offer value to our subscribers: either in the form of educational content or promotions. To drive sales, a promotional campaign is the best format. To create brand recognition and reinforce our expertise in our industry we will use educational newsletters.

2. A quality, permission-based email list will be a vital component of our email marketing campaign. We will ask customers and prospects for permission to add them to our list at every touch-point or use a sign-in sheet.

3. We will listen to our customers by using easy-to-use online surveys to ask specific questions about customers' preferences, interests and satisfaction.

4. We will send only relevant and targeted communications.

5. We will reinforce our brand to ensure recognition of our brand by using a recognizable name in the "from" line of our emails and including our company name, logo and a consistent design and color scheme in every email.

Resources:
https://www.inman.com/2017/06/05/4-tips-for-effective-email-marketing/
https://due.com/blog/ways-take-good-care-email-list/

Every ___ (five?) to ____ (six?) weeks, we will send graphically-rich, permission-based, personalized, email marketing messages to our list of customers who registered on our website or in the office. The emails will alert customers in a ___ (50?)-mile radius to sales and promotions as well as other local events sponsored by the company . This service will be provided by either ExactTarget.com or ConstantContact.com. The email will announce a special event and contain a short sales letter. The message will invite recipients to click on a link to the company website to checkout more information about the event, then print out the page and bring it with them to the event. The software offered by these two companies will automatically personalize each email with the customer's name. The software also provides detailed click-through behavior reports that will enable us to evaluate the success of each message. The software will also allow the company to dramatically scale back its direct mail efforts and associated costs. Our company will send a promotional e-mail about a promotion that the customer indicated was important to them in their preferred membership application. Each identified market segment will get notified of new medical equipment rental services, specials and offers based on past buying patterns and what they've clicked on in our previous e-newsletters or indicated on their surveys. The objective is to tap the right customer's need at the right time, with a targeted subject line and targeted content. Our general e-newsletter may appeal to most customers, but targeted mailings that reach out to our various audience segments will build even deeper relationships, and drive higher sales.

Resources:
www.constantcontact.com/pricing/email-marketing.jsp

Voice Broadcasting

A web-based voice broadcast system will provide a powerful platform to generate thousands of calls to clients and customers or create customizable messages to be delivered to specific individuals. Voice broadcasting and voice mail broadcast will allow our company to instantly send interactive phone calls with ease while managing the entire process right from the Web. We will instantly send alerts, notifications, reminders, GOTV - messages, and interactive surveys with ease right from the Web. The free VoiceShot account will guide us through the process of recording and storing our messages, managing our call lists, scheduling delivery as well as viewing and downloading real-time call and caller key press results. The voice broadcasting interface will guide us through the entire process with a Campaign Checklist as well as tips from the Campaign Expert. Other advanced features include recipient targeting, call monitoring, scheduling, controlling the rate of call delivery and customized text to speech (TTS). Resource: http://www.voiceshot.com/public/outboundcalls.asp

Facebook.com

We will use Facebook to move our businesses forward and stay connected to our customers in this fast-paced world. Content will be the key to staying in touch with our customers and keeping them informed. The content will be a rich mix of information, before and after photos, interactive questions, current trends and events, industry facts, education, promotions and specials, humor and fun. We will use the following step system to get customers from Facebook.com:

1. We will open a free Facebook account at Facebook.com.
2. We will begin by adding Facebook friends. The fastest way to do this is to allow Facebook to import our email addresses and send an invite out to all our customers.
3. We will post a video to get our customers involved with our Facebook page.
  We will post a video called "How to Plan a Successful Temporary Medical Equipment Leasing Program." The video will be first uploaded to YouTube.com and then simply be linked to our Facebook page. Video will be a great way to get people active and involved with our Facebook page.
4. We will send an email to our customers base that encourages them to check out the new video and to post their feedback about it on our Facebook page. Then we will provide a link driving customers to our Facebook page.
5. We will respond quickly to feedback, engage in the dialogue and add links to our response that direct the author to a structured mini-survey.
6. We will optimize our Facebook profile with our business keyword to make it an invaluable marketing tool and become the "go-to" expert in our industry

7. On a weekly basis, we will send out a message to all Facebook fans with a special offer.

8. We will use Facebook as a tool for sharing success stories and relate the ways in which we have helped our customers.

9. We will use Facebook Connect to integrate our Facebook efforts with our regular website to share our Facebook Page activity. This will also give us statistics about our website visitors, and add social interaction to our site.

10. We will use a company called Payvment (www.payvment.com) that has a storefront application for Facebook, that requires a Facebook fan page set up for our dealership. We will install the application on our page, set up the look and feel of the storefront using the tools that Payvment provides, enter information about our dealership, and then start loading products.

Resources:
http://www.facebook.com/advertising/
http://www.socialmediaexaminer.com/how-to-set-up-a-facebook-page-for-business/
http://smallbizsurvival.com/2009/11/6-big-facebook-tips-for-small-business.html

Examples:
https://www.facebook.com/AbilityMedicalSupply
https://www.facebook.com/medonecapital/

Facebook Profiles represent individual users and are held under a person's name. Each profile should only be controlled by that person. Each user has a wall, information tab, likes, interests, photos, videos and each individual can create events.

Facebook Groups are pretty similar to Fan Pages but are usually created for a group of people with a similar interest and they are wanting to keep their discussions private. The members are not usually looking to find out more about a business - they want to discuss a certain topic.

Facebook Fan Pages are the most viral of your three options. When someone becomes a fan of your page or comments on one of your posts, photos or videos, that is spread to all of their personal friends. This can be a great way to get your information out to lots of people...and quickly! In addition, one of the most valuable features of a business page is that you can send "updates" about new products and content to fans and your home building brand becomes more visible.

Facebook Live lets people, public figures and Pages share live video with their followers and friends on Facebook.
Source:
https://live.fb.com/about/
Resources:
https://www.facebook.com/business/a/Facebook-video-ads
http://smartphones.wonderhowto.com/news/facebook-is-going-all-live-video-streaming- your-phone-0170132/

Small Business Promotions
This group allows members to post about their products and services and is a public group designated as a Buy and Sell Facebook group.
Source:
https://www.facebook.com/groups/smallbusinesspronotions/
Resource:
https://www.facebook.com/business/a/local-business-promotion-ads
https://www.facebook.com/business/learn/facebook-create-ad-local-awareness
www.socialmediaexaminer.com/how-to-use-facebook-local-awareness-ads-to-target-customers/

Best social media marketing practices:
1. Assign daily responsibility for Facebook to a single person on your staff with an affinity for dialoguing .
2. Set expectations for how often they should post new content and how quickly they should respond to comments – usually within a couple hours.
3. Follow and like your followers when they seem to have a genuine interest in your area of health and wellness expertise.
4. Post on the walls of not only your own Facebook site, but

also on your most active, influential posters with the largest networks.
5. Periodically post a request for your followers to "like" your page.
6. Monitor Facebook posts to your wall and respond every two hours throughout your business day.

We will use Facebook in the following ways to market our Medical Equipment Rental Company:
1. Promote our blog posts on our Facebook page
2. Post a video of our service people in action.
3. Make time-sensitive offers during slow periods
4. Create a special landing page for coupons or promotional giveaways
5. Create a Welcome tab to display a video message from our owner.
    Resource: Pagemodo.
6. Support a local charity by posting a link to their website.
7. Thank our customers while promoting their businesses at the same time.
8. Describe milestone accomplishments and thank customers for their role.
9. Give thanks to corporate accounts.
10. Ask customers to contribute stories about _____ occurrences.
11. Use the built-in Facebook polling application to solicit feedback.
12. Use the Facebook reviews page to feature positive comments from customers, and to respond to negative reviews.
13. Introduce customers to our staff with resume and video profiles.
14. Create a photo gallery of unusual ____ (requests/jobs?) to showcase our expertise.

We will also explore location-based platforms like the following:
- FourSquare   - GoWalla
- Facebook Places   - Google Latitude

As a Medical Equipment Rental Company serving a local

community, we will appreciate the potential for hyper-local platforms like these. Location-based applications are increasingly attracting young, urban influencers with disposable income, which is precisely the audience we are trying to attract. People connect to geo-location apps primarily to "get informed" about local happenings.

Foursquare.com
A web and mobile application that allows registered users to post their location at a venue ("check-in") and connect with friends. Check-in requires active user selection and points are awarded at check-in. Users can choose to have their check-ins posted on their accounts on Twitter, Facebook, or both. In version 1.3 of their iPhone application, foursquare enabled push-notification of friend updates, which they call "Pings". Users can also earn badges by checking in at locations with certain tags, for check-in frequency, or for other patterns such as time of check-in.]
Resource: https://foursquare.com/business/
Ex: https://foursquare.com/v/binsons-medical-supply-eastpointe-mi/4cf9036a466b6ea83cc2648b

Instagram
Instagram.com is an online photo-sharing, video-sharing and social networking service that enables its users to take pictures and videos, apply digital filters to them, and share them on a variety of social networking services, such as
Facebook, Twitter, Tumblr and Flickr. A distinctive feature is that it confines photos to a square shape, similar to
Kodak Instamatic and Polaroid images, in contrast to the 16:9 aspect ratio now typically used by mobile device cameras. Users are also able to record and share short videos lasting for up to 15 seconds.

We will use Instagram in the following ways to help amplify the story of our brand, get people to engage with our content when not at our store, and get people to visit our store or site:
1.   Let our customers and fans know about specific product availability.
2.   Tie into trends, events or holidays to drive awareness.

3. Let people know we are open and our ambiance is spectacular.
4. Run a monthly contest and pick the winning hashtagged photograph
   to activate our customer base and increase our exposure.

5. Encourage the posting and collection of happy onsite or offsite customer photos.

Examples:
https://www.instagram.com/medstandard/

Note: Commonly found in tweets, a hashtag is a word or connected phrase (no spaces) that begins with a hash symbol (#). They're so popular that other social media platforms including Facebook, Instagram and Google+ now support them. Using a hashtag turns a word or phrase into a clickable link that displays a feed (list) of other posts with that same hashtag. For example, if you click on #_____ in a tweet, or enter #_____ in the search box, you'll see a list of tweets all about _____.

Snapchat.com

This is a photo messaging app for iPhone and Android mobile devices. Users can take a picture or video and add text, drawings, and a variety of filters. They set a designated time limit, 1-10 seconds, and send to selected contacts from their list. Users can also set a "story" – a Snap that pins to their profile and is viewable for 24 hours after posting.

Snapchat photos display for a maximum of 10 seconds (for 24 hours, in the case of a snap story) before becoming permanently inaccessible. The user may choose to save their snaps, but this will only save it to their local device. If the receiver uses the screenshot function on their phone, or chooses to replay a snap, the sender is notified. The point of Snapchat is to be fun and quirky, enticing and engaging your contacts with visual snippets of whatever you are doing. Teen and millennial users enjoy using Snapchat where they would traditionally send a text message. In many cases it's easier and more stimulating to send a quick clip of the equipment you are viewing, for example, than it would be to send a text description.

Snapchat is not useful as a lead generating tool, but it is exceptionally useful for client engagement and retention. When we meet with a client and exchange mobile contact information, we will ask if they use Snapchat and if we can add them to keep them updated on new equipment acquisitions. The beauty of the Snap is that is draws the client into the environment and makes them want to see more. We will use this limitation to our advantage and make our client feel compelled to request and attend more webinars. Snapchat is also a phenomenal tool to engage with existing clients. It will make buyers feel connected to the sales agent and the equipment searching process, which is conducive to converting sales and retaining these clients in the future. While the primary user demographic is in the millennial age range, the app is popular with many adults as well. Incorporating Snapchat into our client communication strategy will aid our ability to close rental deals swiftly and form long term client relationships.

Resources:
https://blog.hootsuite.com/smart-ways-to-use-snapchat-for-business/
http://smallbiztrends.com/2014/10/how-businesses-can-use-snapchat.html
http://nymag.com/selectall/2017/04/the-snapchat-101-the-best-coolest-smartest-weirdest-   accounts.html

LinkedIn.com

LinkedIn ranks high in search engines and will provide a great platform for sending event updates to business associates. To optimize our LinkedIn profile, we will select one core keyword. We will use it frequently, without sacrificing consumer experience, to get our profile to skyrocket in the search engines. Linkedin provides options that will allow our detailed profile to be indexed by search engines, like Google. We will make use of these options so our business will achieve greater visibility on the Web. We will use widgets to integrate other tools, such as importing your blog entries or Twitter stream into your profile, and go market research and gain knowledge with Polls. We will answer questions in Questions and Answers to show our expertise, and ask questions in Questions and Answers to get a feel for what customers and prospects want or think. We will publish our LinkedIn URL on all our marketing collateral, including business cards, email signature, newsletters, and web site. We will grow our network by joining industry and alumni groups related to our business. We will update our status examples of recent work, and link our status updates with our other social media accounts. We will start and manage a group or fan page for our rental company . We will share useful articles that will be of interest to customers, and request LinkedIn recommendations from customers willing to provide testimonials. We will post our presentations on our profile using a presentation application. We will ask our first-level contacts for introductions to their contacts and interact with LinkedIn on a regular basis to reach those who may not see us on other social media sites. We will link to articles posted elsewhere, with a summary of why it's valuable to add to our credibility and list our newsletter subscription information and archives. We will post discounts and package deals. We will buy a LinkedIn <u>direct ad</u> that our target market will see. We will find vendors and contractors through <u>connections.</u>

Examples:
https://www.linkedin.com/company/467209
www.linkedin.com/company/diagnostic-vision/diagnostic-vision-medical-equipment- rental-19786/product?trk=biz_product

Resources:
www.linkedin.com/pulse/20140721060609-349336221-medical-equipment-rental-market

Podcasting

Our podcasts will provide both information and advertising. Our podcasts will allow us to pull in a lot of customers. Our monthly podcasts will be heard by ___ (#) eventual subscribers. Podcasts can now be downloaded for mobile devices, such as an iPod.

Podcasts will give our company a new way to provide information and an additional way to advertise. Podcasting will give our business another connection point with customers. We will use this medium to communicate on important issues, what is going on with a planned event, and other things of interest to our company customers. The programs will last about 10 minutes and can be downloaded for free on iTunes. The purpose is not to be a mass medium. It is directed at a niche market with an above-average educational background and very special child care interests. It will provide a very direct and a reasonably inexpensive way of reaching our targeted audience with relevant information about our Medical medical equipment rental services.

Resources:
www.apple.com/itunes/download/.
www.cbc.ca/podcasting/gettingstarted.html

Examples:
http://www.mddionline.com/podcasts

Blogging

We will use our blog to keep customers and prospects informed about events and services that relate to our Medical Equipment Rental Company business, new releases, contests, and specials. Our blog will show readers that we are a good source of expert information that they can count on. With our blog, we can quickly update our customers anytime our company releases a new service, the holding of a contest for referrals. We will use our blog to communicate the following types of information:
1. Share client testimonials and meaningful success stories.
2. Recognize our employees of the quarter.
3. Confirm our commitment to Healthcare Compliance
4. Document our employee referral program.
5. Share information on how to keep Travelers Mentally and Physically Fit.

Our visitors will be able to subscribe to our RSS feeds and be instantly updated without any spam filters interfering. We will also use the blog to solicit service usage recommendations and future program addition suggestions. Additionally, blogs are free and allow for constant ease of updating.

To get visitors to our blog to take the next action step and contact our firm we will do the following:

1.   Put a contact form on the upper-left hand corner of our blog, right below the   header.
2.   Put our complete contact information in the header itself.
3.   Add a page to our blog and title it, "Become My Client.", giving the reader   somewhere to go for the next sign-up steps.
4.   At the end of each blog post, we will clearly tell the reader what to do next; such as subscribe to our RSS feed, or to sign up for our newsletter mailing list.

Resources: www.blogger.com   www.blogspot.com   www.wordpress.com

Examples:
http://www.medonecapital.com/aboutus/blog
http://eganmedical.blogspot.com/

Twitter

We will use 'Twitter.com' as a way to produce new business from existing clients and generate prospective clients online. Twitter is a free social networking and micro-blogging service that allows its users to send and read other users' updates (otherwise known as tweets), which are text-based posts of up to 140 characters in length. Updates are displayed on the user's profile page and delivered to other users
who have signed up to receive them. The sender can restrict delivery to those in his or
her circle of friends, with delivery to everyone being the default. Users can receive updates via the Twitter website, SMS text messaging, RSS feeds, or email. Twitter will give us the ability to have ongoing two-way conversations with our customers, which will allow us to get better at what we do and offer, while giving us the ability to express our own unique 'personality'. We will use our Twitter account to respond directly to questions, distribute news, solve problems, post updates, circulate information about fundraisers, hold trivia question contests for a chance to win a gift certificate and offer special discounts, known as 'Tweet Deals', on selected products and services. Our posts on Twitter will include our URL (address), our new offers, cooking recipe tips and new service offerings. On a long-term basis, using Twitter consistently and efficiently will help push our website up the rankings on Google.

The intangible, that will only have a positive effect, are the hundreds of impressions that each tweet will get, not to mention the positive statements that will be posted about our service, staff, selection and product knowledge. Using TweetReach, we expect our special promotional offers to receive thousands of impressions.

We will also add our website, company logo, personal photo and/or blog on our profile page. We will provide the following instructions to register as a 'Follower' of _____ (company name) on Twitter:
1.	In your Twitter account, click on 'Find People' in the top right navigation bar, which will redirect to a new page.
2.	Click on 'Find on Twitter' which will open a search box that says 'Who are you looking for?'
3.	Type '_____ (company name) / _____ (owner name)' and click 'search'. This will bring up the results page.
4.	Click the blue '_____' name to read the bio or select the 'Follow' button.
Examples:
htttps://twitter.com/medonecapital
https://twitter.com/CapeMedical

Google Maps
We will first make certain that our business is listed in Google Maps. We will do a search for our business in Google Maps. If we don't see our business listed, then we will add our business to Google Maps. Even if our business is listed in Google Maps, we will create a Local Business Center account and take control of our listing, by adding more relevant information. Consumers generally go to Google Maps for two reasons: Driving Directions and to Find a Business.   Resource: http://maps.google.com/

Bing Maps   www.bingplaces.com/
This will make it easy for customers to find our business.

Apple Maps
A web mapping service developed by Apple Inc. It is the default map system of iOS, macOS, and watchOS. It provides directions and estimated times of arrival for automobile, pedestrian, and public

transportation navigation.

Resources:
http://www.stallcupgroup.com/2012/09/19/three-ways-to-make-your-pawn-business- more-profitable-and-sellable/
http://www.apple.com/ios/maps/
https://en.wikipedia.org/wiki/Apple_Maps

Google Places

Google Places helps people make more informed decisions about where to go for medical equipment rental services. Place Pages connect people to information from the best sources across the web, displaying photos, reviews and essential facts, as well as real-time updates and offers from business owners. We will make sure that our Google Places listing is up to date to increase our online visibility. Google Places is linked to our Google Maps listing, and will help to get on the first page of Google search page results when people search for a Medical Equipment Rental Company in our area.
Resource: www.google/com/places

Yelp.com

We will use Yelp.com to help people find our local business. Visitors to Yelp write local reviews, over 85% of them rating a business 3 stars or higher In addition to reviews, visitors can use Yelp to find events, special offers, lists and to talk with other Yelpers. As business owners, we will setup a free account to post offers, photos and message our customers. We will also buy ads on Yelp, which will be clearly labeled "Sponsored Results". We will also use the Weekly Yelp, which is available in 42 city editions to bring news about the latest business openings and other happenings.
Examples:
http://www.yelp.com/biz/bradford-medical-supply-santa-clara

Manta.com

Manta is the largest free source of information on small companies, with profiles of more than 64 million businesses and organizations. Business owners and sales professionals use Manta's vast database and custom search capabilities to quickly find companies, easily connect with prospective customers and promote their own services.

Manta.com, founded in 2005, is based in Columbus, Ohio.
Examples:
www.manta.com/mb_35_D1160000_000/medical_equipment_rental

HotFrog.com
HotFrog is a fast growing free online business directory listing over 6.6 million US businesses. HotFrog now has local versions in 34 countries worldwide.

Anyone can list their business in HotFrog for free, along with contact details, and products and services. Listing in HotFrog directs sales leads and enquiries to your business. Businesses are encouraged to add any latest news and information about their products and services to their listing. HotFrog is indexed by Google and other search engines, meaning that customers can find your HotFrog listing when they use Google, Yahoo! or other search engines.

Resource: http://www.hotfrog.com/AddYourBusiness.aspx

Local.com
Local.com owns and operates a leading local search site and network in the United States. Its mission is to be the leader at enabling local businesses and consumers to find each other and connect. To do so, the company uses patented and proprietary technologies to provide over 20 million consumers each month with relevant search results for local businesses, products and services on Local.com and more than 1,000 partner sites. Local.com powers more than 100,000 local websites. Tens of thousands of small business customers use Local.com products and services to reach consumers using a variety of subscription, performance and display advertising and website products.

Resource: http://corporate.local.com/mk/get/advertising-opportunities

Autoresponder
An autoresponder is an online tool that will automatically manage our mailing list and send out emails to our customers at preset intervals. We will write a short article that is helpful to potential

medical equipment rental clients. We will load this article into our autoresponder. We will let people know of the availability of our article by posting to newsgroups, forums, social networking sites etc. We will list our autoresponder email address at the end of the posting so they can send a blank email to our autoresponder to receive our article and be added to our mailing list. We will then email them at the interval of our choosing with special offers. We will load the messages into our autoresponder and set a time interval for the messages to be mailed out.

Resource: www.aweber.com

Pay-Per-Click Advertising

Google AdWords, Yahoo! Search Marketing, and Microsoft adCenter are the three largest network operators, and all three operate under a bid-based model. Cost per click (CPC) varies depending on the search engine and the level of competition for a particular keyword. Google AdWords are small text ads that appear next to the search results on Google. In addition, these ads appear on many partner web sites, including NYTimes.com (The New York Times), Business.com, Weather.com, About.com, and many more. Google's text advertisements are short, consisting of one title line and two content text lines. Image ads can be one of several different Interactive Advertising Bureau (IAB) standard sizes. Through Google AdWords, we plan to buy placements (ads) for specific search terms through this "Pay-Per-Click" advertising program. This PPC advertising campaign will allow our ad to appear when someone searches for a keyword related to our business, organization, or subject matter. More importantly, we will only pay when a potential customer clicks on our ad to visit our website. For instance, since we operate a Medical Equipment Rental Company in _ (city), _(state), we will target people using search terms such as "Medical Equipment Rental Company, Clinical Medical Equipment, Medical Compliance, Medical IT, wheelchair rentals, Medical technology, Medical Equipment Leasing, Medical state-of-the-art technology in ____ (city), ____ (state)". With an effective PPC campaign our ads will only be displayed when a user searches for one of these keywords. In short, PPC advertising will be the most cost-effective and measurable form of advertising for our Medical

Equipment Rental Company.
Resources:
http://adwords.google.com/support/aw/?hl=en
www.wordtracker.com

Yahoo Local Listings

We will create our own local listing on Yahoo. To create our free listing, we will use our web browser and navigate to http://local.yahoo.com. We will first register for free with Yahoo, and create a member ID and password to list our business. Once we have accessed http://local.yahoo.com, we will scroll down to the bottom and click on "Add/Edit a Business" to get onto the Yahoo Search Marketing Local Listings page. In the lower right of the screen we will see "Local Basic Listings FREE". We will click on the Get Started button and log in again with our new Yahoo ID and password. The form for our local business listing will now be displayed. When filling it out, we will be sure to include our full web address (http://www.companyname.com). We will include a description of our medical equipment rental services in the description section, but avoid hype or blatant advertising, to get the listing to pass Yahoo's editorial review. We will also be sure to select the appropriate business category and sub categories.
Examples:
https://local.yahoo.com/info-14110800-care-medical-equipment-scooter-rental-orlando-   orlando

Sales Reps/Account Executives

_____ (company name) will use independent commissioned sales reps to penetrate markets outside of _____ (city/state). Management will work to keep in constant communication with the sales reps to ensure that their placement service is professional and timely. Independent sales representatives will provide the best mode for distribution in order to maintain pricing controls and higher margins. Independent sales reps are not full-time employees, thus benefits are not necessary. Independent sales reps receive a flat commission based on gross sales. Our sales reps are set at a commission rate of __ (15?)% of gross sales. The average sales rep can service up to __ (#) accounts with the average location generating around $____ per year. We expect to have ___(#) independent sales reps covering ___ (#) states in place to sell the company's medical equipment rental services. In addition to field calls, sales reps will represent our company at all regional tradeshows, with the marketing director attending all national tradeshows.

Advertorials

An advertorial is an advertisement written in the form of an objective article, and presented in a printed publication—usually designed to look like a legitimate and independent news story. We will use quotes as testimonials to back up certain claims throughout our copy and break-up copy with subheadings to make the material more reader-friendly. We will include the "call to action" and contact information with a 24/7 voicemail number and a discount coupon. The advertorial will have a short intro about a client's experience with our medical equipment rental services and include quotes, facts, and statistics. We will present helpful information about different leasing programs.

Affiliate Marketing

We will create an affiliate marketing program to broaden our reach. We will first devise a commission structure, so affiliates have a reason to promote our business. We will give them ___ (10)% of whatever sales they generate. We will go after medical practice bloggers or webmasters who get a lot of web traffic for our keywords. These companies would then promote our Medical Equipment Rental Company services, and they would earn commissions for the sales they generated. We will work with the following services to handle the technical aspects of our program.

ConnectCommerce https://www.connectcommerce.com/
Commission Junction https://members.cj.com
ShareASale http://www.shareasale.com/

Share Results
LinkShare

Online Directory Listings
The following directory listings use proprietary technology to match customers with industry professionals in their geographical area. The local search capabilities for specific niche markets offer an invaluable tool for the customer. These directories help member businesses connect with purchase-ready buyers, convert leads to sales, and maximize the value of customer relationships. Their online and offline communities provide a quick and easy low or no-cost solution for customers to find a rental company quickly. We intend to sign-up with all no cost directories and evaluate the ones that charge a fee.

Medical Devices Directory
    www.medicaldevices.org/?memberdirectory
Medicare
    www.medicare.gov/supplierdirectory/search.html
Medical Devices   www.medicaldevicedirectory.com/
Rent It Today   www.rentittoday.com
Qualified Suppliers   www.qmed.com/
Wellness   www.wellness.com/find
BBB Example:
www.bbb.org/charlotte/accredited-business-directory/medical-equipment-sales-and-rental

Other General Directories Include:

Listings.local.yahoo.com	Switchboard Super Pages
YellowPages.com	MerchantCircle.com
Bing.com/businessportal	Local.com
Yelp.com	BrownBook.com
InfoUSA.com	iBegin.com
Localeze.com	Bestoftheweb.com
YellowBot.com	HotFrog.com
InsiderPages.com	MatchPoint.com

CitySearch.com
Profiles.google.com/me
Jigsaw.com
Whitepages.com

YellowUSA.com
Manta.com
LinkedIn.com
PowerProfiles.com

Get Listed   http://getlisted.org/enhanced-business-
listings.aspx
Universal Business Listing   https://www.ubl.org/index.aspx
                                    www.UniversalBusinessListing.org

Universal Business Listing (UBL) is a local search industry service dedicated to acting as a central collection and distribution point for business information online. UBL provides business owners and their marketing representatives with a one-stop location for broad distribution of complete, accurate, and detailed listing information.

Testimonial Marketing

We will either always ask for testimonials immediately after a completed project or contact our clients once a quarter for them. We will also have something prepared that we would like the client to say that is specific to a service we offer, or anything relevant to advertising claims that we have put together. For the convenience of the client we will assemble a testimonial letter that they can either modify or just sign off on. Additionally, testimonials can also be in the form of audio or video and put on our website or mailed to potential clients in the form of a DVD or Audio CD. A picture with a testimonial is also excellent. We will put testimonials directly on a magazine ad, slick sheet, brochure, or website, or assemble a complete page of testimonials for our sales presentation folder.

Examples:
http://www.medonecapital.com/resources/testimonials

We will collect customer testimonials in the following ways:
1.   Our website – A page dedicated to testimonials (written and/or video).

2. Social media accounts – Facebook fan pages offer a review tab, which makes it easy to receive and display customer testimonials.
3. Google+ also offers a similar feature with Google+ Local.
4. Local search directories – Ask customers to post more reviews on Yelp and Yahoo Local.
5. Customer Satisfaction Survey Forms

We will pose the following questions to our customers to help them frame their testimonials:
1. What was the obstacle that would have prevented you from buying this product?
2. "What was your main concern about buying this product?"
3. What did you find as a result of buying this product?
4. What specific feature did you like most about this product?
5. What would be three other benefits about this product?
6. Would you recommend this product? If so, why?
7. Is there anything you'd like to add?

Reminder Service

We will use a four-tier reminder system in the following sequence: email, postcard, letter, phone call. We will stress the importance of staying in touch in our messages and keeping their profile updated with their activities. We will also try to determine the reason for the non-response or inactivity and what can be done to reactivate the client. The reminder service will also work to the benefit of regular clients, that want to be reminded of an agreed upon special date or coming event.

Resource: http://www.easyivr.com/reminder-service.htm

Business Logo

Our logo will graphically represent who we are and what we do, and it will serve to help brand our image. It will also convey a sense of uniqueness and professionalism. The logo will represent our company image and the message we are trying to convey. Our business logo will reflect the philosophy and objectives of rental company . Our logo will incorporate the following design guidelines:

1.	It will relate to our industry, our name, a defining characteristic of our company or a competitive advantage we offer.
2.	It will be a simple logo that can be recognized faster.
3.	It will contain strong lines and letters which show up better than thin ones.
4.	It will feature something unexpected or unique without being overdrawn.
5.	It will work well in black and white (one-color printing).
6.	It will be scalable and look pleasing in both small and large sizes.
7.	It will be artistically balanced and make effective use of color, line density and shape.
8.	It will be unique when compared to competitors.
9.	It will use original, professionally rendered artwork.
10.	It can be replicated across any media mix without losing quality.
11.	It appeals to our target audience.
12.	It will be easily recognizable from a distance if utilized in outdoor advertising.

Resources:	www.freelogoservices.com/
	www.hatchwise.com
		www.logosnap.com
	www.99designs.com
		www.fiverr.com
	www.freelancer.com
		www.upwork.com

Logo Design Guide:
www.bestfreewebresources.com/logo-design-professional-guide
www.creativebloq.com/graphic-design/pro-guide-logo-design-21221

Fundraisers

Community outreach programs involving charitable fundraising and showing a strong interest in the local school system will serve to elevate our status in the community as a "good corporate citizen" while simultaneously increasing store traffic. We will execute a

successful fundraising program for our liquor store and build goodwill in the community, by adhering to the following guidelines:
1. Keep It Local
When looking for a worthy cause, we will make sure it is local so the whole neighborhood will support it.
2. Plan It
We will make sure that we are organized and outline everything we want to accomplish before planning the fundraiser.
3. Contact Local Media
We will contact the suburban newspapers to do stories on the event and send out press releases to the local TV and radio stations.
4. Contact Area Businesses
We will contact other businesses and have them put up posters in their stores and pass out flyers to promote the event.
5. Get Recipient Support
We will make sure the recipients of the fundraiser are really willing to participate and get out in the neighborhood to invite everyone into our store for the event, plus help pass out flyers and getting other businesses to put up the posters.
6. Give Out Bounce Backs
We will give a "bounce-back" coupon that allows for both a discount and an additional donation in exchange for customer next purchase. (It will have an expiration date of two weeks to give a sense of urgency.)
7. Be Ready with plenty of product and labor on hand for the event.

Examples:
http://www.standris.com/Fundraisers.html

Fundraiser Action Plan Checklist:
1. Choose a good local cause for your fundraiser.
2. Calculate donations as a percentage for normal sales.
3. Require the group to promote and support the event.
4. Contact local media to get exposure before and after the event.
5. Ask area businesses to put up flyers and donate printing of

materials.
6. Use a bounce-back coupon to get new customers back.
7. Be prepared with sufficient labor and product.

Resource: www.thefundraisingauthority.com/fundraising-basics/fundraising-event/

Seminars

Seminars present the following marketing and bonding opportunities:
1. Signage and branding as a presenting sponsor.
2. Opportunity to provide logo imprinted handouts.
3. Media exposure through advertising and public relations.
4. The opportunity for one-on-one interaction with a targeted group of consumers to demonstrate an understanding of their needs and our matching expert solutions.
5. Use of sign-in sheet to collect names and email addresses for database build.
6. Present opportunity to sell products, such as workbooks.

Possible seminar funding sources:
1. Small registration fee to cover the cost of hand-outs and refreshments.
2. Get sponsorship funding from partner/networking organizations.
3. Sponsorship classified ads in the program guide or handouts.

We will establish our expertise and trustworthiness by offering free seminars on the following topics:
1. How to Locate and Evaluate Medical Equipment Rental Companies
2. How to Work with a Medical Equipment Rental Company to Reduce Costs
3. The Growing Demand for Medical Equipment Rentals

Seminar target groups include the following:
1. Corporations
2. Computer Companies
3. Medical Practices
4. Hospital

Managers
5.   Daycare Centers   6.   Real Estate Agents
7.   Support Groups   8.   AARP Groups

Seminar marketing approaches include:
1.   Posting to website and enabling online registrations.
2.   Email blast to in-house database using www.constantcontact.com
3.   Include seminar schedule in newsletter and flyer.
4.   Classified ads using craigslist.org

Seminar Objectives:
Seminar Topic   Target Audience   Handout
    Target Date

_____
_____

Webinars

A webinar is a presentation, lecture, workshop or seminar that is transmitted over the Web. A key feature of a Webinar is its interactive elements -- the ability to give, receive and discuss information. Webinars will be used as an effective vehicle for communicating a message, building awareness and buy-in about a particular topic, and offering an interactive educational experience.

Our Webinars will be educational in nature and allow our clinic to demonstrate the value of our Medical Equipment Rental Company services and expertise, directly to prospects or existing clients without spending money to meet with them. Webinars allow prospects to listen to experts discuss uses, benefits and demand for certain products and services while gleaning insights about the unique benefits businesses provide. Webinars, like other forms of content marketing, should convey succinct messages and focus on one topic of interest. Webinars tend to run an hour, including Q&A time. Webinars are generally in the form of slide decks. While webinar marketing is a great tool for lead generation, the webinars, themselves, must be informative and cater to the learning needs of customers or prospects. Pairing webinars with blog posts and other website content, as well as placing calls to action at the end of the presentations, can direct prospects through conversion funnels.

Sample Webinar
Title: How to Evaluate the Benefits of Working with a Medical Equipment Rental Company
As a result of the webinar participants will be able to: Evaluate their cost savings.
Prerequisite: None
Target Audience: Hospital and Clinic Administrators
Resources:
www.gotomeeting.com/fec/webinar/secure_webinar_software
www.webex.com/WebEx-Meetings-Purchase-FAQ.html?TrackID=1030070&hbxref=&goid=webex-meetings-FAQ

Cold Calling

Cold calling is the process of approaching prospective customers or clients, typically via telephone or actual visits, who were not expecting such an interaction.

1. Requires visiting business premises and obtaining contact details of the person who is the responsible decision maker for hiring medical professionals.
2. Involves outgoing telemarketing operations. A script will be developed with the objective of establishing a contact name and setting an appointment for a visit by our sales rep. Requires researching the prospects current pain points to offer remedies. We will send out a personalized letter that introduces our placement services and informs the prospect that we will be calling on a certain date.
3. May involve walking in cold with a business suit and making introductions to both the gatekeeper and 'The Decision Maker' with the aid of small token gifts, such as a logo imprinted paperweight or pen set.

Autoresponder

An autoresponder is an online tool that will automatically manage our mailing list and send out emails to our customers at preset intervals. We will write a short article that is helpful to potential Medical Equipment Rental Company clients. We will load this article into our autoresponder. We will let people know of the availability of our article by posting to newsgroups, forums, social networking sites etc. We will list our autoresponder email address at the end of the posting so they can send a blank email to our autoresponder to receive our article and be added to our mailing list. We will then email them at the interval of our choosing with special offers. We will load the messages into our autoresponder and set a time interval for the messages to be mailed out.
Resource: www.aweber.com

Database Marketing

Database marketing is a form of direct marketing using databases of customers or prospects to generate personalized communications in order to promote a product or service for marketing purposes. The method of communication can be any addressable medium, as in direct marketing. With database marketing tools, we will be able to implement customer nurturing, which is a tactic that attempts to communicate with each customer or prospect at the right time, using the right information to meet that customer's need to progress through the process of identifying a problem, learning options available to resolve it, selecting the right solution, and making the purchasing decision. We will use our databases to learn more about customers, select target markets for specific campaigns, through customer segmentation, compare customers' value to the company, and provide more specialized offerings for customers based on their transaction histories, demographic profile and surveyed needs and wants. This database will gives us the capability to automate regular promotional mailings, to semi-automate the telephone outreach process, and to prioritize prospects as to interests, timing, and other notable delineators. The objective is to arrange for first meetings, which are meant to be informal introductions, and valuable fact-finding and needs-assessment events.

We will use sign-in sheets, coupons, surveys and newsletter subscriptions to collect the following information from our clients:
1. Name
2. Telephone Number
3. Email Address
4. Address
5. Equipment Needs
6. Specialties

We will utilize the following types of contact management software to generate leads and stay in touch with customers to produce repeat business and referrals:
1. Act   www.act.com
2. Front Range Solutions   www.frontrange.com
3. The Turning Point   www.turningpoint.com
4. Acxiom   www.acxiom.com/products_and_services/

We will utilize contact management software, such as ACT and Goldmine, to track the following:
1. Dates for follow-ups.
2. Documentation of prospect concerns, objections or comments.
3. Referral source.
4. Marketing Materials sent.
5. Log of contact dates and methods of contact.
6. Ultimate disposition.

Cause Marketing

Cause marketing or cause-related marketing refers to a type of marketing involving the cooperative efforts of a "for profit" business and a non-profit organization for mutual benefit. The possible benefits of cause marketing include positive public relations, improved customer relations, and additional marketing opportunities. Cause marketing sponsorship by American businesses is rising at a dramatic rate, because customers, employees and stakeholders prefer to be associated with a company that is considered socially responsible. Our business objective will be to generate highly cost-effective public relations and media coverage for the launch of a marketing campaign focused on _____ (type of cause), with the help of the _____ (non-profit organization name) organization.

Resources:
www.causemarketingforum.com/
www.cancer.org/AboutUs/HowWeHelpYou/acs-cause-marketing

Example:
SoldierStrong (www.turnsfortroops.com), previously known as SoldierSocks, helps American patriots literally take their new steps forward. Through educational scholarships and by harnessing the most innovative technology in advanced rehabilitation, we help our returning service men and women to continue moving in the only direction they should know – forward. Nearly every dollar SoldierStrong receives from United Rentals goes towards direct support of American patriots so that they can re-acclimate to civilian life. Our organization works to remind those men and women who sacrificed so much that we are forever thankful.
Source:
https://globenewswire.com/news-release/2017/05/11/982474/0/en/United-Rentals-and-Rahal-Letterman-Lanigan-Racing-Renew-Support-for-SoldierStrong-Through-Turns-for-Troops-Charitable-Program.html

Courtesy Advertising
We will engage in courtesy advertising, which refers to a company or corporation "buying" an advertisement in a nonprofit dinner program, event brochure, and the like. Our company will gain visibility this way while the nonprofit organization may treat the advertisement revenue as a donation. We will specifically advertise in the following non-profit programs, newsletters, bulletins and event brochures: _____

_____

_____

Speaking Engagements
We will consider a "problem/solution" format where we describe a

challenge and tell how our expertise achieved an exceptional solution. We will use speaking engagements as an opportunity to expose our areas of expertise to prospective clients. By speaking at conferences and forums put together by professional and industry trade groups, we will increase our firm's visibility, and consequently, its prospects for attracting new business. Public speaking will give us a special status, and make it easier for our speakers to meet prospects. Attendees expect speakers to reach out to the audience, which gives speakers respect and credibility. We will identify speaking opportunities that will let us reach our targeted audience. We will designate a person who is responsible for developing relationships with event and industry associations, submitting proposals and, most importantly, staying in touch with contacts. We will tailor our proposals to the event organizers' preferences.

Speaking Proposal Package:
1. Speech Topic/Agenda/Synopsis
2. Target Audience: Community and Civic Groups
3. Speaker Biography
4. List of previous speaking engagements
5. Previous engagement evaluations

Possible Targets:
1. Hospitals
2. Nursing Homes
3. Government Agencies
4. Home Healthcare Services
5. Adult Daycare Centers
6. Assisted living residences
7. Schools
8. Physician practices
9. Camps
10. Ambulatory Centers
11. Rehabilitation Centers
12. Laboratory Services

Possible Speech Topics:
1. The Benefits of Using a Medical Equipment Rental Company
2. The ROI from Medical Equipment Maintenance

Speech Tracking Form

Group/Class Date	Subject/ Target Topic	Business Development Potential	Resources Needed

We will use the following techniques to leverage the business development impact of our speaking engagements:

1. Send out press releases to local papers announcing the upcoming speech. We will get great free publicity by sending the topic and highlights of the talk to the newspaper.
2. Produce a flyer with our picture on it, and distribute it to our network.
3. Send publicity materials to our prospects inviting them to attend our presentation.
4. Whenever possible, get a list of attendees before the event. Contact them and introduce yourself before the talk to build rapport with your audience. Arrive early and don't leave immediately after your presentation.
5. Always give out handouts and a business card. Include marketing materials and something of value to the recipient, so that it will be retained and not just tossed away. You might include tips or secrets you share in your talk.
6. Give out an evaluation form to all participants. This form should request names and contact information. Offer a free consultation if it's appropriate. Follow up within 72 hours with any members of the audience who could become ideal clients.
7. Have a place on the form where participants can list other groups that might need speakers, along with the name of the program chairperson or other contact person.
8. Offer a door prize as incentive for handing in the evaluation. When you have collected all of the evaluations, you can select a winner of the prize.

9. Meet with audience members, answer their questions and listen to their concerns. Stay after your talk and mingle with the audience. Answer any questions that come up and offer follow-up conversations for additional support.
10. Request a free ad in the group's newsletter in exchange for your speech.
11. Send a thank-you note to the person who invited you to speak. Include copies of some of the evaluations to show how useful it was.

Speaking Engagement Package
1. Video or DVD of prior presentation.
2. Session Description
3. Learning Objectives
4. Takeaway Message
5. Speaking experience
6. Letters of recommendation
7. General Biography
8. Introduction Biography

Resource: www.toastmasters.com

Meet-up Group
We will form a meet-up group to encourage people to participate in our recruiting programs.
Resource: http://www.meetup.com/create/
Examples: http://www.meetup.com/INpact/

BBB Accreditation
We will apply for BBB Accreditation to improve our perceived trustworthiness. BBB determines that a company meets BBB accreditation standards, which include a commitment to make a good faith effort to resolve any consumer complaints. BBB Accredited Businesses pay a fee for accreditation review/monitoring and for support of BBB services to the public. BBB accreditation does not mean that the business' products or services have been evaluated or

endorsed by BBB, or that BBB has made a determination as to the business' product quality or competency in performing services. We will place the BBB Accreditation Logo in all of our ads. Examples: www.bbb.org/dallas/accredited-business-directory/medical-equipment-and-supplies

Sponsor Events

The sponsoring of events, such as health fairs, medical conventions and golf tournaments, will allow our company to engage in what is known as experiential marketing, which is the idea that the best way to deepen the emotional bond between a company and its customers is by creating a memorable and interactive experience. We will ask for the opportunity to prominently display our company signage and the set-up of a booth from which to handout sample products and sales literature. We will also seek to capitalize on networking, speech giving and workshop presenting opportunities.

Sponsorships

We will sponsor a local team, such as our child's little league team, the local soccer club or a bowling group. We will then place our company name on the shirts in exchange for providing the equipment and uniforms.

Patch.com

A community-specific news and information platform dedicated to providing comprehensive and trusted local coverage for individual towns and communities.
Patch makes it easy to: Keep up with news and events, Look at photos and videos from around town, Learn about local businesses, Participate in discussions and Submit announcements, photos, and reviews.

Mobile iPhone Apps

We will use new distribution tools like the iPhone App Store to give us unprecedented direct access to consumers, without the need to necessarily buy actual mobile *ads* to reach people. Thanks to Apple's iPhone and the App Store, we will be able to make cool mobile apps that may generate as much goodwill and purchase intent as a banner ad. We will research Mobile Application Development, which is the process by which application software is developed for small low-power handheld devices, such as personal digital assistants, enterprise digital assistants or mobile phones. These applications are either pre-installed on phones during manufacture, or downloaded by customers from various mobile software distribution platforms. iPhone apps make good marketing tools. The bottom line is iPhones and smartphones sales are continually growing, and people are going to their phones for information. Apps will definitely be a lead generation tool because it gives potential clients easy access to our contact and business information and the ability to call for more information while they are still "hot". Our apps will contain: directory of staffers, publications on relevant issues, office location, videos, etc.

We will especially focus on the development of apps that can accomplish the following:
1.   **Mobile Reservations:** Customers can use this app to access mobile reservations   linked directly to your in-house calendar. They can browse open slots and book   appointments easily, while on the go.
2.   **Appointment Reminders:** You can send current customers reminders of regular   or special appointments through your mobile app to increase your yearly revenue   per customer.
3.   **Style Libraries**
        Offer a style library in your app to help customers to pick out a _____ style.
        Using a simple photo gallery, you can collect photos of various styles, and have   customers browse and select specific _____.
4.   **Customer Photos**
        Your app can also have a feature that lets customers take photos and email them   to you. This is great for creating a database of customer photos for testimonial   purposes, advertising, or just easy reference.
5.   **Special Offers**

239

Push notifications allow you to drive activity on special promotions, deals, events, and offers. If you ever need to generate revenue during a down time, push notifications allow you to generate interest easily and proactively.

6. Loyalty Programs

A mobile app allows you to offer a mobile loyalty program (buy ten ___, get one free, etc.). You won't need to print up cards or track anything manually – it's all done simply through users' mobile devices.

7. Referrals

A mobile app can make referrals easy. With a single click, a user can post to a social media account on Facebook or Twitter about their experience with your business. This allows you to earn new business organically through the networks of existing customers.

8. Product Sales

We can sell used products through our mobile app. Customers can browse products, submit orders, and make payments easily, helping you open up a new revenue stream.

Resources: http://www.apple.com/iphone/apps-for-iphone/

http://iphoneapplicationlist.com/apps/business/
Software Development: http://www.mutualmobile.com/
http://www.avenuesocial.com/mob-app.php#

http://www.biznessapps.com/
Resource: http://www.appolicious.com/pages/services
Example: https://itunes.apple.com/us/app/bms-medical-supply/id600718553?mt=8

Transit Ads

According to the Metropolitan Transportation Authority, MTA subways, buses and railroads provide billions of trips each year to residents. Marketing our medical equipment rental company in subway cars and on the walls of subway stations will be a great way to advertise our business to a large, captive audience.

Restroom billboard advertising (Bathroom Advertising)

We will target a captive audience by placing restroom billboard advertising in select high-traffic venues with targeted demographics. A simple, framed ad on the inside of a bathroom stall door or above a urinal gets at least a minute of viewing, according to several studies. The stall door ads are a good choice for venues with shorter waiting times, such as small businesses, while large wall posters are well-suited to airports or movie theatres where people are more likely to be standing in line near the entrance or exit. Many new restroom based ad agencies that's specialize in restroom advertisement have also come about, such as; Zoom Media, BillBoardZ , Flush Media , Jonny Advertising, Insite Advertising, Inc, Wall AG USA, ADpower, NextMedia, and Alive Promo (American Restroom Association, 9/24/2009).
Resources:
http://www.indooradvertising.org/
http://www.stallmall.com/
http://www.zoommedia.com/

Tumblr.com

Tumblr will allow us to effortlessly share anything. We will be able to post text, photos, quotes, links, music, and videos, from our browser, phone, desktop, email, or wherever we happen to be. We will be able to customize everything, from colors, to our theme's HTML.
Examples:
http://jonottmedical.tumblr.com/

thumbtack.com

A directory for finding and booking trustworthy local services, which is free to consumers.
Resource: www.thumbtack.com/postservice

Publish e-Book

Ebooks are electronic books which can be downloaded from any website or FTP site on the Internet. Ebooks are made using special software and can include a wide variety of media such as HTML, graphics, Flash animation and video. We will publish an e-book to establish our medical equipment rental expertise, and reach people who are searching for ebooks on how to make better use our products and/or services. Included in our ebook will be links back to our website, product or affiliate program. Because users will have permanent access to it, they will use our ebook again and again, constantly seeing a link or banner which directs them to our site. The real power behind ebook marketing will be the viral aspect of it and the free traffic it helps to build for our website. ebook directories include:

  www.e-booksdirectory.com/
  www.ebookfreeway.com/p-ebook-directory-list.html
  www.quantumseolabs.com/blog/seolinkbuilding/top-5-free-ebook-directories-subscribers/
Resource: www.free-ebooks.net/

e-books are available from the following sites:
 Amazon.com   Createspace.com
 Lulu.com   Kobobooks.com
 BarnesandNoble.com Scribd.com
 AuthorHouse.com

Business Card Exchanges
We will join our Chamber of Commerce or local retail merchants association and volunteer to host a mixer or business card exchange. We will take the opportunity to invite social and business groups to our store to enjoy wine tastings, and market to local businesses that will be looking for medical rental solutions. We will also build our email database by collecting the business cards of all attendees.

Hubpages.com
HubPages has easy-to-use publishing tools, a vibrant author community and underlying revenue-maximizing infrastructure. Hubbers (HubPages authors) earn money by publishing their Hubs (content-rich Internet pages) on topics they know and love, and earn recognition among fellow Hubbers through the community-wide

HubScore ranking system. The HubPages ecosystem provides a search-friendly infrastructure which drives traffic to Hubs from search engines such as Google and Yahoo, and enables Hubbers to earn revenue from industry-standard advertising vehicles such as Google AdSense and the eBay and Amazon Affiliates program. All of this is provided free to Hubbers in an open online community.
Resource:
http://hubpages.crabbysbeach.com/blogs/
http://hubpages.com/learningcenter/contents

Trivok.com
A totally free online directory that aims to provide information on businesses in USA and help its users find the best company.

Pinterest.com
The goal of this website is to connect everyone in the world through the 'things' they find interesting. They think that a favorite book or article topic can reveal a common link between two people. With millions of new pins added every week, Pinterest is connecting people all over the world based on shared tastes and interests. What's special about Pinterest is that the boards are all visual, which is a very important marketing plus. When users enter a URL, they select a picture from the site to pin to their board. People spend hours pinning their own content, and then finding content on other people's boards to "re-pin" to their own boards. We will use Pinterest for remote personal appointments. When we have a customer with specific needs, we will create a board just for them with resources we handle that would meet their needs, along with links to other tips and content. We will invite our customer to check out the board on Pinterest, and let them know we created it just for them.

Examples:
www.pinterest.com/eganmedical/
www.pinterest.com/explore/medical-equipment/

Resources:
www.copyblogger.com/pinterest-marketing/

www.shopify.com/infographics/pinterest
www.pinterest.com/entmagazine/retail-business/
www.pinterest.com/brettcarneiro/ecommerce/
www.pinterest.com/denniswortham/infographics-retail-online-shopping/
www.cio.com/article/3018852/e-commerce/how-to-use-pinterest-to-grow-your-business.html

Pinterest usage recommendation include:
1. Conduct market research by showing photos of potential products or test launches, asking the customer base for feedback.
2. Personalize the brand by showcasing style and what makes the brand different, highlighting new and exciting things through the use of imagery.
3. Add links from Pinterest photos to the company webstore, putting price banners on each photo and providing a link where users can buy the products directly.

Topix.com
Topix is the world's largest community news website. Users can read, talk about and edit the news on over 360,000 of our news pages. Topix is also a place for users to post their own news stories, as well as comment about stories they have seen on the Topix site. Each story and every Topix page comes with the ability to add your voice to the conversation.

Survey Marketing
We will conduct a survey in our target area to illicit opinions to our proposed business model. This will provide valuable feedback, lead to prospective clients and serve to introduce our Medical Equipment Rental Company, before we begin actual operations.

Google Calendar   www.google.com/calendar
We will use Google Calendar to organize our mobile Medical Equipment Rental Company seminar schedule and share events with friends.

'Green' Marketing

We will target environmentally friendly customers to introduce new customers to our business and help spread the word about going "green". We will use the following 'green' marketing strategies to form an emotional bond with our customers:

1. We will use clearly labeled 'Recycled Paper' and Sustainable Packaging, such as receipts and storage containers.
2. We will use "green", non-toxic cleaning supplies.
3. We will install a 'green' lighting and heating systems to be more eco-friendly.
4. We will use web-based Electronic Mail and Social Media instead of using paper advertisements.
5. We will find local suppliers to minimize the carbon footprint that it takes for deliveries.
6. We will use products that are made with organic ingredients and supplies.
7. We will document our 'Green' Programs in our sales brochure and website.
8. We will be a Certified Energy Star Partner.
9. We will install new LED warehouse lighting, exit signs, and emergency signs.
10. We will install motion detectors in low-traffic areas both inside and outside of warehouses.
11. We will implement new electricity regulators on HVAC units and compressors to lower energy consumption.
12. We will mount highly supervised and highly respected recycling campaigns.
13. We will start a program for waste product to be converted into sustainable energy sources.
14. We will start new company-wide document shredding programs.
15. We will use of water-based paints during the finishing process to reduce V.O.C.'s to virtually zero.

Sticker Marketing

Low-cost sticker, label and decal marketing will provide a cost-effective way to convey information, build identity and promote our company in unique and influential ways. Stickers can be affixed to almost any surface, so they can go and stay affixed where other marketing materials can't; opening a world of avenues through which we can reach our target audience. Our stickers will be simple in design, and convey an impression quickly and clearly, with valuable information or coupon, printed optionally as part of its backcopy. Our stickers will handed out at trade shows and special events, mailed as a postcard, packaged with product and/or included as part of a mailing package. We will insert the stickers inside our product or hand them out along with other marketing tools such as flyers or brochures. Research has found that the strongest stickers are usually less than 16 square inches, are printed on white vinyl, and are often die cut. Utilizing a strong design, in a versatile size, and with an eye-catching shape, that is, relevant to our business, will add to the perceived value of our promotional stickers.

We will adhere to the following sticker design tips:
1. We will strengthen our brand by placing our logo on the stickers and using company colors and font styles.
2. We will include our phone number, address, and/or website along with our logo to provide customers with a call to action.
3. We will write compelling copy that solicits an emotional reaction.
4. We will use die-cut stickers using unusual and business relevant shapes to help draw attention to our business.
5. We will consider that size matters and that will be determined by where they will be applied and the degree of desired visibility to be realized.
6. We will be aware of using color on our stickers as color can help create contrast in our design, which enables the directing of prospect eyes to images or actionable items on the stickers.
7. We will encourage customers to post our stickers near their phones, on yellow page book covers, on event invitations, on notepads, on book covers, on gift boxes and packaging, etc.
8. We will place our stickers on all the products we sell and marketing materials we distribute.

ZoomInfo.com
Their vision is to be the sole provider of constantly verified information about companies and their employees, making our data indispensible — available anytime, anywhere and anyplace the customer needs it. Creates just-verified, detailed profiles of 65 million businesspeople and six million businesses. Makes data available through powerful tools for lead generation, prospecting and recruiting.
Examples:
http://www.zoominfo.com/c/Medmark-Medical-Equipment/368752928

CitySlick.net
CitySlick.net's unique approach to *online local advertising* helps distribute search traffic for local businesses. We will get more local customers through the internet via CitySlick's local citation network.

Zipslocal.com
Provides one of the most comprehensive ZIP Code-based local search services, allowing visitors to access information through our online business directories that cover all ZIP Codes in the United States. Interactive local yellow pages show listings and display relevant advertising through the medium of the Internet, making it easy for everyone to find local business information

Hold Biggest Fan Contest
Do you love _____ (company name)? Do you have a great story about how the team at _____ (company Name) helped you "get there" to achieve your goals? Well, then _____ (company name) wants to hear from you! _____ (company name) has launched the "Biggest Fan Contest" on its Facebook Page at the beginning of _____ (month), inviting current and former customers to share why they are _____'s (company name) "Biggest Fan." Participants are eligible to win a number of prizes including: _____.
To enter, visit www.facebook.com/_____ (company name),

"like" the page, and click the "Biggest Fan Contest" tab on the right hand side. Participants are then asked to write a short blurb or upload a photo sharing why they love _____ (company name).
If you have a story to tell or photo to share, enter today. Contest ends _____ (date).
See contest tab for full details.

BusinessVibes   www.businessvibes.com/about-businessvibes

A growing B2B networking platform for global trade professionals. BusinessVibes uses a social networking model for businesses to find and connect with international partner companies. With a network of over 5000+ trade associations, 20 million companies and 25,000+ business events across 100+ major industries and 175 countries, BusinessVibes is a decisive source to companies looking for international business partners, be they clients, suppliers, JV partners, or any other type of business contact.
Examples:
https://www.businessvibes.com/companyprofile/Daves-Medical-Equipment-Rental-LLC

Yext.com

Lets companies manage their digital presence in online maps, directories and apps. Over 400,000 businesses make millions of monthly updates across 85+ exclusive global partners, making Yext the global market leader. Digital presence is a fundamental need for all 50 million businesses in the world, and Yext's mission is perfect location information in every hand. Yext is based in the heart of New York City with 350 employees and was named to Forbes Most Promising Companies lists for 2015 and 2017, as well as the Fortune Best Places to Work 2015 list.

Google+

We will pay specific attention to Google+, which is already playing a more important role in Google's organic ranking algorithm. We will create a business page on Google+ to achieve improved local search visibility. Google+ will also be the best way to get access to

Google Authorship, which will play a huge role in SEO. Aside from having all the necessary information like hours and contact information, quality photos and visuals will be essential on our Google+ local page. To go above the basics, we will have a local Google photographer visit and create a virtual tour.

Resources:
https://plus.google.com/pages/create
http://www.google.com/+/brands/
https://www.google.com/appserve/fb/forms/plusweekly/
https://plus.google.com/+GoogleBusiness/posts
http://marketingland.com/beyond-social-benefits-google-business-73460
http://searchenginewatch.com/sew/how-to/2124899/seo-for-google-profiles-and-pages

Examples:
https://plus.google.com/+Medonecapital

Inbound Marketing

Inbound marketing is about pulling people in by sharing relevant medical equipment rental information, creating useful content, and generally being helpful. It involves writing everything from buyer's guides to blogs and newsletters that deliver useful content. The objective will be to nurture customers through the buying process with unbiased educational materials that turn consumers into informed buyers.
Resource:
www.Hubspot.com

Google My Business Profile
www.google.com/business/befound.html

We will have a complete and active Google My Business profile to give our medical equipment rental company a tremendous advantage over the competition, and help potential customers easily find our firm and provide relevant information about our business.

Sampling Program
We will give each sample with a mini-survey to enable customers to rate the product or service, and supply constructive feedback.

Reddit.com
An online community where users vote on stories. The hottest stories rise to the top, while the cooler stories sink. Comments can be posted on every story, including stories about startup medical equipment rental companies.
Examples:
www.reddit.com/r/bestof/comments/3umkms/redditor_who_works_in_medical_supplies_ company/

Exterior Signage
We will make effective use of the following types of signage:
(select)
1. **Channel Letter**
Channel letters can be illuminated by LED or neon and come in a variety of colors and sizes. Front-lit signs are illuminated from the letter face, while reverse- lit signs are lit from behind the sign. Open-face channel letters lit by exposed neon work well to create a night presence.
2. **Monument Signs**
Monument signs are usually placed at the entrance to a parking lot or a building. This sign can easily be installed on a median or lawn. The size for a monument sign is typically based on city regulations for the specific location. These signs can be illuminated or non-illuminated, single- or double-sided.
3. **Pylon Signs**
Also known as pole signs, they soar high above a business location to set the business apart from other businesses. They get attention from highway motorists who are still a distance away.
4. **Cabinet Signs**
Commonly called "wall" or "box" signs, they are a traditional form of signage. They effectively use a large copy area and eye-popping graphics. This type of signage can highlight our business day or night because we have the option to add

illumination. The background can be the element that lights up, and the copy can   be lit or non-lit.

6.4.1   Strategic Alliances

We will form strategic alliances to accomplish the following objectives:
1. To share marketing expenses.
2. To realize bulk buying power on wholesale purchases.
3. To engage in barter arrangements.
4. To collaborate with industry experts.
5. To set-up mutual referral relationships.

_____ (company name) will provides medical equipment rentals to a wide range of facilities and medical practices including hospitals, ambulatory surgery centers, government facilities, correctional facilities, rehabilitation facilities, school systems, long-term care facilities, assisted living facilities, home health agencies and medical clinics. We plan to develop the largest network of physicians, nurses and allied Medical providers to meet the clinical medical equipment rental needs of almost any facility.

We will develop strategic alliances with the following service providers by conducting introductory 'cold calls' to their offices and making them aware of our capabilities by distributing our corporate brochures and business cards:

1.	Adult Daycare Centers	2.	Health Clubs
3.	Hospitals	4.	Nursing Homes
5.	Assisted living residences	6.	Schools
7.	Physician practices	8.	Camps
9.	Ambulatory Centers	10.	Rehabilitation Centers
11.	Home Medical Centers Services	12.	Laboratory
13.	Pharmacies	14.	Retirement homes

15. Skilled Nursing Facilities Departments
16. Health
17. Insurance Companies Healthcare Companies
18. Home
19. Government Agencies Centers
20. Radiology
21. Urgent Care Centers institutions
22. Educational
23. Home Healthcare Agencies
24. Nursing Homes
25. Outpatient Clinics Centers
26. Acute Care
27. Long term Treatment Care Centers
28. Hospices
29. Health Care providers Practitioners
30. Private
31. Geriatric Care providers one-on-one
32. Private families

We will assemble and present a sales presentation package that includes sales brochures, business cards, and a DVD presentation of basic temp hiring tips, and client testimonials. We will include coupons that offer a discount or other type of introductory deal. We will ask to set-up a take-one display for our sales brochures at the business registration counter.

We will promptly give the referring business any one or combination of the following agreed upon reward options:
1. Referral fees
2. Free services
3. Mutual referral exchanges

We will monitor referral sources to evaluate the mutual benefits of the alliance and make certain to clearly define and document our referral incentives prior to initiating our referral exchange program.

6.4.2 Monitoring Marketing Results

To monitor how well _____ (company name) is doing, we will measure how well the advertising campaign is working by taking customer surveys. What we would like to know is how they heard of us and how they like and dislike about our medical equipment rental services. In order to get responses to the surveys, we will be give discounts as thank you rewards.

Response Tracking Methods

Coupons: ad-specific coupons that easily enable tracking
Landing Pages: unique web landing pages for each advertisement
800 Numbers: unique 1-800-# per advertisement
Email Service Provider: Instantly track email views, opens, and clicks
Address inclusion of dept # or suite #.

Our financial statements will offer excellent data to track all phases of sales. These are available for review on a daily basis.
_____ (company name) will benchmark our objectives for sales promotion and advertising in order to evaluate our return on invested marketing dollars, and determine where to concentrate our limited advertising dollars to realize the best return. We will also strive to stay within our marketing budget.

Key Marketing Metrics

We will use the following two marketing metrics to evaluate the cost-effectiveness of our marketing campaign:

1. The cost to acquire a new customer: The average dollar amount invested to get one new client. Example: If we invest $3,000 on marketing in a single month and end the month with 10 new customers, our cost of acquisition is $300 per new customer.

2. The lifetime value of the average active customer. The average dollar value of an average customer over the life of their business with you. To calculate this metric for a given period of time, we will take the total amount of revenue our business generated during the time period and divide it by the total number of customers we had from the beginning of the time period.

3. We will track the following set of statistics on a weekly basis to keep informed of the progress of our practice:
    A. Number of total referrals.
    B. Percentage increase of total referrals (over baseline).
    C. Number of new referral sources.

D. Number of new customers/month.
E. Number of Leads

Key Marketing Metrics Table

We've listed some key metrics in the following table. We will need to keep a close eye on these, to see if we meet our own forecasted expectations. If our numbers are off in too many categories, we may, after proper analysis, have to make substantial changes to our marketing efforts.

Key Marketing Metrics	2017	2018	2019
Revenue			
Leads			
Leads Converted			
Avg. Transaction per Customer			
Avg. Dollars per Customer			
Number of Referrals			
Number of PR Appearances			
Number of Testimonials			
Number of New Club Members			
Number of Returns			
Number of BBB Complaints			
Number of Completed Surveys			
Number of Blog readers			

Number of Twitter followers

Number of Facebook Fans

Metric Definitions
1.   Leads: Individuals who step into the store to consider a purchase.
2.   Leads Converted: Percent of individuals who actually make a purchase.
3.   Average Transactions Per Customer: Number of purchases per customer per   month. Expected to rise significantly as customers return for more and more _____ items per month
4.   Average $ Per Customer: Average dollar amount of each transaction. Expected to rise along with average transactions.
5.   Referrals: Includes customer and business referrals
6.   PR Appearances: Online or print mentions of the business that are not paid   advertising. Expected to be high upon opening, then drop off and rise again until   achieving a steady level.
7.   Testimonials: Will be sought from the best and most loyal customers. Our   objective is ___ (#) per month) and they will be added to the website. Some will   be sought as video testimonials.
8.   New Loyalty Club Members: This number will rise significantly as more   customers see the value in repeated visits and the benefits of club membership.
9.   Number of Returns/BBB Complaints: Our goal is zero.
10.   Number of Completed Surveys: We will provide incentives for customers to   complete customer satisfaction surveys.

6.4.3   Word-of-Mouth Marketing

We plan to make use of the following techniques to promote

word-of-mouth advertising:
1. Repetitive Image Advertising
2. Provide exceptional customer service.
3. Make effective use of loss leaders.
2. Schedule in-store activities, such as demonstrations or special events.
3. Make trial easy with a coupon or introductory discount.
4. Initiate web and magazine article submissions
5. Utilize a sampling program
6. Add a forward email feature to our website.
7. Share relevant and believable testimonial letters
8. Publish staff bios.
9. Make product/service upgrade announcements
10. Hold contests or sweepstakes
12. Have involvement with community events.
13. Pay suggestion box rewards
14. Distribute a monthly newsletter
15. Share easy-to-understand information (via an article or seminar).
16. Make personalized marketing communications.
17. Structure our referral program.
18. Sharing of Community Commonalities
19. Invitations to join our community of shared interests.
20. Publish Uncensored Customer Reviews
21. Enable Information Exchange Forums
22. Provide meaningful comparisons with competitors.
23. Clearly state our user benefits.
24. Make and honor ironclad guarantees
25. Provide superior post-sale support

26. Provide support in the pre-sale decision making process.
27. Host Free Informational Seminars or Workshops
28. Get involved with local business organizations.
29. Issue Press Release coverage of charitable involvements.
30. Hold traveling company demonstrations/exhibitions/competitions.

6.4.4 Customer Satisfaction Survey

We will design a customer satisfaction survey to measure the "satisfaction quotient" of our Medical Equipment Rental Company customers. By providing a detailed snapshot of our current customer base, we will be able to generate more repeat and referral business and enhance the profitability of our leasing company.

Our Customer Satisfaction Survey will including the following basics:
1. How do our customers rate our medical equipment rental business?
2. How do our customers rate our competition?
3. How well do our customers rate the value of our products or services?
4. What new customer needs and trends are emerging?
5. How loyal are our customers?
6. What can be done to improve customer loyalty and repeat business?
7. How strongly do our customers recommend our business?
8. What is the best way to market our business?
9. What new value-added services would best differentiate our business from that of our competitors?
10. How can we encourage more referral business?
11. How can our pricing strategy be improved?

Our customer satisfaction survey will help to answer these questions and more. From the need for continual new products and services to improved customer service, our satisfaction surveys will allow our business to quickly identify problematic and underperforming areas, while enhancing our overall customer satisfaction.

Examples:
http://www.heartlandmedequip.com/customer-satisfaction-survey/

Resources:
https://www.survata.com/
https://www.google.com/insights/consumersurveys/use_cases
https://www.surveymonkey.com/mp/customer-satisfaction-survey-questions/
http://www.smetoolkit.org/smetoolkit/en/content/en/6708/Customer-Satisfaction-Survey- Template-
http://smallbusiness.chron.com/common-questions-customer-service-survey-1121.html
http://smallbiztrends.com/2014/11/tailoring-survey-questions-for-your-industry.html
http://www.amplituderesearch.com/customer-satisfaction-surveys.shtml

6.4.5 Marketing Training Program

Our Marketing Training Program will include both an initial orientation and training, as well as ongoing continuing education classes. Initial orientation will be run by the owner until an HR manager is hired. For one week, half of each day will be spent in training, and the other half shadowing the operation's manager. Training will include:

- Learning the entire selection of Medical Equipment Rental Company services.
- Understanding our Mission Statement, Value Proposition, Position Statement and Unique Selling Proposition.
- Appreciating our competitive advantages.
- Understanding our core message and branding approach.
- Learning our store's policies; returns processing, complaint handling, etc.
- Learning our customer services standards of practice.

Learning our customer and business referral programs.
Learning our Membership Club procedures, rules and benefits.
Becoming familiar with our company website, and online ordering options.
Service procedures specific to the employee's role.

Ongoing workshops will be based on customer feedback and problem areas identified by mystery buyers, which will better train employees to educate customers. These ongoing workshops will be held ____ (once?) a month for ____ (three?) hours.

6.5   Sales Strategy

The development of our sales strategy will start by developing a better understanding of our customer needs. To accomplish this task we will pursue the following research methods:
1.   Join the medical trade associations that our target customers belong to.
2.   Contact the membership director and establish a relationship to understand their   member's needs, challenges and concerns.
3.   Identify non-competitive suppliers who sell to our customer to learn their   challenges and look for partnering solutions.
4.   Work directly with our customer and ask them what their needs are and if our   business may offer a possible solution.

The Management of our company will focus on weekly sales revenue goals, and explaining any variances. Best value services will be identified to assist customers with smart purchase selections. The situation will be monitored to insure that the company invests adequately in its own operations.

Sales feedback will be elicited to stimulate ideas, approaches, relate success stories, instruct in new techniques, share news, and implement improvements. Major corporate accounts will be solicited through networking, neighborhood solicitations via sales agents, and opportunistic encounters at any time by management.

_____ (company name) will keep its placement prices competitive with other Medical Equipment Rental Companies in a ___ (#) mile radius of our office. Customers that purchase more than $___ (10000) worth of combined services will be given ___ (5)% coupon on future purchases.

Our focus will be on making the medical equipment rental services we offer of the highest possible quality. Only when those services are well-established, will we consider expanding our range of services offered. We will become a one-stop shop for medical equipment rental services, and specialized program offerings. We will also be very active in the community, building a solid reputation with professionals and community leaders.

Our clients will be primarily obtained through word-of-mouth referrals, but we will also advertise introductory offers to introduce people to our frequent buyer and preferred club membership programs. The combination of the perception of higher quality, exceptional customer service, innovative medical equipment rental services and the recognition of superior value should turn referral leads into satisfied customers.

The company's sales strategy will be based on the following elements:
- Advertising in the Yellow Pages - two inch by three inch ads describing our services will be placed in the local Yellow Pages.
- Placing classified advertisements in the regional editions of trade magazines.
- Word of mouth referrals - generating sales leads in the local community through customer referrals.

Our basic sales strategy is to:
- Develop a website for lead generation by _____ (date).
- Provide exceptional customer service.
- Accept payment by all major credit cards, cash, PayPal and check.
- Survey our customers regarding medical equipment rental

services they would like to see added.

Sponsor charitable and other community events.

Provide tours of the company so customers can learning how to be discriminating customers and build a trust bond with our operations.

Motivate employees with a pay-for-performance component to their straight salary compensation package, based on profits and customer satisfaction rates.

Build long-term customer relationships by putting the interests of customers first.

Establish mutually beneficial relationship with local businesses serving the child caring and socializing needs of local residents.

6.5.1   Customer Retention Strategy

We will use the following post-purchase techniques to improve customer retention, foster referrals and improve the profitability of our business:

1. Keep the office sparkling clean and well-organized.
2. Use only well-trained sales associates.
3. Actively solicit customer feedback and promptly act upon their inputs.
4. Tell customers how much you appreciate their business.
5. Call regular customers by their first names.
6. Send thank you notes.
7. Offer free new product and service samples.
8. Change displays and sales presentations on a regular basis.
9. Practice good phone etiquette
10. Respond to complaints promptly.
11. Reward referrals.
12. Publish a monthly opt-in direct response newsletter with customized content, dependent on recipient stated information preferences .
13. Develop and publish a list of frequently asked questions.
14. Issue Preferred Customer Membership Cards.

15. Hold informational seminars and workshops.
16. Provide an emergency hotline number.
17. Publish code of ethics and our service guarantees.
18. Help customers to make accurate competitor comparisons.
19. Build a stay-in-touch (drip marketing) communications calendar.
20. Keep marketing communications focused on our competitive advantages.
21. Offer repeat user discounts and incentives.
22. Be supportive and encouraging, and not judgmental.
23. Measure customer retention and look at recurring revenue and customer surveys.
24. Build a community of shared interests by offering a website forum or discussion group for professionals and patients to allow sharing of knowledge.
25. Offer benefits above and beyond those of our competitors.
26. Issue reminder emails and holiday gift cards.

We will also consider the following Customer Retention Programs:
    Type of Program
    Customer Rewards

Type of Program	Customer Rewards
Frequency Purchase Loyalty Program	Special Discounts
'Best Customer' Program	Free Product or Services
Affinity Programs	Special Recognition/Treatment/Offers
Credit Card Points	Sharing of Common Interests
Customer Community Programs	Accumulate Participation
Auto-Knowledge Building Programs	Special Event
Profile Building Programs	Purchase
Transaction History	Recommendations based On Past

Recommendations Based on Stated Customer Profile Information.

6.5.2 Sales Forecast

Our sales projections are based on the following:
1. Actual sales volumes of local competitors
2. Interviews with other Medical Equipment Rental Company owners and managers
3. Observations of office sales and traffic at competitor establishments.
4. Government and industry trade statistics
5. Local demographics and projections.

With _____ (community name) growing from a base of ____ (#) to _____ (#) residents, we expect Medical equipment rental revenue from Medical organizations in a range of $_____ to $_____ over the course of the next _____ (#) years.

The balance of our forecasted rental sales, representing some ____ (20)% of total sales, will come from sources external to _____ (community name), including corporate consulting services.

Our sales forecast is an estimated projection of expected sales over the next three years, based on our chosen marketing strategy, economic conditions and assumed competitive environment.

Sales are expected to be below average during the first year, until a regular customer base has been established. It has been estimated that it takes the average Medical Equipment Rental Company a minimum of two years to establish a significant customer base. After the customer base is built, sales will grow at an accelerated rate from word-of-mouth referrals and continued networking efforts. We expect sales to steadily increase as our marketing campaign, employee training programs and contact management system are executed.

By using advertising, especially discounted introductory coupons, as a catalyst for this prolonged process, ____(company name) plans to attract more customers sooner. Throughout the first year, it is forecasted that sales will incrementally grow until profitability is reached toward the end of year ___(one?). Year two reflects a conservative growth rate of ____ (20?) percent. Year three reflects a growth rate of _____ (25?) percent. We expect to be open for business on ____ (date), and start with an initial enrollment of ____ (#) parents. With our unique household rental service offerings, along with our thorough and aggressive marketing strategies, we believe that sales forecasts are actually on the conservative side.

Table: Sales Forecast

Sales	2017	Annual Sales 2018	Sales 2019
Equipment Rental Services			
Equity Rental Services			
Operating Lease Services			
Capital Lease Services			
Refurbish Equipment			
Customized Solutions			
Asset Management Services			
Equipment Maintenance Services			
Consulting/Seminars			
Supply Sales			

Misc.

Total Unit Sales

Direct Cost of Sales:
Equipment Rental Services

Equity Rental Services

Operating Lease Services

Capital Lease Services

Refurbish Equipment

Customized Solutions

Asset Management Services

Equipment Maintenance Services

Consulting/Seminars

Supply Sales

Misc.

Subtotal Direct Cost of Sales

6.6 Merchandising Strategy

Merchandising is that part of our marketing strategy that is involved with promoting the sales of our merchandise, as by consideration of the most effective means of selecting, pricing, displaying, and advertising items for sale in our Medical Equipment Rental

Company business. Through proper product placement, space allocation, and in-store promotion, sales space will be geared towards high profit margin products.

The décor of the merchandising area is extremely important to sales. Display units are primary, but lighting, furniture, wall surfaces, window treatments, carpeting, accessories and countertops will all play important supporting roles.

We will monitor our sales figures and data to confirm that products in demand are well-stocked and slow moving software products are phased-out. We will improve telephone skills of employees to boost phone orders. We will attach our own additional business labels to all products to promote our line of services and location.

6.7 Pricing Strategy

When setting prices, we will consider the following factors:
1. Direct Costs: labor, time and supplies
2. Indirect Costs: rent, utilities, taxes and expenses.
3. Demand: economic conditions, demographics, consumer behavior, etc.
4. Marketing Promotions
5. Level of Competition
6. Positioning Image
7. Goals: profit objectives, return on investment, growth objectives.

Pricing will be based on competitive parity guidelines. Prices will be consistent with those of the other medical equipment rental companies in the area, with the exception of very high-volume operations who have more powerful pricing leverage. Pricing will be monitored continuously against neighborhood and other competitive sources who we can readily research.

We are not interested in being the low price leader, as our pricing strategy plays a major role in whether we will be able to create and maintain customers for a profit. Our revenue structure must support our cost structure, so the salaries we pay to our staff are balanced by the revenue we collect.

Example of Medical Equipment Rental Rates
www.mccannsmedical.com/medical-equipment-rental

Sample Rental Rate Schedule
www.hhdepot.com/sites/327/uploaded/files/Rental_Rate_Sheet.pdf

The number of competitors in the area largely determines what type of pricing we will have. We don't want to be known as the highest price company in town but it is equally important not to be the cheapest. We will continuously try to expand our rental service offerings.

Price List Comparison

Competitor	Service	Our Price	Competitor Price
B/(W) Competitor			

We will adopt the following pricing guidelines:
1. We must insure that our price plus service equation is perceived to be an exceptional value proposition.
2. We must refrain from competing on price, but always be price competitive.
3. We must develop value-added services, and bundle those with our products to create offerings that cannot be easily price compared.
4. We must focus attention on our competitive advantages.
5. Development of a pricing strategy based on our market positioning strategy, which is ____ (mass market value leadership/exceptional premium niche value?)

6. Our pricing policy objective, which is to _____ (increase profit margins/achieve revenue maximization to increase market share/lower unit costs).
7. We will use marketplace intelligence and gain insights from competitor pricing.
8. We will solicit pricing feedback from customers using surveys and interviews.
9. We will utilize limited time pricing incentives to penetrate niche markets
10. We will conduct experiments at prices above and below the current price to determine the price elasticity of demand. (Inelastic demand or demand that does not decrease with a price increase, indicates that price increases may be feasible.)
11. We will keep our offerings and prices simple to understand and competitive, based on market intelligence.
12. We will consider a price for volume strategy on certain items, and study the effects of price on volume and of volume on costs, as in a recession, trying to recover these costs through a price increase can be fatal.

Determining the costs of servicing business is the most important part of covering our expenses and earning profits. We will factor in the following pricing formula:

Product Cost + Materials + Overhead + Labor + Profit + Tax = Price

Materials are those items consumed in the delivering of the service.

Overhead costs are the variable and fixed expenses that must be covered to stay in business. Variable costs are those expenses that fluctuate including vehicle expenses, rental expenses, utility bills and supplies. Fixed costs include the purchase of equipment, service ware, marketing and advertising, and insurance. After overhead costs are determined, the total overhead costs are divided among the total number of transactions forecasted for the year.

Labor costs include the costs of performing the services. Also included are Social Security taxes (FICA), vacation time, retirement and other benefits such as health or life insurance. To determine labor costs per hour, keep a time log. When placing a value on our time, we will consider the following: 1) skill and reputation; 2) wages paid by employers for similar skills and 3) where we live. Other pricing factors include image, inflation, supply and demand, and competition.

Profit is a desired percentage added to our total costs. We will need to determine the percentage of profit added to each service. It will be important to cover all our costs to stay in business. We will investigate available computer software programs to help us price our services and keep financial data for decision-making purposes. Close contact with customers will allow our company to react quickly to changes in demand.

We will develop a pricing strategy that will reinforce the perception of value to the customer and manage profitability, especially in the face of rising inflation. To ensure our success, we will use periodic competitor and customer research to continuously evaluate our pricing strategy. We intend to review our profit margins every six months.

6.8 Differentiation Strategies

We will use differentiation strategies to develop and market unique services for different customer segments. To differentiate ourselves from the competition, we will focus on the assets, creative ideas and competencies that we have that none of our competitors has.
The goal of our differentiation strategies is to be able to charge a premium price for our unique products and services and/or to promote loyalty and assist in retaining our customers.

Differentiation in our medical equipment rental business will be achieved in the following types of ways, including:

                                                                  Explanation

  Product features

Complementary services
_____

Technology embodied in design
_____

Location
_____

Service innovations
_____

Superior service
_____

Creative advertising
_____

Better supplier relationships
_____

Source: http://scholarship.sha.cornell.edu/cgi/viewcontent.cgi?article=1295&context=articles

Differentiating will mean defining who our perfect target market is and then catering to their needs, wants and interests better than everyone else. It will be about using surveys to determine what's most important to our targeted market and giving it to them consistently. It will not be about being "everything to everybody"; but rather, "the absolute best to our chosen targeted group".

In developing our differentiation strategy will we use the following form to help define our differences:

1. Targeted customer segments
_____

2. Customer characteristics
_____

3. Customer demographics
_____

4. Customer behavior
_____

5. Geographic focus
_____

6. Ways of working

7. Service delivery approach

8. Customer problems/pain points

9. Complexity of customers' problems

10. Range of services

We will use the following approaches to differentiate our products and services from those of our competitors to stand apart from standardised offerings:

1. Superior quality
2. Unusual or unique product features
3. More responsive customer service
4. Rapid product or service innovation
5. Advanced technological features
6. Engineering design or styling
7. Additional product features
8. An image of prestige or status

Specific Differentiators will include the following:
1. Being a Specialist in one procedure
2. Utilizing advanced/uncommon technology
3. Possessing extensive experience
4. Building an exceptional facility
5. Consistently achieving superior results
6. Having a caring and empathetic personality
7. Giving customer s WOW experience, including a professional customer welcome   package.
8. Enabling convenience and 24/7 online accessibility
9. Calling customers to express interest in their challenges.
10. Keeping to the appointment schedule.
11. Remembering customer names and details like they were family
12. Assuring customer fears.
13. Building a visible reputation and recognition around our

community
14. Acquiring special credentials or professional memberships
15. Providing added value services, such as taxi service, longer hours, financing plans, and post-sale services.

Primary Differentiation Strategies:
1. Beyond a marketing tool, we will use the web as a way to build an online community both among Medical professionals and between Medical organizations.
2. Technology will be a key differentiator, because being able to provide customized usage reports, sophisticated compliance systems, and real-time information on equipment performance are valuable services for today's Medical organizations.
3. We will utilize software systems that will enable us to personalize each customer's leasing experience, including easy access to customer transaction history, profile search criteria and information about all the services of interest to that particular client.
4. We will develop a referral program that turns our clients into referral agents.
5. We will use regular client satisfaction surveys to collect feedback, improvement ideas, referrals and testimonials.
6. We will promote our "green" practices, such as establishing a recycling program, purchasing recycled-content office goods and responsibly handling hazardous wastes.
7. We will customize our proposals according to the language, cultural influences, customs, interests and preferences of our local market to create loyalty and increase sales.
8. We will develop the expertise to satisfy the needs of targeted market segments with customized and exceptional maintenance and support services.
9. We take the time to understand our clients' business cultures, objectives and goals.
10. We will work with our customers to reduce the customer's cost of managing our interface with them and contribute positively to the customer's bottom line.
11. We will develop the ability of our customers to evaluate and improve the profitability and performance of contribution to their

profitability.

12. We will acquire the software to generate proposals in real-time.

6.9 Milestones (select)

The Milestones Chart is a timeline that will guide our company in developing and growing our business. It will list chronologically the various critical actions and events that must occur to bring our business to life. We will make certain to assign real, attainable dates to each planned action or event.

_____ (company name) has identified several specific milestones which will function as goals for the company. The milestones will provide a target for achievement as well as a mechanism for tracking progress. The dates were chosen based on realistic delivery times and necessary construction times. All critical path milestones will be completed within their allotted time frames to ensure the success of contingent milestones. The following table will provide a timeframe for each milestone.

Table: Milestones

Milestones Budget Responsibility	Start Date	End Date
Business Plan Completion		
Secure Permits/Licenses		
Locate & Secure Space		
Obtain Insurance Coverage		
Secure Additional Financing		

Get Start-up Supplies Quotes

Obtain County Certification

Purchase Office Equipment

Renovate Facilities

Define Marketing Programs

Install Equipment/Displays

Technology Systems

Set-up Accounting System

Develop Office Policies

Develop Procedures Manual

Arrange Support Service Providers

Finalize Media Plan

Create Facebook Business Page

Open Twitter Account

Conduct Blogger Outreach

Develop Personnel Plan

Develop Staff Training Programs

Hire/Train Staff

Implement Marketing Plan

Get Website Live

Conduct SEO Campaign

Form Strategic Alliances

Purchase Start-up Inventory/Supplies

Press Release Announcements

Advertise Grand Opening

Kickoff Advertising Program

Join Community Orgs./Network

Conduct Satisfaction Surveys

Evaluate/Revise Plan

Monitor Social Media Networks

Respond Positively to Reviews

Measure Return on Marketing $$$

Devise Growth Strategy

Revenues Exceed $_____

Reach Profitability

Totals:

7.0 Website Plan Summary

_____ (company name) is currently developing a website at the URL address www. (company name).com. We will focus on updating our website, adding new services, features and functions for our clients. We understand the special training, licensing and compliance requirements in Medical, as well as the need for skilled, motivated and productive employees and our website needs to reflect that knowledge and experience. Our site will also have enhanced search functions to assist physicians, nurses, laboratory technicians and other Medical professionals search for jobs in their local communities or in different areas of the country.

The website will be developed to offer customers a product catalog for online orders. The overriding design philosophy of the site will be ease of use. We want to make the process of placing an order as easy and fast as possible thereby encouraging increased sales. We will incorporate special features such as a section that is specific to each customer so the customer can easily make purchases of repeat items. Instead of going through the website every month and locating their monthly needs, the site will capture regularly ordered items for that specific customer, significantly speeding up the ordering process. This ease-of-use feature will help increase sales as customers become more and more familiar with the site and appreciate how easy it is to place an order.

We will also provide multiple incentives to sign-up for various benefits, such as our newsletters and promotional sale notices. This will help us to build an email database, which will supply our automated customer follow-up system. We will create a personalized drip marketing campaign to stay in touch with our customers and prospects.

We will develop our website to be a resource for web visitors who are seeking knowledge and information about brand comparisons, with a goal to service the knowledge needs of our customers and generate leads. Our home page will be designed to be a "welcome mat" that clearly presents our service offerings and provides links through which visitors can gain easy access to the information they seek. We will use our website to match the problems our customers face with the solutions we offer.

We will use the free tool, Google Analytics (http://www.google.com/analytics), to generate a history and measure our return on investment. Google Analytics is a free tool that can offer insight by allowing the user to monitor traffic to a single website. We will just add the Google Analytics code to our website and Google will give our firm a dashboard providing the number of unique visitors, repeat traffic, page views, etc.
This will help to stop wasting our company's money on inefficient marketing. Using an analytic program will show exactly which leads are paying off, and which ones to do without. We will find out what's bringing our site the most traffic and how to improve upon that.

To improve the readability of our website, we will organize our website content in the following ways.
1. Headlines
2. Bullet points
3. Callout text
4. Top of page summaries

To improve search engine optimization, we will maximize the utilization of the following;
1. Links
2. Headers
3. Bold text
4. Bullets
5. Keywords
6. Meta tags

This website will serve the following purposes:
About Us   How We Work/Our Philosophy
Our Clients
Service Team
Personnel Benefits and Incentives
Contact Us   Customer service contact info
Our Leasing Service Options   Medical
Equipment Rentals
Request a Quote   Form
Lease Application   Form

Financial Forms	
Mobile Apps	
Equipment Manuals	
Community Outreach Programs	
Frequently Asked Questions	FAQs
Articles	Interview Tips
Club Membership	Sign-up
Newsletter Sign-up	Join Mailing List
Newsletter Archives	Articles
Upcoming Events Schedule	Wine Tasting
Testimonials	Letters w/photos
Referral Rewards Program	Details
Customer Satisfaction Survey	Feedback
Press Releases	Community Involvement
Strategic Alliance Partners	Links
Tradeshow Schedule	
Training Programs	Password Login
Resources	Professional
Associations	
RentalBlog comments	Accept
Refer-a-Friend	Viral marketing
YouTube Video Clips	Seminar
Presentation/Testimonials	
Service Guarantees	
Code of Ethics	Compliance
Privacy Policy	
Customer Service Policy	
Report a Compliance Concern	Form
Join Our Staff Opportunities	Career
Client Access	Make a Payment
Social Networking Pages MySpace/Facebook/Twitter	
Heathcare News	
Classified Ads	

Classified Ads
By joining and incorporating a classified ad affiliate program into our website, we will create the ultimate win-win-win. We will provide our guests with a free benefit, increase our rankings with the search engines by incorporating keyword hyperlinks into our site, attract additional markets to expose to our product, create an additional income source as they upgrade their ads, and provide our prospects a reason to return to our web site again and again Resources:

    App Themes
    www.appthemes.com/themes/classipress/
    e-Classifieds   http://www.e-classifieds.net/
    Noah's Classifieds   http://www.noahsclassifieds.org/
    Joom Prod   http://www.joomprod.com/
    Flynax   http://www.flynax.com/
    Market Grabber   http://www.marketgrabber.com/

7.1 Website Marketing Strategy

Our online marketing strategy will employ the following distinct mechanisms:

1. Search Engine Submission
   This will be most useful to people who are unfamiliar with _____ (company name), but are looking for a local Medical Equipment Rental Company. There will also be searches from customers who may know about us, but who are seeking additional information.

2. Website Address (URL) on Marketing Materials
   Our URL will be printed on all marketing communications, business cards, letterheads, faxes, and invoices and product labels. This will encourage a visit to our website for additional information

3. Online Directories Listings
   We will make an effort to list our website on relevant, free and paid online directories and manufacturer website product

locators.

The good online directories possess the following features:
Free or paid listings that do not expire and do not require monthly renewal.
Ample space to get your advertising message across.
Navigation buttons that are easy for visitors to use.
Optimization for top placement in the search engines based on keywords that people typically use to find Medical Equipment Rental Companies.
Direct links to your website, if available.
An ongoing directory promotion campaign to maintain high traffic volumes to the directory site.

4. Strategic Business Partners

We will use a Business Partners page to cross-link to prominent _____ (city) area Medical web sites as well as the city Web sites and local recreational sites.   We will also cross-link with brand name suppliers.

5.   YouTube Posting

We will produce a video of testimonials from several of our satisfied clients and   educate viewers as to the range of our leasing services and products. Our research   indicates that the YouTube video will also serve to significantly improve our   ranking with the Google Search Engine.

6.   Exchange of links with strategic marketing partners.

We will cross-link to non-profit businesses that accept our gift donations as in-   house run contest prize awards.

7.   E-Newsletter

Use the newsletter sign-up as a reason to collect email addresses and limited profiles, and use embedded links in the newsletter to return readers to website.

8.   Create an account for your photos on flickr.com

Use the name of your site on flickr so you have the same keywords and your   branded.

9.   Geo Target Pay Per Click (PPC) Campaign

Available through Google Adwords program. Example keywords include Health   Care Equipment, Medical Equipment

Rental Company, equity leasing and _(city).

10. Post messages on Internet user groups and forums.
Get involved with Medical rentalrelated discussion groups and forums and develop a descriptive signature paragraph.
Ex: www.smallbusinessonlinecommunity.bankofamerica.com/message/97573

11. Write up your own MySpace.com and Facebook.com bios.
Highlight your background and professional interests.

12. Facebook.com Brand-Building Applications:
- Upload Videos of new seminars.   - Download wallpaper for cell phones.
- Sign-up for latest news and mailing list.   - Enter Contests
- Link to company website.   - Discussion Boards/ Solicit Feedback
- Post testimonials

13. Blog to share our success stories and solicit comments
Blogging will be a great way for us to share information, expertise, and news, and start a conversation with our customers, the media, suppliers, and any other target audiences. Blogging will be a great online marketing strategy because it keeps our content fresh, engages our audience to leave comments on specific posts, improves search engine rankings and attracts links. In the blog we will share Medical Professional screening tips. We will also provide a link to our Facebook.com page. Resource: www.blogger.com www.blogspot.com

7.2 Development Requirements

A full development plan will be generated as documented in the milestones. Costs that ____ (company name) will expect to incur with development of its new website include:

Development Costs
User interface design $_____.

Site development and testing	$_____
Site Implementation	$._____

Ongoing Costs

Website name registration	$_____ per year.
Site Hosting	$_____ or less per month.

Site design changes, updates and maintenance are considered part of Marketing.

The site will be developed by _____ (company name), a local start-up company. The user interface designer will use our existing graphic art to come up with the website logo and graphics. We have already secured hosting with a local provider, _____ (business name). Additionally, they will prepare a monthly statistical usage report to analyze and improve web usage and return on investment.

The plan is for the website to be live by ___(date). Basic website maintenance, including update and data entry will be handled by our staff. Site content, such as images and text will be maintained by _____ (owner name). In the future, we may need to contract with a technical resource to build the trackable article download and newsletter capabilities.

Resource: www.1and1.com

7.3   Sample Frequently Asked Questions

We will use the following guidelines when developing the frequently asked questions for our the ecommerce section of the website:

1.   Use a Table of Contents: Offer subject headers at the top of the FAQ page with a hyperlink to that related section further down on the page for quick access.

2.   Group Questions in a Logical Way and group separate specific questions related   to a subject together.

3.   Be Precise With the Question: Don't use open-ended questions.

4. Avoid Too Many Questions: Publish only the popular questions and answers.
5. Answer the Question with a direct answer.
6. Link to Resources When Available: via hyperlinks so the customer can continue with self-service support.
7. Use Bullet Points to list step-by-step instructions.
8. Focus on Customer Support and Not Marketing.
9. Use Real and Relevant Frequently Asked Questions from actual customers.
10. Update Your FAQ Page as customers continue to communicate questions.

The following frequently asked questions will enable us to convey a lot of important information to our clients in a condensed format. We will post these questions and answers on our website and create a hardcopy version to be included on our sales presentation folder.

What are your office hours?
Monday through Friday from 8:30 AM to 5 PM and 9 AM to 4 PM on Saturday, with afterhours voicemail, including holidays.

Is the equipment medically necessary?
Medicare will only cover medical equipment products and services that are considered medically necessary, i.e., are needed for the diagnosis or treatment of your medical condition. For some special equipment, such as home oxygen and patient lifts, Medicare requires a Certificate of Medical Necessity from your physician's office before coverage is approved.

Should I reserve equipment in advance?
We will accept reservations up to a year in advance. Once your plans are firm then make your equipment reservation.

What makes ___ (company name) stand apart from other rental companies?
Our commitment to not compromise on equipment inspection procedures, our professionalism, our ability to listen and respond to our clients and our availability is the best around. From the feedback we get from clients, they say that we are the most responsive

company with whom they have ever worked.

What is the difference between a standard hospital bed and luxury hospital bed?

A luxury hospital bed has all of the functionality of a standard full electric hospital bed but comes standard with an upgraded 10″ foam innerspring mattress. By comparison, standard full or semi electric hospital beds come with 7″ innerspring or foam mattress. Luxury beds are also distinguished from standard hospital beds by the base unit the upgraded mattress rests upon. Standard hospital bed frames are metallic and have to be assembled in two pieces. Luxury bed base units are one piece and padded.

Sample Home Medical Rental Questions and Answers
http://www.kindredathome.com/resources/durable-medical-equipment-faqs/

7.4 Website Performance Summary

We will use web analysis tools to monitor web traffic, such as identifying the number of site visits. We will analyze customer transactions and take actions to minimize problems, such as incomplete sales and abandoned shopping carts. We will use the following table to track the performance of our website:

Category	2017 Fcst	2017 Act	2018 Fcst	2018 Act	2019 Fcst	2019 Act
No. of Customers						
New Newsletter Subscribers						
Unique Visitors						
Avg. Time on Site						

Pages per Visit _____

Percent New Visits _____

Bounce Rate _____

No. of Products _____

Product Categories _____

Number of Incomplete Sales _____

Conversion Rate _____

Affiliate Sales _____

Customer Satisfaction Score _____

8.0 Operations Plan

Operations include the business aspects of running our business, such as conducting quality assessment and improvement activities, auditing functions, cost-management analysis, and customer service. Our operations plan will present an overview of the flow of the daily activities of the business and the strategies that support them. It will focus on the following critical operating factors that will make the business a success:

1.   We will enjoy the following advantages in the sourcing of our inventory:

   _____

   _____

2.   We will utilize the following technological innovations in the customer   relationship management (CRM) process:

   _____

   _____

3.   We will make use of the following advantages in our distribution process:

   _____

   _____

4. We will develop the following in-house training program to improve worker productivity:

_____

5. We will utilize the following system to better control inventory carrying costs.

_____

_____

6. We will implement the following quality control plan:

_____

_____

Quality Control Plan
Our Quality Control Plan will include a review process that checks all factors involved in our operations. The main objectives of our quality control plan will be to uncover defects and bottlenecks, and reporting to management level to make the decisions on the improvement of the whole production process. Our review process will include the following activities:
    Quality control checklist
    Finished product/service review
    Structured walkthroughs
    Statistical sampling
    Testing process

Operations Planning
We will use Microsoft Visio to develop visual maps, which will piece together the different activities in our organization and show how they contribute to the overall "value stream" of our business. We will rightfully treat operations as the lifeblood of our business. We will develop a combined sales and operations planning process where sales and operations managers will sit down every month to review sales, at the same time creating a forward-looking 12-month rolling plan to help guide the product development and manufacturing processes, which can become disconnected from sales. We will approach our operations planning using a three-step process that analyzes the company's current state, future state and the initiatives it will tackle next. For each initiative, such as launching a new product or service, the company will examine the related financials, talent and operations needs, as well as target customer

profiles. Our management team will map out the cost of development and then calculate forecasted return on investment and revenue predictions.

The Operating Plan will focus on creating a retail infrastructure by establishing permanent offices and forging strategic alliances with key customer groups.

Start-up Business Manuals

Our Operations Manuals will be a comprehensive blueprint for structuring our company for efficiency, reliability, and profit maximization. They will also include 'how-to' guides and training programs, which contain the forms and procedures we can use to run our full-service Medical Equipment Rental Company.

Staff Filing System

Our rental company will maintain files containing the following types of documents for all our employment candidates:
1. Driver's license copy
2. Social security card copy
3. Employment application
4. Resume
5. W-2 forms
6. Performance Appraisal
7. Employment Contract
8. Screening and Placement Tests
9. Background Check Reports
10. Proof of CPR Certification
11. Copy of State License
12. TB Skin Test Results
13. Annual Training Status Matrix
14. Updated Skills Checklist

We will conduct a quality improvement plan, which consists of an ongoing process of improvement activities and includes periodic samplings of activities not initiated solely in response to an identified problem. Our plan will be evaluated annually and revised as necessary. Our client satisfaction survey goal is a ___ (98.0)% satisfaction rating.

We plan to write and maintain an operations manual and a personnel policies handbook. The Operating Manual will be a comprehensive document outlining virtually every aspect of the business. The operating manual will include management and accounting procedures, hiring and personnel policies, and daily operations procedures, such as opening and closing the store, and how to _____. The manual will cover the following topics:

- Community Relations   - Customer Relations
- Media Relations   - Employee Relations
- Vendor Relations   - Government Relations
- Competition Relations   - Equipment Maintenance Checklist
- Environmental Concerns   - Screening Techniques
- Intra Company Procedures   - Accounting and Billing
- Banking and Credit Cards   - Financing
- Computer Procedures   - Scheduling Tips
- Quality Controls   - Safety Procedures
- Open/Close Procedures   - Security Procedures
- Software Documentation   - Skills Checklist

We will also develop a personnel manual. Its purpose is to set fair and equal guidelines in print for all to abide. It's the playbook detailing specific policies, as well as enforcement, thereby preventing any misinterpretation, miscommunication or ill feelings. This manual will reflect only the concerns that affect our personnel. A companion policy and procedure manual will cover everything else.

We plan to create the following business manuals:

Manual Type	Key Elements
1. Operations Manual	Process flowcharts
2. Employee Manual	Benefits/Appraisals/Practices
3. Managers Manual	Job Descriptions
4. Customer Service Policies	Inquiry Handling Procedures

We plan to develop and install a computerized customer tracking system that will enable us to target customers who are likely to have an interest in a particular type of store promotional event.

Resources:
Accounting Software   www.quickbooks.com

9.0 Management Summary

The Management Plan will reveal who will be responsible for the various management functions to keep the business running efficiently. It will further demonstrate how that individual has the experience and/or training to accomplish each function. It will address who will do the planning function, the organizing function, the directing function, and the controlling function.

At the present time _____ (owner name) will run all operations for _____ (company name). _____ (His/Her) background in _____ (business management?) indicates an understanding of the importance of financial control systems. There is not expected to be any shortage of qualified staff from local labor pools in the market area.

_____ (owner name) will be the owner and operations manager of _____ (company name). His/her general duties will include the following:
1. Oversee the daily operations
2. Ordering inventory and supplies.
3. Develop and implementing the marketing strategy
4. Purchasing equipment.
5. Arranging for the routine maintenance and upkeep of the facility.
6. Hiring, training and supervision of new recruiters.
7. Scheduling and planning of seminars and other special events.
8. Creating and pricing products and services.
9. Managing the accounting/financial aspect of the business.
10. Contract negotiation/vendor relations.

9.1 Owner Personal History

The owner has been working in the _____ industry for over _____ (#) years, gaining personal knowledge and experience in all phases of the industry. _____ (owner name) is the founder and operations manager of _____ (company name). The owner

holds a degree from the University of _____ at _____ (city). He/she began his/her career as a _____. Over the last _ (#) years, ____ (owner name) became quite proficient in a wide range of management activities and responsibilities, becoming an operations manager for ___ (former employer name) from __to _ (dates). There he/she was able to achieve _____.
For ____ years he/she has managed a business similar to _____ (company name).
_____ (His/her) duties included ____. Specifically, the owner brings _____ (#) years of experience as a ____ , as well as certification as a _____ from the _____ (National _____ Association). He/she is an experienced entrepreneur with ____ years of small business accounting, finance, marketing and management experience. Education includes college course work in business administration, banking and finance, investments, and commercial credit management. The owner will draw an annual salary of $___ from the business although most of this goes to repay loans to finance business start-up costs. These loans will be paid-in-full by _____ (month) of _____ (year).

9.2 Management Team Gaps

Despite the owner's and manager's experience in the _____ (?) industry, the company will also retain the consulting services of _____ (consultant company name). This company has over _____ (#) years of experience in the _____ industry, and has successfully opened dozens of Medical Equipment Rental Companies across the country. The Consultants will be primarily used for certification approval, market research, customer satisfaction surveys and to provide additional input in the evaluation of new business opportunities. The company also expects to retain the services of a local CPA to help the owner manage cash flow. Additionally the business will make use of the following advisory board to provide support for strategic planning and human resource related issues.

The Board of Advisors will provide continuous mentoring support on business matters. Expertise gaps in legal, tax, marketing and personnel will be covered by the Board of Advisors. The owner will actively seek free business advice from SCORE, a national non-profit organization with a local office. This is a group of retired executives and business owners who donate their time to serve as business counselors to new business owners.

Advisory Resources Available to the Business Include:

                                  Name   Address   Phone

CPA/Accountant

_____
___
Attorney

_____
___
Insurance Broker

_____
___
Banker

_____
___
Business Consultant

_____
___
Wholesale Suppliers

_____
___
Trade Association

_____
___
Realtor

_____
___
SCORE.org

_____
___
Other

9.2.1 Management Matrix

Note: See appendix for attached management resumes.

Name   Title   Credentials   Functions   Responsibilities

9.2.2 Outsourcing Matrix

Company Name   Functions   Responsibilities   Cost

9.3.0 Employee Requirements

1. Recruitment

Experience suggests that personal referrals are an excellent source for experienced associates We will also place newspaper ads, and use our Yellow Page Ad to indicate what types of staff we use and what types of customers we serve. We will also make effective use of our newsletter to post positions available and contact local trade schools for possible job candidates. We will target the following groups:

- Skilled but yet-inexperienced workers looking to get a foot in the door at prestigious companies.

- "Drifters" or those who tend to rapidly drift from job to job because they have the opportunity to work on short-term projects and move on without

the negative repercussions.
- Retirees seeking rewarding mental enjoyment and extra income.
- Students looking to gain valuable experience working with a technical company.

2. **Training and Supervision**
Training is largely accomplished through hands-on experience and by manufacturer product reps with supplemental instruction. Additional knowledge is gained through our policy and operations manuals, and attending manufacturer and trade association seminars. We will foster professional development and independence in all phases of our business. Supervision is task-oriented and the quantity is dependent on the complexity of the job assignment.

Employees are called team members because they are part of Team _____ (company name). To help them succeed and confidently handle customer questions, employees will receive assistance with our internal certification program. They will also participate in our written training modules and receive regular samples to evaluate.

3. **Salaries and Benefits**
Staff will be basically paid a salary plus commission basis on product sales. Good training and incentives, such as cash bonuses handed out monthly to everyone for reaching goals, will serve to retain good employees. An employee discount of __ percent on personal sales is offered. As business warrants, we hope to put together a benefit package that includes insurance, and paid vacations. The personnel plan also assumes a 5% annual increase in salaries.

9.4.0   Job Descriptions

Job Description— Company Director
This position plans, organizes, and directs the operations of the

Medical Equipment Rental Company. They order supplies, monitor and evaluate cost effectiveness and efficiency of operations, and prepare and balance daily reports and maintain. Incumbents provide customer service and specialized information regarding laws, policies, and procedures governing Medical Professional related issues. Incumbents utilize effective public relations to provide services to customers, respond to inquiries, handle complaints or resolve problems. This position is responsible for the efficient operations of the company . Incumbents determine medical equipment rental needs, prepare work schedules, establish and implement work procedures and priorities, and recommend changes to policies. They supervise staff including recruiting and training employees, assigning work, preparing and conducting performance evaluations, and handling employee problem solving issues. The Director must possess proven management skills, and the ability to drive sales. Must have a passion for people development and delivering excellent customer service. Must be capable of delivering performance through their teams and drive customer service through high placement standards, availability and presentation.

Key Accountabilities:
- Exceptional customer focus.
- Excellent Interpersonal skills.
- Effective planning and organizational skills.
- Influencing and negotiation skills.
- Budget management
- Supportive and persuasive management style.
- Tactical and strategic planning and implementation skills are a must.
- Clear vision and a determination to succeed.

Job Description -- Medical Sales Rep

Responsible for selling medical products and rental services to hospitals, clinics, doctors' offices, and healthcare professionals. Sells products such as medicines, drugs, and medical equipment to be used in general practices, primary care trusts, hospitals and pharmacies.

PRIMARY RESPONSIBILITIES

- Travel to defined geographies to sell medical equipment rental contracts.
- Contact potential customers at hospitals, clinics, doctors' offices, rehab facilities, and nursing homes to sell medical products and rental equipment.
- Arrange appointments with doctors, pharmacists and hospital medical teams.
- Cold-call or go door-to-door.
- Deliver presentations to doctors, practice staff and nurses in GP surgeries, hospital doctors and pharmacists in the retail sector.
- Build relationships with medical staff.
- Provide competitive information such as bid situations, pricing data, or bundling arrangements in order to establish negotiated pricing contracts for assigned products.
- Perform product demonstrations, installations, and application support.
- Improve product knowledge and sales techniques.
- Travel throughout assigned territory to call on regular and prospective customers to solicit orders or talks with customers on sales floor or by phone.
- Research competitors.
- Gathers, analyzes and delivers information from the field to allow the company to develop strategies and products appropriated to the Quality and Safety Testing market.
- Coordinate all issues with key clients between sales, service, support, customer services, marketing and finance.
- Take orders and disburse receipts.
- Estimate time and date of delivery.
- Help in the installation and set-up of equipment.
- Stay informed about the activities of health services in a particular area.

Job Description -- Medical Equipment Preparer

1. Organize and assemble routine and specialty equipment and supplies, filling special requests as needed.
2. Clean equipment in order to prepare them for sterilization.
3. Operate and maintain steam autoclaves, keeping records of loads completed, items in loads, and maintenance procedures

performed.
4. Record sterilizer test results.
5. Disinfect and sterilize equipment such as respirators, hospital beds, and oxygen and dialysis equipment, using sterilizers, aerators, and washers.
6. Start equipment and observe gauges and equipment operation, in order to detect malfunctions and to ensure equipment is operating to prescribed standards.
7. Examine equipment to detect leaks, worn or loose parts, or other indications of disrepair.
8. Report defective equipment to appropriate supervisors or staff.
9. Check sterile supplies to ensure that they are not outdated.
10. Maintain records of inventory and equipment usage.
11. Attend hospital in-service programs related to areas of work specialization.
12. Purge wastes from equipment by connecting equipment to water sources and flushing water through systems.
13. Deliver equipment to specified hospital locations or to patients' residences.
14. Install and set up medical equipment using hand tools.

Job Description -- Medical Supply Clerk

Prepares requisitions for supplies and equipment to keep adequate stock on hand; orders or requisitions special items as requested; orders certain standard items directly from approved vendor; receives and inspects items by contacting purchasing department or vendor; receives and inspects supplies and equipment; checks items against invoices or freight bills for proper quantity; checks items for damage and notifies purchasing department, vendor or transportation company of unacceptable items; marks discrepancies on invoices; accepts delivery on items and records items received; stores items received on shelves, in bins or in other storage areas; fills requests for supplies and equipment; describes items in stock and suggest substitutes; maintains inventory records showing items received, issued and standard stock levels; establishes reorder points for a variety of items; prepares departmental charges for items requisitioned and sends totals by division to accounting personnel for billing; maintains a perpetual inventory system; takes annual inventory of supplies and equipment and reconciles against perpetual inventory and other records; arranges for office equipment repairs; may make minor repairs to items carried in stock; may direct others in taking inventory or in moving or storage of equipment and supplies.

9.4.1 Job Description Format

Our job descriptions will adhere to the following format guidelines:

1.	Job Title	2.	Reports to:
3.	Pay Rate	4.	Job Responsibilities
5.	Travel Requirements	5.	Supervisory Responsibilities
6.	Qualifications	7.	Work Experience
8.	Required Skills	10.	Salary Range
11.	Benefits	12.	Opportunities

9.5 Personnel Plan

1. We will develop a system for recruiting, screening and interviewing employees.
2. Background checks will be performed as well as reference checks and drug tests.
3. We will develop an assistant training course.
4. We will keep track of staff scheduling.
5. We will develop client satisfaction surveys to provide feedback and ideas.
6. We will develop and perform semi-annual employee evaluations.
7. We will "coach" all of our employees to improve their abilities and range of skills.
8. We will employ temporary employees via a local staffing agency to assist with

one-time special projects.
9. Each employee will be provided an Employee Handbook, which will include detailed
job descriptions and list of business policies, and be asked to sign these documents as
a form of employment contract.
10. Incentives will be offered for reaching quarterly financial and enrollment goals,
completing the probationary period, and passing county inspections.
11. Customer service awards will be presented to those employees who best exemplify
our stated mission and exceed customer expectations.
12. Independent Contractors will be utilized to perform the following functions in compliance with IRS rules:

Our Employee Handbook will include the following sections:
1. Overview
2. Introduction to the Company
3. Organizational Structure
4. Employment and Hiring Policies
5. Performance Evaluation and Promotion Policies
6. Compensation Policies
7. Time Off Policies
8. Training Programs and Reimbursement Policies
9. General Rules and Policies
10. Termination Policies.

We will go to great lengths to conduct thorough background checks, competency assessments and evaluations of all our Associates, which is why the client can be completely confident all our Associates meet or exceed the highest standards and competencies in their respective fields.

Continuing competency is assessed through a review of client evaluations, audits and continuing education. When appropriate, we also conduct interviews with managers who work with our medical leasing professionals.

9.6   Staffing Plan

The following table summarizes our personnel expenditures for the first three years, with compensation costs increasing from $_____ in the first year to about $_____ in the third year, based on ____ (5?) % payroll increases each year. The payroll includes tuition reimbursement, pay increases, vacation pay, bonuses and state required certifications.

Table: Personnel Plan

	Number of Employees	Hourly Rate	Annual Salaries 2017	2018	2019
Company Director					
Assistant Director					
Warehouse Manager					
Project Manager					
Medical Equipment Preparer					
Medical Supply Clerk					
Medical Sales Reps					
Receptionist					
Scheduler					
Marketing Coordinator					
Bookkeeper					

Janitor

Other _____

Total People: Headcount

Total Annual Payroll

Payroll Burden (Fringe Benefits)   (+)

Total Payroll Expense   (=)

Professional Certifications
The Medical Device Body of Knowledge, created by the World Medical Device Organization, is an accrediting body that provides online multimedia medical device training. It offers three levels of qualification:

1. Certified Medical Device Associate (CMDA) – A basic level of knowledge that covers legislation, medical directives, assessment, classification, standards and the role of notified bodies.
2. Certified Medical Device Professional (CMDP) – This intermediate accreditation teaches the latest standards as applicable in the product life cycle. This course offers training in diverse aspects of medical device knowledge, including project management, worldwide device regulatory systems, clinical investigation submission, and clinical project financing and reporting.
3. Master Medical Device Professional (MMDP) – This qualification facilitates a more in-depth understanding of regulatory systems and strategies, and also involves training in ethics, reviewing clinical research, post-market assessment, traceability and product recall.

10.0 Risk Factors

Risk management is the identification, assessment, and prioritization of risks, followed by the coordinated and economical application of resources to minimize, monitor, and control the probability and/or impact of unfortunate events or to maximize the realization of opportunities. For the most part, our risk management methods will consist of the following elements, performed, more or less, in the following order.
1. Identify, characterize, and assess threats
2. Assess the vulnerability of critical assets to specific threats
3. Determine the risk (i.e. the expected consequences of specific types of attacks on specific assets)
4. Identify ways to reduce those risks
5. Prioritize risk reduction measures based on a strategy

Types of Risks:
_____ (company name) faces the following kinds of risks:

1. **Financial Risks**

Our quarterly revenues and operating results are difficult to predict and may fluctuate significantly from quarter to quarter as a result of a variety of factors. Among these factors are:
- Changes in our own or competitors' pricing policies.
- Recession pressures.
- Fluctuations in expected revenues from advertisers, sponsors and strategic relationships.
- Timing of costs related to acquisitions or payments.

2. **Legislative / Legal Landscape.**

Our participation in the Medical Equipment Rental Company arena presents unique risks:
- Service and other related liability.
- State regulations on licensing, privacy and insurance.

3. **Operational Risks**

For the past __ (#) years the owner has been dealing with computers so he is comfortable with technology and understands a wide array of software applications. However, the biggest potential problem will be equipment malfunction. To minimize the potential for problems, the owner will be taking equipment repair training from the manufacturer and will deal with basic troubleshooting and minor repairs. Beyond that, we have identified a service technician who is located close-by.

To attract and retain client to the _____ (company name) community, we must continue to provide differentiated and quality services. This confers certain risks including the failure to:
- Anticipate and respond to consumer preferences for partnerships and service.
- Attract, excite and retain a large audience of customers to our community.
- Create and maintain successful strategic alliances with quality partners.
- Deliver high quality, customer service.
- Build our brand rapidly and cost-effectively.
- Compete effectively against better-established

4. **Human Resource Risks**

The most serious human resource risk to our business, at least in the initial stages, would be my inability to operate the business due to illness or disability. The owner is currently in exceptional health and would eventually seek to replace himself on a day-to-day level by developing systems to support the growth of the business.

5. **Marketing Risks**

Advertising is our most expensive form of promotion and there will be a period of testing headlines and offers to find the one that works the best. The risk, of course, is that we will exhaust our advertising budget before we find an ad that works. Placing greater emphases on sunk-cost marketing, such as our storefront and on existing relationships through direct selling will minimize our initial reliance on advertising to bring in a large percentage of business in the first year.

6. **Business Risks**

A major risk to retail service businesses is the performance of the economy and the small business sector. Since economists are predicting this as the fastest growing sector of the economy, our risk of a downturn in the short-term is minimized. The entrance of one of the major chains into our marketplace is a risk. They offer more of the latest equipment, provide a wider array of products and services, competitive prices and 24-hour service. This situation would force us to lower our prices in the short-term until we could develop an offering of higher margin, value-added services not provided by the large chains. It does not seem likely that the relative size of our market today could support the overhead of one of those operations. Projections indicate that this will not be the case in the future and that leaves a window of opportunity for ___ (company name) to aggressively build a loyal client base. We will also not pursue big-leap, radical change misadventures, but rather strive to hit stepwise performance benchmarks, with a planned consistency over a long period of time.

To combat the usual start-up risks we will do the following:
1.   Utilize our industry experience to quickly establish desired strategic relationships.
2.   Pursue business outside of our immediate market area.
3.   Diversify our range of product and service offerings.
4.   Develop multiple distribution channels.
5.   Monitor our competitor actions.
6.   Stay in touch with our customers and suppliers.
7.   Watch for trends which could potentially impact our business.
8.   Continuously optimize and scrutinize all business processes.
9.   Institute daily financial controls using Business Ratio Analysis.
10. Create pay-for-performance compensation and training programs to reduce   employee turnover.

Further, to attract and retain customers the Company will need to continue to expand its market offerings, utilizing third party strategic relationships. This could lead to difficulties in the management of relationships, competition for specific services and products, and/or adverse market conditions affecting a particular partner.

The Company will take active steps to mitigate risks. In preparation of the Company's pricing, many factors will be considered. The Company will closely track the activities of all third parties, and will hold monthly review meetings to resolve issues and review and update the terms associated with strategic alliances.

Additionally, we will develop the following kinds of contingency plans:
   Disaster Recovery Plan
   Business Continuity Plan
   Business Impact and Gap Analysis
   Testing & Maintenance

The Company will utilize marketing and advertising campaigns to promote brand identity and will coordinate all expectations with internal and third party resources prior to release. This strategy should maximize customer satisfaction while minimizing potential costs associated with unplanned expenditures and quality control issues.

10.1 Business Risk Reduction Strategy

We plan to implement the following strategies to reduce our start-up business risk:
1. Implement our business plan based on go, no-go stage criteria.
2. Develop employee cross-training programs.
3. Regularly back-up all computer files/Install ant-virus software.
4. Arrange adequate insurance coverage with higher deductibles.
5. Develop a limited number of prototype samples.
6. Test market offerings to determine level of market demand and appropriate pricing strategy.
7. Thoroughly investigate and benchmark to competitor offerings.
8. Research similar franchised businesses for insights into successful prototype business/operations models.
9. Reduce operation risks and costs by flowcharting all structured systems & standardized manual processes.
10. Use market surveys to listen to customer needs and priorities.
11. Purchase used equipment to reduce capital outlays.
12. Use leasing to reduce financial risk.
13. Outsource manufacturing to job shops to reduce capital at risk.
14. Use subcontractors to limit fixed overhead salary expenses.
15. Ask manufacturers about profit sharing arrangements.
16. Pay advertisers with a percent of revenues generated.
17. Develop contingency plans for identified risks.
18. Set-up procedures to control employee theft.
19. Do criminal background checks on potential employees.
20. Take immediate action on delinquent accounts.
21. Only extend credit to established account with D&B rating
22. Get regular competitive bids from alternative suppliers.
23. Check that operating costs as a percent of rising sales are lower as a result of productivity improvements.
24. Request bulk rate pricing on fast moving supplies.
25. Don't tie up cash in slow moving inventory to qualify for bigger discounts.

26. Reduce financial risk by practicing cash flow policies.
27. Reduce hazard risk by installing safety procedures.
28. Use financial management ratios to monitor business vitals.
29. Make business decisions after brainstorming sessions.
30. Focus on the products with biggest return on investment.
31. Where possible, purchase off-the-shelf components.
32. Request manufacturer samples and assistance to build prototypes.
33. Design production facilities to be flexible and easy to change.
34. Develop a network of suppliers with outsourcing capabilities.
35. Analyze and shorten every cycle time, including product development.
36. Develop multiple sources for every important input.
37. Treat the business plan as a living document and update it frequently.
38. Conduct a SWOT analysis and use determined strengths to pursue opportunities.
39. Conduct regular customer satisfaction surveys to evaluate performance.

10.2 Reduce Customer Perceived Risk Tactics

We will utilize the following tactics to help reduce the new customer's perceived risk of starting to do business with our company.

Status
1. Publish a page of testimonials.
   _____
2. Secure Opinion Leader written endorsements.
   _____
3. Offer an Unconditional Satisfaction Money Back Guarantee. _____
4. Long-term Performance Guarantee (Financial Risk).
   _____

5. Guaranteed Buy Back (Obsolete time risk)

6. Offer free trials and samples.

7. Brand Image (consistent marketing image and performance)

8. Patents/Trademarks/Copyrights

9. Publish case studies

10. Share your expertise (Articles, Seminars, etc.)

11. Get recognized Certification

12. Conduct responsive customer service

13. Accept Installment Payments

14. Display product materials composition or ingredients.

15. Publish product test results.

16. Publish sales record milestones.

17. Foster word-of-mouth by offering an unexpected extra.

18. Distribute factual, pre-purchase information.

19. Reduce consumer search costs with online directories.

20. Reduce customer transaction costs.

21. Facilitate in-depth comparisons to alternative services.

22. Make available prior customer ratings and comments.

23. Provide customized info based on prior transactions.

24. Become a Better Business Bureau member.

25. Publish overall customer satisfaction survey results.

26. Offer plan options that match niche segment needs.

27. Require client sign-off before proceeding to next phase.

28. Document procedures for dispute resolution.

29. Offer the equivalent of open source code.

30. Stress your compatibility features (avoid lock-in fear).

31. Create detailed checklists & flowcharts to show processes

32. Publish a list of frequently asked questions/answers.

33. Create a community that enables clients to connect with each other and share common interests.

34. Inform customers as to your stay-in-touch methods.

35. Conduct and handover a detailed needs analysis worksheet.

36. Offer to pay all return shipping charges and/or refund all original shipping and handling fees.

37. Describe your product testing procedures prior to shipping.

38. Highlight your competitive advantages in all marketing materials.

11.0 Financial Plan

The over-all financial plan for growth allows for use of the significant cash flow generated by operations. We are basing projected sales on the market research, industry analysis and competitive environment. ___ (company name) expects a profit margin of over __ % starting with year one. By year two, that number should slowly increase as the law of diminishing costs takes hold, and the day-to-day activities of the business become less expensive. Sales are expected to grow at __% per year, and level off by year _____.
Our financial statements will show consistent growth in earnings, which provides notice of
the durability of our company's competitive advantage.

The initial investment in _____ (company name) will be provided by _____
(owner name) in the amount of $ _____. The owner will also seek a ___ (#) year bank
loan in the amount of $ _____ to provide the remainder of the required initial funding.
The funds will be used to renovate the space and to cover initial operating expenses. The owner financing will become a return on equity, paid in the form of dividends to the
owner. We expect to finance steady growth through cash flow. The owners do not intend to
take any profits out of the business until the long-term debt has been satisfied.

Our financial plan includes:

Moderate growth rate with a steady cash flow.
Investing residual profits into company expansion.
Company expansion will be an option if sales projections are met.
Marketing costs will remain below ___ (5?) % of sales.
Repayment of our loan calculated at a high A.P.R. of ___ (10?) percent and at a 5-year-payback on our $_____ loan.

11.1 Important Assumptions

Since this is a start-up operation, a steady increase in sales is forecast over three years, as consumer awareness and regular repeat business grows with a strong and consistent increase in the local population, from an initial ___(#) residents to about __ (#) residents upon completion. A solid business plan and the management skills and experience of the managing partners should be sufficient to orchestrate the necessary growth to make this a successful launch with steady increases in sales over the first three years.

Operating expenses are based on an assessment of operational needs for a company of this size. Observations of ____ (city) Medical Equipment Rental Company staffing, direct experience at _____ Medical agencies, and interviews with company owners and suppliers are the basis for these projections. Rent is based on negotiated lease agreement with the landlord. Other estimates are based on experience in operating a _____ (#) square foot _____ (city) office space, and on vendor quotes and estimates. Collection days should remain fairly short, given the substantial cash revenues, and standard credit card collection periods.

Financial Plan Assumptions
1. All operating costs are based on the management's research of similar operating companies.
2. Automated informational systems will reduce the staff requirements.
3. Developmental start-up costs are amortized over a five-year

period.
4. Home office or other apartment expenses are not included.
5. Overhead and operations costs are calculated on an annual basis.
6. The founders' salary is based on a fixed monthly salary expense basis.
7. All fixed and variable labor costs are scheduled to rise annually at __ (5?) percent.
8. All revenues are figured to rise annually at __ (10?) percent.
9. Administrative and office expenses rise at an annual rate of 2.5 percent.
10. Operating costs increase at __ (5) percent annually.
11. Loan amount interest rate at ____(10) percent.

Other Assumptions:

1. The economy will grow at a steady slow pace, without another major recession.
2. There will be no major changes in the industry, other than those discussed in the
   trends section of this document.
3. The State will not enact 'impact' legislation on our industry.
4. Sales are estimated at minimum to average values, while expenses are estimated
   at above average to maximum values..
5. Payroll expansions will be driven by increased sales.
6. Materials expenses will not increase dramatically over the next several years, but
   will grow at a rate that matches increasing consumption.
7. We assume access to equity capital and financing sufficient to maintain our
   financial plan as shown in the tables.
8. The amount of the financing needed from the bank will be approximately $_____
   and this will be repaid over the next 10 years at $_____ per month.
9. We assume that the area will continue to grow at present rate of __ % per year.
10. Interest rates and tax rates are based on conservative assumptions.
11. The Medical Equipment Rental Company will have an

annual revenue growth   rate of ___(10)% per year.

Revenue Assumptions:
　　　　Year　　　　Sales/Month　　　　Growth Rate
1. _____
2. _____
3. _____

Resource:
www.score.org/resources/business-plans-financial-statements-template-gallery

11.2　　Break-even Analysis

Break-Even Analysis will be performed to determine the point at which revenue received equals the costs associated with generating the revenue. Break-even analysis calculates what is known as a margin of safety, the amount that revenues exceed the break-even point. This is the amount that revenues can fall while still staying above the break-even point. The two main purposes of using the break-even analysis for marketing is to (1) determine the minimum number of sales that is required to avoid a loss at a designated sales price and (2) it is an exercise tool so that you can tweak the sales price to determine the minimum volume of sales you can reasonably expect to sell in order to avoid a loss.

Definition:　　Break-Even Is the Volume Where All Fixed Expenses Are Covered.

Three important definitions used in break-even analysis are:
- **Variable Costs** (Expenses) are costs that change directly in proportion to changes in activity (volume), such as raw materials, labor and packaging.

- **Fixed Costs** (Expenses) are costs that remain constant (fixed) for a given time period despite wide fluctuations in activity (volume), such as rent, loan payments, insurance, payroll and utilities.

- **Unit Contribution Margin** is the difference between your product's unit selling price and its unit variable cost.
  Unit Contribution Margin = Unit Sales Price - Unit Variable Cost

For the purposes of this breakeven analysis, the assumed fixed operating costs will be approximately $ _____ per month, as shown in the following table.

Averaged Monthly Fixed Costs:		**Variable Costs:**	
Payroll	_____	Cost of Inventory Sold	
Rent	_____	Labor	
Insurance	_____	Supplies	
Utilities	_____		
Security.	_____	Other	
Legal/Technical Help	_____		
Other	_____		
Total:	_____	Total	

A break-even analysis table has been completed on the basis of average costs/prices. With monthly fixed costs averaging $_____ , $_____ in average sales and $_____ in average variable costs, we need approximately $_____ in sales per month to break-even.

Based on our assumed ___ % variable cost, we estimate our breakeven sales volume at around $ ____ per month. We expect to reach that sales volume by our _____ month of operations. Our break-even analysis is shown in further detail in the following table.

Breakeven Formulas:
Break Even Units = Total Fixed Costs / (Unit Selling Price - Variable Unit Cost)

_____ = _____ / (_____ - _____)

BE Dollars = (Total Fixed Costs / (Unit Price – Variable Unit Costs))/ Unit Price

_____ = (_____ / (_____ - _____)) / _____

BE Sales = Annual Fixed Costs / (1- Unit Variable costs / Unit Sales Price)

_____ = _____ / (1 - _____ / _____)

Table: Break-even Analysis

Monthly Units Break-even	_____
Monthly Revenue Break-even	$ _____
Assumptions:	
Average Per-Unit Revenue	$ _____
Average Per-Unit Variable Cost	$ _____
Estimated monthly Fixed Cost	$ _____

Ways to Improve Breakeven Point:
1. Reduce Fixed Costs via Cost Controls
2. Raise unit sales prices.
3. Lower Variable Costs by improving employee productivity or getting lower competitive bids from suppliers.
4. Broaden product/service line to generate multiple revenue streams.

11.3 Projected Profit and Loss

Pro forma income statements are an important tool for planning our future business operations. If the projections predict a downturn in profitability, we can make operational changes such as increasing prices or decreasing costs before these projections become reality.

Our monthly profit for the first year varies significantly, as we aggressively seek improvements and begin to implement our marketing plan. However, after the first ___ months, profitability should be established.

We predict advertising costs will go down in the next three years as word-of-mouth about our company gets out to the public and we are able to find what has worked well for us and concentrate on those advertising methods, and corporate affiliations generate sales without the need for extra advertising.

Our net profit/sales ratio will be low the first year. We expect this ratio to rise at least _____ (15?) percent the second year. Normally, a startup concern will operate with negative profits through the first two years. We will avoid that kind of operating loss on our second year by knowing our competitors and having a full understanding of our target markets.

Our projected profit and loss is indicated in the following table. From our research of the medical rental industry, our annual projections are quite realistic and conservative, and we prefer this approach so that we can ensure an adequate cash flow.

Key P & L Formulas:

Gross Profit Margin = Total Sales Revenue - Cost of Goods Sold

Gross Margin % = (Total Sales Revenue - Cost of Goods Sold) / Total Sales Revenue
This number represents the proportion of each dollar of revenue that the company retains as gross profit.

EBITDA =Revenue - Expenses (exclude interest, taxes, depreciation & amortization)

PBIT = Profit (Earnings) Before Interest and Taxes = EBIT
A profitability measure that looks at a company's profits before the company has to pay corporate income tax and interest expenses. This measure deducts all operating expenses from revenue, but it leaves out the payment of interest and tax. Also referred to as "earnings before interest and tax ".

Net Profit = Total Sales Revenues - Total Expenses

Pro Forma Profit and Loss

	Formula	2017	2018	2019
Gross Revenue:				
Equipment Rental Services				
Equity Rental Services				
Operating Lease Services				

Capital Lease Services

Refurbish Equipment

Customized Solutions

Asset Management Services

Equipment Maintenance Services

Consulting/Seminars

Supply Sales

Misc.

Total Revenue   A

Cost of Sales
Cost of Goods Sold

Other

Total Costs of Sales   D

Gross Margin   A-D=E

Gross Margin %   E / A

Operating Expenses:
Payroll

Payroll Taxes

Sales & Marketing

Conventions/Trade Shows

Depreciation

License/Permit Fees

Dues and Subscriptions

Rent

Utilities

Deposits

Repairs and Maintenance

Janitorial Supplies

Office Supplies

Classroom Supplies

Leased Equipment

Buildout Costs

Insurance

Location Rental

Van Expenses

Contracted Therapists

Professional Development

Resource Library

Merchant Fees

Bad Debts

Miscellaneous

Total Operating Expenses   F

Profit Before Int. & Taxes   E - F = G

Interest Expenses   H

Taxes Incurred   I

Net Profit   G - H - I = J

Net Profit / Sales   J / A = K

11.4 Projected Cash Flow

The Cash Flow Statement shows how the company is paying for its operations and future growth, by detailing the "flow" of cash between the company and the outside world. Positive numbers represent cash flowing in, negative numbers represent cash flowing out.

We are positioning ourselves in the market as a medium-risk concern with steady cash flows. Accounts payable is paid at the end of each month while sales are in cash and short-term credit card collectibles. Cash balances will be used to reduce outstanding line of credit balances, or will be invested in a low-risk liquid money market fund to decrease the opportunity cost of cash held. Surplus cash balances during the critical first year of operations will function as protection against unforeseen changes in the timing of disbursements required to fund operations.

The first year's monthly cash flows are will vary significantly, but we do expect a solid cash balance from day one. We expect that the majority of our sales will be done in cash or by credit card and that will be good for our cash flow position. Additionally, we will stock only slightly more than one month's inventory at any time. Consequently, we do not anticipate any problems with cash flow,

once we have obtained sufficient start-up funds.
A __ year commercial loan in the amount of $_____, sought by the owner will be used to cover our working capital requirement. Our projected cash flow is summarized in the following table, and is expected to meet our needs. In the following years, excess cash will be used to finance our growth plans.

Cash Flow Management:
We will use the following practices to improve our cash flow position:
1. Perform credit checks and become more selective when granting credit.
2. Seek deposits or multiple stage payments.
3. Reduce the amount/time of credit given to clients.
4. Reduce direct and indirect costs and overhead expenses.
5. Use the 80/20 rule to manage inventories, receivables and payables.
6. Invoice as soon as the project has been completed.
7. Generate regular reports on receivable ratios and aging.
8. Establish and adhere to sound credit practices.
9. Use more pro-active collection techniques.
10. Add late payment fees where possible.
11. Increase the credit taken from suppliers.
12. Negotiate purchase prices and extended credit terms from vendors.
13. Use some barter arrangements to acquire goods and service.
14. Use leasing to gain access to the use of productive assets.
15. Covert debt into equity.
16. Regularly update cash flow forecasts.
17. Defer projects which cannot achieve acceptable cash paybacks.
18. Require a 50% deposit upon the signing of the contract and the balance in full, due five days before the event.
19. Speed-up the completion of projects to get paid faster.
20. Ask for extended credit terms from major suppliers.
21. Put ideal bank balances into interest-bearing (sweep) accounts.
22. Charge interest on client installment payments.
23. Check the accuracy of invoices to avoid unnecessary rework

delays.

24. Include stop-work clauses in contracts to address delinquent payments.

Cash Flow Formulas:
Net Cash Flow = Incoming Cash Receipts - Outgoing Cash Payments
Equivalently, net profit plus amounts charged off for depreciation, depletion, and amortization. (also called cash flow).

Cash Balance = Opening Cash Balance + Net Cash Flow
We are positioning ourselves in the market as a medium risk concern with steady cash flows. Accounts payable is paid at the end of each month, while sales are in cash, giving our company an excellent cash structure.

Pro Forma Cash Flow

	Formula	2017
2018 2019		

Cash Received
Cash from Operations
Cash Sales   A

_____

Cash from Receivables   B

_____

Subtotal Cash from Operations   A + B = C

_____

Additional Cash Received
Non Operating (Other) Income

_____

Sales Tax, VAT, HST/GST Received

_____

New Current Borrowing

_____

New Other Liabilities (interest fee)

_____

New Long-term Liabilities

_____

Sales of Other Current Assets

_____

Sales of Long-term Assets

_____

New Investment Received

_____

Total Additional Cash Received   D

Subtotal Cash Received   C + D = E

Expenditures
Expenditures from Operations
Cash Spending   F

Payment of Accounts Payable   G

Subtotal Spent on Operations   F+G = H

Additional Cash Spent
Non Operating (Other) Expenses

Sales Tax, VAT, HST/GST Paid Out

Principal Repayment Current Borrowing

Other Liabilities Principal Repayment

Long-term Liabilities Principal Repayment

Purchase Other Current Assets

Dividends

Total Additional Cash Spent   I

Subtotal Cash Spent   H + I = J

Net Cash Flow   **E - J = K**

Cash Balance

11.5   Projected Balance Sheet

Pro forma Balance Sheets are used to project how the business will be managing its assets in the future. As a pure start-up business, the opening balance sheet may contain no values.

As the business grows, our investment in inventory increases. This reflects sales volume increases and the commensurate ability to secure favorable volume discount terms with our distributors.

The projected accounts receivable position is relatively low and steady due to the nature of the business, in which up to 50% of our sales are cash, and the balance are consumer credit card purchases. No other consumer credit terms are envisioned or necessary for the operation of this business.

Capital assets of $_____ are comprised of a quoted $_____ for the build-out of the store (depreciating straight line over the 15 year term of the lease), $_____ for start-up costs (amortized over five years), and $_____ for the landlord's security deposit (about eight months rent).

Long-term liabilities are projected to decrease steadily, reflecting repayment of the original seven year term loan required to finance the business. It is important to note that part of the retained earnings may become a distribution of capital to the owners, while the balance would be reinvested in the business to replenish depreciated assets and to support further growth.

Note: The projected balance sheets must link back into the projected income statements and cash flow projections.

_____ (company name) does not project any real

trouble meeting its debt obligations, provided the revenue predictions are met. We are very confident that we will meet or exceed all of our objectives in the Business Plan and produce a slow but steady increase in net worth.

All of our tables will be updated monthly to reflect past performance and future assumptions. Future assumptions will not be based on past performance but rather on economic cycle activity, regional industry strength, and future cash flow possibilities. We expect a solid growth in net worth by the year _____.

The Balance Sheet table for fiscal years 2017, 2018, and 2019 follows. It shows managed but sufficient growth of net worth, and a sufficiently healthy financial position.

Excel Resource:
www.unioncity.org/ED/Finance%20Tools/Projected%20Balance%20Sheet.xls

Key Formulas:

Paid-in Capital = Capital contributed to the corporation by investors on top of the par value of the capital stock.

Retained Earnings = The portion of net income which is retained by the corporation and used to grow its net worth, rather than distributed to the owners as dividends.
Retained Earnings = After-tax net earnings - (Dividends + Stock Buybacks)

Earnings = Revenues - (Cost of Sales + Operating Expenses + Taxes)

Net Worth = Total Assets - Total Liabilities
   Also known as 'Owner's Equity'.

Pro Forma Balance Sheet

	Formulas	2017	2018	2019

Assets
Current Assets

Cash
_____

Accounts Receivable
_____

Inventory
_____

Other Current Assets
_____

Total Current Assets   A
_____

Long-term Assets
Long-term Assets   B
_____

Accumulated Depreciation   C
_____

Total Long-term Assets   B - C = D
_____

Total Assets   **A + D = E**
_____

Liabilities and Capital

Current Liabilities
Accounts Payable
_____

Current Borrowing
_____

Other Current Liabilities
_____

Subtotal Current Liabilities   **F**
_____

Long-term Liabilities
Notes Payable
_____

Other Long-term Liabilities

Subtotal Long-term Liabilities	G
Total Liabilities	F + G = H
Capital	
Paid-in Capital	I
Retained Earnings	J
Earnings	K
Total Capital	I - J + K = L
Total Liabilities and Capital	H + L = M
Net Worth	E - H = N

11.6 Business Ratios

Our comparisons to the SIC Industry profile are very favorable and we expect to maintain healthy ratios for profitability, risk and return. Use Business Ratio Formulas provided to assist in calculations.

Key Business Ratio Formulas:

EBIT = Earnings Before Interest and Taxes
EBITA = Earnings Before Interest, Taxes & Amortization.
(Operating Profit Margin)

Sales Growth Rate = ((Current Year Sales - Last Year Sales)/(Last Year Sales)) x 100
Ex: **Percent of Sales = (Advertising Expense / Sales) x 100**

Net Worth = Total Assets - Total Liabilities

Acid Test Ratio = Liquid Assets / Current Liabilities
Measures how much money business has immediately available. A ratio of 2:1 is good.

Net Profit Margin = Net Profit / Net Revenues
The higher the net profit margin is, the more effective the company is at converting revenue into actual profit.

Return on Equity (ROE) = Net Income / Shareholder's Equity
The ROE is useful for comparing the profitability of a company to that of other firms in the same industry. Also known as "return on net worth" (RONW).

Debt to Shareholder's Equity = Total Liabilities / Shareholder's Equity
A ratio below 0.80 indicates there is a good chance the company has a durable competitive advantage, with the exception of financial institutions, which are highly leveraged institutions.

Current Ratio = Current Assets / Current Liabilities
The higher the current ratio, the more capable the company is of paying its obligations. A ratio under 1 suggests that the company would be unable to pay off its obligations if they came due at that point.

Quick Ratio = Current Assets - Inventories / Current Liabilities
The quick ratio is more conservative than the current ratio, because it excludes inventory from current assets.

Pre-Tax Return on Net Worth = Pre-Tax Income / Net Worth
Indicates stockholders' earnings before taxes for each dollar of investment.

Pre-Tax Return on Assets = (EBIT / Assets) x 100
Indicates much profit the firm is generating from the use of its assets.

Accounts Receivable Turnover = Net Credit Sales / Average Accounts Receivable
A low ratio implies the company should re-assess its credit policies in order to ensure the timely collection of imparted credit that is not earning interest for the firm.

Net Working Capital = Current Assets - Current Liabilities
Positive working capital means that the company is able to pay off its short-term liabilities. Negative working capital means that a company currently is unable to meet its short-term liabilities with its current assets (cash, accounts receivable and inventory).

Interest Coverage Ratio = Earnings Before Interest & Taxes /Total Interest Expense
The lower the ratio, the more the company is burdened by debt expense. When a company's interest coverage ratio is 1.5 or lower, its ability to meet interest expenses may be questionable. An interest coverage ratio below 1 indicates the company is not generating sufficient revenues to satisfy interest expenses.

Collection Days = Accounts Receivables / (Revenues/365)
A high ratio indicates that the company is having problems getting paid for services.

Accounts Payable Turnover = Total Supplier Purchases/Average Accounts Payable
If the turnover ratio is falling from one period to another, this is a sign that the company is taking longer to pay off its suppliers than previously. The opposite is true when the turnover ratio is increasing, which means the firm is paying of suppliers at a faster rate.

Payment Days = (Accounts Payable Balance x 360) / (No. of Accounts Payable x 12)

The average number of days between receiving an invoice and paying it off.

Total Asset Turnover = Revenue / Assets
Asset turnover measures a firm's efficiency at using its assets in generating sales or revenue - the higher the number the better.

Sales / Net Worth = Total Sales / Net Worth

Dividend Payout = Dividends / Net Profit

Assets to Sales = Assets / Sales

Current Debt / Totals Assets = Current Liabilities / Total Assets

Current Liabilities to Liabilities = Current Liabilities / Total Liabilities

Business Ratio Analysis

	2017	2018	2019
Sales Growth			

Percent of Total Assets
Accounts Receivable

Inventory

Other Current Assets

Total Current Assets

Long-term Assets

Total Assets

Current Liabilities

Long-term Liabilities

Total Liabilities

Net Worth

Percent of Sales
Sales

Gross Margin

Selling G& A Expenses

Advertising Expenses

Profit Before Interest & Taxes

Main Ratios
Current

Quick

Total Debt to Total Assets

Pre-tax Return on Net Worth

Pre-tax Return on Assets

Additional Ratios
Net Profit Margin

Return on Equity

Activity Ratios
Accounts Receivable Turnover

Collection Days

Inventory Turnover

Accounts Payable Turnover

Payment Days

Total Asset Turnover

Inventory Productivity

Sales per sq/ft.

Gross Margin Return on Inventory (GMROI)

Debt Ratios
Debt to Net Worth

Current Liabilities to Liabilities

Liquidity Ratios
Net Working Capital

Interest Coverage

Additional Ratios
Assets to Sales

Current Debt / Total Assets
_____

Acid Test
_____

Sales / Net Worth
_____

Dividend Payout
_____

Business Vitality Profile
Sales per Employee
_____ Survival Rate
_____

12.0   Summary

_____ (company name) will be successful. This business plan has documented that the establishment of _____ (company name) is feasible. All of the critical factors, such as industry trends, marketing analysis, competitive analysis, management expertise and financial analysis support this conclusion.

Project Description: (Give a brief summary of the product, service or program.)
_____

_____
Description of Favorable Industry and Market Conditions.
_____

_____
Summary of Earnings Projections and Potential Return to Investors:
_____

_____
Summary of Capital Requirements:
_____

_____
Security for Investors & Loaning Institutions:
_____

_____
Summary of expected benefits for people in the community beyond the immediate business concern:
_____

_____
Means of Financing:
A. Loan Requirements: $_____
B. Owner's Contribution: $ $_____
C. Other Sources of Income: $_____

Total Funds Available: $_____

13.0   Potential Exit Scenarios

Two potential exit strategies exist for the investor:
1. **Initial Public Offering. (IPO)**
We seek to go public within ___ (#) years of operations. The funds used will both help create liquidity for investors as well as allow for additional capital to develop our _____ (international/national?) roll out strategy.
2. **Acquisition Merger with Private or Public Company.**
Our most desirable option for exit is a merger or buyout by a large corporation. We believe with substantial cash flows and a loyal customer base our company will be attractive to potential corporate investors within five years. Real value has been created through the novel combination of medical equipment rental services as well as partnering with key referral groups. The value of this company will far exceed the amount of money invested into the start-up. By positioning ourselves in the market, as a special needs rental service, we will gain the interest of hospitals, physicians, not to mention larger rental agencies. Either we will run the business to generate positive cash flow or our firm would be acquired by another firm for its value chain and client base.

APPENDIX

Purpose: Supporting documents used to enhance your business proposal.

- Tax returns of principals for the last three years, if the plan is for new business
- A personal financial statement, which should include life insurance and endowment policies, if applicable
- A copy of the proposed lease or purchase agreement for building space, or zoning information for in-home businesses, with layouts, maps, and blueprints
- A copy of licenses and other legal documents including partnership, association, or shareholders' agreements and copyrights, trademarks, and patents applications
- A copy of résumés of all principals in a consistent format, if

- possible
- Copies of letters of intent from suppliers, contracts, orders, and miscellaneous.
- In the case of a franchised business, a copy of the franchise contract and all supporting documents provided by the franchisor
- Newspaper clippings that support the business or the owner, including something about you, your achievements, business idea, or region
- Promotional literature for your company or your competitors
- Product/Service Brochures of your company or competitors
- Photographs of your product. equipment, facilities, etc.
- Market research to support the marketing section of the plan
- Trade and industry publications when they support your intentions
- Quotations or pro-forma invoices for capital items to be purchased, including a list of fixed assets, company vehicles, and proposed renovations
- References/Letters of Recommendation
- All insurance policies in place, both business and personal
- Operation Schedules
- Organizational Charts
- Job Descriptions
- Additional Financial Projections by Month
- Customer Needs Analysis Worksheet
- Sample Sales Letters
- Copies of Software Management Reports
- Copies of Standard Business Forms
- Equipment List
- Personal Survival Budget

Helpful Resources:

Healthcare Publications, Journals and News

AHA News - bi-weekly from American Hospital Association
American Journal of Managed Care / AJMC - clinical, economic, policy, finance & delivery
American Journal of Maternal Child Nursing / MCN - perinatal, neonatal, midwifery, & pediatric specialties
American Journal of Nursing / AJN - award-winning, peer-reviewed, monthly journal
American Medical News / AMNews - news effecting medical practice, AMA
Anesthesia & Pain Management Coding Alert - Coding Institute, expert coding advice
Applied Clinical Trials - practical hands-on information
Business Insurance - for those who purchase insurance
Cardiology Coding Alert - Coding Institute, expert coding & compliance advice
CIN / Computers, Informatics, Nursing - dedicated to computers in nursing practice
Clinical Examples in Radiology - guide to CPT coding & billing, AMA
CodeManager - software, data, quarterly updates from AMA
CPT Changes - companion to CPT Assistant
Critical Care Nurse - cardiac care, pharmacology, nutrition, pulmonary care, neurology
ED Coding Alert - Coding Institute, expert coding advice
eHealthcare Strategies & Trends - internet strategies for healthcare
Family Practice Coding Alert - Coding Institute, expert compliance & coding advice
Gastroenterology Coding Alert - Coding Institute, expert coding & compliance tools
General Surgery Coding Alert - Coding Institute, compliance & coding advice
Group Practice Journal - AMGA, American Medical Group Association
Healthcare Design - medical building & facilities design
Health Care Management Review - by leading health care

executives, peer-reviewed
Health Care Manager - for professionals in managerial or supervisory roles
Healthcare Marketing Report - HMR Publications Group
Health Facilities Management - from AHA, ASHE & ASHES, facility management
Health Information Compliance Alert - monthly guide, HIPAA mandates, compliance
HealthLeaders - coverage of industry problems, issues, trends
Health Management Technology - for CIOs, IT Managers and other medical executives
Home Care Week - reimbursement, industry trends, fraud & abuse, contracting
Home Health ICD-9 Alert - monthly newsletter
Hospitals & Health Networks / H&HN - from American Hospital Association
Internal Medicine Coding Alert - Coding Institute, expert compliance & reimbursement advice
JONA's Healthcare Law Ethics & Regulation - nursing care management
Journal for Nurses in Staff Development - issues & innovations impacting staff development
Journal of Ambulatory Care Management / JACM - issues in ambulatory care
Journal of Nursing Administration / JONA - geared to top-level nurse executives
Journal of Nursing Care Quality - quality principles & concepts in practice
Journal of Public Health Management & Practice - design, implementation, health programs
Lippincott's Case Management - managing the process of patient care
Long-Term Care Report - issues shaping the long-term industry
Long-Term Care Survey Alert - The Joint Commission & state survey guidance
Managed Care Report - regulatory updates, business strategies, litigation, etc.
Managed Healthcare Executive - insight & analysis, apply industry trends to operating strategies

Marketing Health Services / MHS - from American Marketing Association, healthcare strategies
Maternal Child Nursing / MCN - perinatal, neonatal, midwifery, & pediatric specialties
Medical Marketing & Media / MM&M - articles on marketing & promotion
Medical Office Billing & Collections Alert - Coding Institute, optimizing billing, collections, medical practices
Medicare Part B Insider - Coding Institute, newsletter, billing, reimbursement
Modern Healthcare - the only health care business news weekly
Neurology Coding Alert - Coding Institute, compliance advice from experts
Neurosurgery Coding Alert - Coding Institute, expert coding techniques
Nurse Educator - peer-reviewed, developments, innovations in nursing education
Nursing - comprehensive range of nursing topics
Nursing Home Law & Litigation Report - recent cases & settlements in long-term care
Nursing Management - success strategies for health care managers & leaders
Nursing Research - more depth, more detail, more of what today's nurses demand
OASIS Alert - requirements, strategies, home health billing
OB-GYN Coding Alert - Coding Institute, expert coding advice
Oncology & Hematology Coding Alert - Coding Institute, compliance guidance from experts
Ophthalmology Coding Alert - Coding Institute, expert up-to-date coding advice
Optometry Coding & Billing Alert - Coding Institute, compliance & reimbursement
Orthopedic Coding Alert - Coding Institute, tools to optimize reimbursement
Otolaryngology Coding Alert - Coding Institute, coding & compliance
Outpatient Physical Therapy Coding Alert - monthly coding guidance for PT, OT, rehab
Pain Management Coding Alert - Coding Institute, expert coding

alerts
Part B Insider - Coding Institute, news, analysis, Medicare Part B, regulation, reimbursement
Pathology / Lab Coding Alert - Coding Institute, reimbursement & compliance strategies
Pediatric Coding Alert - Coding Institute, expert coding advice
Physical Medicine & Rehab Coding Alert - Coding Institute, compliance & reimbursement advice
Physician Referral & Telephone Triage Times - marketing, technology, protocols, legal issues
Podiatry Coding & Billing Alert - Coding Institute, reimbursement & compliance
Professional Case Management - managing the process of patient care
Psychiatric Times - widely read publication in behavioral health & psychiatry
Pulmonology Coding Alert - Coding Institute, reimbursement, coding, compliance
Quality Management in Health Care - peer-reviewed, quarterly
Radiology Coding Alert - Coding Institute, reimbursement & compliance
Rehab Report - mastering the business side of rehab
Strategic Health Care Marketing - marketing strategies & plans
Trustee - for governing boards of health care systems & hospitals
Urology Coding Alert - Coding Institute, reimbursement & compliance tips

Online Publications
Many of these publications will only give access to abstracts of articles unless you purchase the full print subscription, which usually includes access to the online versions. American Hospital Association News - online version of print publication
American Medical News - online version of print publication
British Medical Journal - full text online version of print publication
Business Journals - links to numerous city business journals
CNN - Health Page - health news, mostly for popular consumption
Harvard Business Review
Health Affairs - from Project Hope
Health Care/Hospitals News - compilation of headlines, by Yahoo

Health Facilities Management - for facilities and environmental managers
Health Services and Outcomes Research Methodology
Hospitals & Health Networks - from American Hospital Association
JAMA - Journal of the American Medical Association, online version
Journal of Health Politics, Policy & Law - by Duke Univ. Press, abstracts only
Journal of Health Services Research & Policy - Royal Society of Medicine, not full access
Journal of the National Medical Association - articles online
Journal of Public Health Policy
Materials Management in Health Care - for purchasing depts.
MEDLINE - published med info, by National Library of Medicine
Milbank Quarterly - abstracts only, health policy
MMWR - Morbidity and Mortality Weekly Report
New England Journal of Medicine - medical research papers primarily
New York Times - daily newspaper with business news
Nurse Week - magazine for nurses
The Informatics Review - journal of Assoc. of Med. Directors of Info. Systems
Wall Street Journal - daily newspaper with healthcare business news

Miscellaneous:
Vista Print Free Business Cards   www.vistaprint.com
Free Business Guides
        www.smbtn.com/businessplanguides/
Open Office
        http://download.openoffice.org/
US Census Bureau   www.census.gov
Federal Government   www.business.gov
US Patent & Trademark Office   www.uspto.gov
US Small Business Administration   www.sba.gov
National Association for the Self-Employed   www.nase.org
International Franchise Association   www.franchise.org
Center for Women's Business Research   www.cfwbr.org

Advertising Plan Worksheet

Ad Campaign Title:
_____
Ad Campaign Start Date: _____ End Date: _____

What are the features (what product has) and hidden benefits (what product does for consumer) of my products/services?

Who is the targeted audience?

What problems are faced by this targeted audience?

What solutions do you offer?

Who is the competition and how do they advertise?

What is your differentiation strategy?

What are your bullet point competitive advantages?

What are the objectives of this advertising campaign?

What are your general assumptions?

What positioning image do you want to project?
    ___ Exclusiveness   ___ Low Cost
    ___ High Quality
    ___ Speedy Service   ___ Convenient
    ___ Innovative

What is the ad headline?

What is the advertising budget for this advertising campaign?

What advertising methods will be used?
    ___ Radio   ___ TV/Cable

___ Yellow Pages
___ Coupons   ___ Telemarketing
___ Flyers
___ Direct Mail   ___ Magazines
___ Newspapers
___ Press Release   ___ Brochures
___ Billboards
___ Other

When will each advertising method start and what will it cost?
　　Method　　　　Start Date　　　　Frequency
　　Cost

_____

_____

_____

Indicate how you will measure the cost-effectiveness of the advertising plan?
Formula:　Return on Investment (ROI) = Generated Sales / Ad Costs.

Marketing Action Plan

Month:

_____

—

Target Market:

_____

Responsibilities:

_____

Allocated Budget:

_____

Objectives

_____

Strategies

_____

Implementation
_____

Tactics
_____

Results
_____

Evaluation
_____

_____
_____
_____
_____
_____
_____
_____
_____
_____
_____
_____
_____
_____
_____
_____
_____
_____

Lessons Learned:
_____

Viral Marketing

Definition: Also known as word-of-mouth advertising.
Objective: To prompt your customers to deliver your sales message to others.
Strategy: Encourage and enable communication recipients to pass the offer
or message along to others.
Benefit: Provides an excellent advertising return on investment and builds the trust factor.

Methodologies:
1. Encourage blog comments and two-way dialogue.
2. Use surveys to solicit feedback.
3. Use refer-a-friend forms or scripts.
4. Provide discount coupon or logo imprinted giveaway rewards for telling a friend.
5. Utilize pre-existing social networks.
6. Participate in message boards or forums.
7. Add a signature line with a refer-a-friend tagline to all posts and emails.
8. Enable unrestricted access.
9. Facilitate website content sharing.
10. Write articles and e-books, and encourage free reprints with byline mention.
11. Submit articles with 'about the author' box to article directories, such as www.articlecity.com.
12. Develop attention-grabbing product line extensions to stay connected.
13. Do the unexpected by offering a surprise benefit.
14. Deliver a remarkable offering that exceeds customer

expectations.
15. Provoke a strong emotional response by getting involved with a cause that is important to your customers.
16. Provide referral incentives.
17. Get free samples into the hands of respected opinion leaders.
18. Educate customers, as to your product benefits and competitive advantages, to act as spokespersons for your company.

Explain Your Viral Marketing Program
_____
_____
_____
_____
_____
_____
_____
_____

Marketing on Social Networking Websites

1. Place banner ads or Pay-Per-Click ads on social networking sites.
2. Create an account on the website and add your company logo.
3. Encourage word-of-mouth exchanges by posting comments on friend's profiles.
4. Post surveys on your social networking pages to solicit feedback.
5. Create a profile that subtly and humbly tells

everyone about you and your gift basket products and services.
6. Include links to your gift basket business website.
7. Make your profile keyword rich with keyword phases from your business specialty.
8. Use a soft sell approach, and focus on establishing your credibility and expertise as a gift basket marketing guru, to be trusted by prospective clients.
9. Name your social networking page exactly as your organization is named.
10. Have a strong presence in one channel rather than all of them.
11. Make sure you give visitors a strong call to action to supply
    their email address, so you can contact them later.
12. Include a signature line with your website contact info.
13. Blog often, but make certain that instead of selling, you are
    sharing your gift industry expertise.

Helpful Resources:
http://en.wikipedia.org/wiki/List_of_social_networking_websites

Examples:	Facebook.com	Myspace.com
	LinkedIn.com	Ryse.com

Explain Your Online Social Networking Strategy
_____
_____
_____

Integrate Marketing into Daily Operations

Objective: To seamlessly integrate marketing processes into daily, routine operations.

Strategies:
1. Develop form to ask for referrals upon new customer registration and annual renewal.
2. Present a sales presentation folder upon registration or contract sign-up with needs analysis worksheets, testimonials, new product introduction flyers, innovative application ideas, etc.
3. Develop a second sales presentation folder version for presentation upon job completion or sale, with referral program details, warranty service contract blank, and accessory suggestions.
4. Include business cards and coupons with all product deliverables.
5. Install company yard signs during job set-up.
6. Include a thank you note/comment card with all deliverables.
7. Include flyers and helpful articles in all customer correspondence, especially mailed invoices and statements.
8. Attach logo and contact info to all finished products.
9. Conduct customer satisfaction surveys while clients are waiting to be served.
10. Develop enclosed warranty card to build customer database and feed drip marketing program.
11. Provide competitor product/service comparisons that highlight your strengths.

12. Incorporate feedback cards into merchandise displays.
13. Train all employees to also be sales and customer service agents.
14. Print your Mission Statement or slogan on all forms and correspondence.
15. _____
16. _____

Indicate how you will incorporate marketing into daily operations.

Sales Stage	Incorporate Techniques	Business Processes	Opportunities to Marketing
Pre-sale	_____	_____	_____
	_____	_____	_____
	_____	_____	_____
Transaction	_____	_____	_____
	_____	_____	_____
	_____	_____	_____

353

Post Sale

_____
_____

_____
_____

_____
_____

Monthly Marketing Calendar

Instruction: Use to plan your monthly marketing events or activities and evaluate individual event results and marketing lessons learned for the month.

Month/Year:

_____
_____

Event/   Responsibility   Cost   Comments   Date
        Results
Activity
      Evaluation

_____
_____
_____
_____
_____
_____
_____
_____
_____
_____
_____

_____
_____
_____
_____
_____
_____
_____
_____
_____
_____
_____
_____
_____
_____
_____
_____
_____

Monthly Evaluation of Lessons Learned:
_____
_____
_____
_____

Form Strategic Marketing Alliances

Definition: A collaborative relationship between two or more non-competing firms with the intent of accomplishing mutually compatible and beneficial goals that would be difficult for each to

accomplish alone.
Also referred to as 'Collaboration Marketing'.

Note: Usually, potential alliance partners sell distinct or complementary products and/or services to the same target market audience.

Advantages: Improve marketing efficiency by achieving synergy in resource allocation with strategic partners.
Improve marketing effectiveness by creating a one-stop or wraparound shopping experience.
A way to inexpensively test the market for growth potential.

Types of Co-Ventures:
1. Informal Strategic Alliances
2. Contractual Relationships (Attorney review recommended)
3. New Business Entity (Set-up by attorney)

Informal Strategic Alliances
1. Most involve consultations regarding:
    a. Mutual Referrals
    b. Research for product improvements
    c. Promotion of products or services (affiliate programs).
    d. Creative product bundling arrangements.
2. May or may not require a written agreement.
3. May or may not require compensation.

Topics to be Covered:
1. The specific strategic goals and objectives of the alliance.
2. The performance expectations of the parties..
3. The scope of the alliance.

4. The period of performance.
5. Termination and renewal procedures.
6. Strategic marketing plan to promote the alliance.
7. Dispute resolution procedures.
8. Performance tracking methods.
9. Periodic evaluation of reciprocal benefits realized.
10. Website pages/links to promote alliance partners.

Example: The mutual referral relationship between a sports bar and a fitness club or physical fitness trainer.

Strategic Marketing Alliance Worksheet

Methodology:
1. Identify the assets and capabilities you can provide to the alliance.
2. Identify the assets and capabilities that the proposed partner will bring to the alliance.
3. Determine the benefits you are seeking from the alliance.
4. Determine the gaps in your offerings that the alliance partner can fill.
5. List any conflicting relationships with other businesses and benefits received.
6. Research the potential alliance for strategic fit and other opportunities.
7. List the ways in which your customers will benefit from this alliance.
8. Assess any alliance risks.
9. Determine the ongoing actions needed to maintain the alliance.
10. Design a marketing plan to promote the alliance.
11. Develop a Mission Statement for the alliance.
12. Develop the Management Plan for the alliance.

13. Design the alliance appraisal and renewal procedures.

| Potential Benefits Alliance Partner | Partner Alliance Strengths Risks Offered | Your Offering Gaps Filled | Customer |

_____
_____
_____
_____
_____
_____
_____
_____
_____
_____
_____
_____
_____

Referral Program Tips

Objective: To formalize your referral program so that it can be easily and consistently integrated into your operating processes.

1. Define the stages in the sales process when you will ask for a referral. Ex: Registration, Renewals, Annual Drive, etc.)

2. Document your referral asking script (include objection handling responses).

3. Include a request for referrals in your customer satisfaction survey and your registration forms.

4. Stress the dependence of your business on referrals in all your marketing communications.

5. Set-up a follow-up procedure and tracking form to convert referral leads into actual customers.

6. Publish your referral incentives, awards criteria and timetable for settlement.

7. Customize your referral program to the motivational needs of a select number of potential 'Bird Dogs' or 'Big Hitters'.

8. Educate potential referral agents as to the characteristics of your ideal prospect. (Develop Ideal Prospect Profile)

9. Set-up special, mutual referral arrangements with strategic business alliance partners and track the reciprocity of efforts.

10.   Join or start a local lead group.

11.   Set-up 'thank-you note' templates to facilitate your
        expression of gratitude.

12.   Use logo imprinted giveaways, such as T-sheets, as
        referral thank you expressions.

Seminar Outline Worksheet

Objective: To establish your expertise on the subject matter, and produce future possible networking contacts by offering a newsletter sign-up and/or business card exchange.

Warning: Make seminar information rich and not a sales presentation.

1. Start with Attention-Grabbing Headline
   Ex: Hard-hitting Quotation, Thought Provoking Question, Startling Fact

   _____

   _____

2. Introduce Yourself and Establish Your Credentials

   _____

   _____

3. Present Seminar Overview

   _____

   _____

4. Discuss Attendee Participation Guidelines

   _____

   _____

5. Solicit a sampling of attendee interests, backgrounds and concerns.

   _____

6.   Establish Learning Objectives

7.   Preview the Bulleted Topics To be Covered

8.   Share a Relevant Success Story (Case Study).

9.   Use analogies and comparisons to create reference points.

10.   Use statistics to support your position.

11.   Conclusion: - Summarize Benefits for Attendees / Appeal to Action

12.   Hold Question and Answer Session

13.   Final Thoughts
        - Appreciation for Help Received
        - Indicate after-seminar availability

14.   Handout A Remembrance
        - Business Cards   -
Glossary of Terms
        - Seminar Outline   -

Feedback Survey

YouTube Marketing Tips

Definition: An online video destination to watch and share original video clips.

(World-wide approx. 55 million unique users/month)

1. Focus on something that is funny or humorous, so that people will feel compelled to share it with friends and family.
2. Make the video begin and end with a black screen and include the URL of your originating website to bring traffic to your site.
3. Put your URL at the bottom of the entire video.
4. Clearly demonstrate how your product works.
5. Create how-to videos to share your expertise and develop a following.
6. Build contests and events around special holidays and occasions.
7. Run a search on similar content by keyword, and use the info to choose the right category and tags for your video.
8. Make sure the video is real, with no gimmicks or tricks.
9. Add as many keywords as you can.
10. Make sure that your running time is five minutes or less.
11. Break longer videos into several clips, each with a clear title, so that they can be selectively viewed.
12. Encourage viewer participation and support.
13. Take advantage of YouTube tags, use adjectives to target people searching based on interests, and match your title and description to the tags.
14. Use the flexibility provided by the medium to experiment.
15. Use the 'Guru Account' sign-up designation to highlight info videos and how-to guides.

16. Create 'Playlists' to gather individual clips into niche-targeted context so viewers can easily find related content.
17. Use 'Bulletins' to broadcast short messages to the world via Your YouTube Channel.
18. Email 'The Robin Good YouTube Channel' to promote a new video release.
19. Join a 'YouTube Group' to post videos or comments to the group discussion area and build your network of contacts.
20. Use 'YouTube Streams' to join or create a room where videos are shared and discussed in real-time.
21. Use 'Active Sharing' to broadcast the videos that you are currently watching, and drive traffic to your profile.
22. Use the 'Share Video' link found under each video you submit and then check the box 'Friends' to send your video to all your friends.
23. Create your own YouTube Channel when you sign-up for a new YouTube account.

Basic Monthly Marketing Plan Checklist

1. Send birthday greetings to existing clients. ____

2. Contact referral sources and express appreciation for their referrals. ____

3. Implement program to develop new referral sources. ____
4. Research new ways to solve more problems of your

target clients.
_____

5. Research possible new target audience needs. _____
6. Make your friends/family/associates/social contacts
aware of your expanding capabilities.
_____

7. Train all employees to assist in marketing efforts. _____
8. Conduct selected client interviews to assess performance, changing needs and suggestions. _____
9. Forward copies of articles of interest to contacts. _____
10. Take contact to breakfast, lunch or dinner. _____
11. Invite contact to sporting or cultural event.
_____

12. Distribute articles that demonstrate your expertise. _____
13. Invite contacts to an informative seminar.
_____

14. Send personal notes of congratulation.
_____

15. Join organizations important to your contacts. _____
16. Update your mailing list.
_____

17. Issue a press release on a firm accomplishment or
planned marketing event.
_____

18. Update your firm's list of competitive advantages. _____
19. Attend a networking event. _____
20. Update the helpful content on your website. _____
21. Arrange to speak on your area of expertise. _____
22. Become actively involved in the community. _____
23. Track your ad results to determine resource focus. _____
24. Develop alliances with complementary businesses. _____
25. Conduct customer satisfaction surveys. _____
26. Implement client needs analysis checklist. _____
27. Distribute newsletter featuring clients. _____
28. _____ _____ _____
29. _____ _____ _____
30. _____ _____ _____

Networking Insights
Definition: A reciprocal process in which you share ideas,

leads, information, and advice to build mutually beneficial relationships.

Networking Tips:
1. Start your own local referral group with other business owners.
2. Understand your long-term networking goals.
3. Become a helpful resource to networking members.
4. Research people and companies to know their goals and interests.
5. Offer referrals, resources and recommendations to receive same in return.
6. Consistently try to meet new people and make new friends.
7. Develop good listening skills.
8. Frequently express your gratitude for assistance.
9. Know what interests, strengths and availability you bring to the table.
10. Stay in touch with a newsletter, blog, postcards or email messages.
11. Keep asking questions to get others to tell you more about themselves.
12. Show warmth, display confidence, smile and shake hands firmly.
13. Explore organizations that offer accreditation and directory listings.

Entrepreneur Networking Possibilities
1. Meet Up
    www.meetup.com
2. FaceBook, Friendster, Myspace
    www.facebook.com
3. LinkedIn
    www.linkedIn.com
4. Ryze
    www.ryze.com
5. Int'l Virtual Women's Chamber of Commerce
    www.ivwcc.org
6. Business Network International

www.BNI.com
7. Club E Network
    www.clubENetwork.com
8. Local Chamber of Commerce
9. Rotary Club
    www.rotary.org
10. Lion's Club
    www.lionsclubs.org
11. Jaycees
12. Toastmasters
    www.toastmasters.com
13. Woman Owned Network
    wwwwomanowned.com
14. Alumni Associations
15. Parent Teacher Associations (PTA)
16. Trade Shows
    www.tsnn.com
17. Trade Associations
    www.associationscentral.com
18. EONetwork
    www.eonetwork.org
19. Prof. Organizations, Economic Clubs, Charities, Churches, Museums, etc.

Perfect Your Elevator Pitch

A brief, focused message aimed at a particular person or niche segment that summarizes why they should be interested in your products and/or services.

I am a/we are _____(profession) **and we help** _____(target market description) **to**_____(primary problem solved).

Press Release Cover Letter Worksheet

Instructions: Use this form to build a ready-to-use cover letter.

Your Letterhead.

Date

Dear _____,

As a company located in your coverage area, we thought the attached Press Release would be of special concern to your readers/viewers, as it touches upon something that we all have in common, an interest in
_____
_____.

Brief overview purpose of the press release.
_____
_____.

I have also enclosed a media kit to give you background information on _____ Company and myself. I hope to follow-up with you shortly.

I also possess expertise in the following related areas:
- _____
- _____
- _____

Should you wish to speak to me or require additional information, I can be reached at _____ or via email at _____.
Additional assistance with company supplied photos can be requested at the same number. This Press Release can also be downloaded from my company website at
www. _____.

Thank you for your time and attention,

Contact Name
Company Title
Phone Number
Email Address

New Release Template

News Release

For Immediate Release
(Or Hold For Release Until …(date)….)

Contact:
Contact Person _____
Contact Title _____
Company Name _____
Phone Number _____
Fax Number _____
Email Address _____
Website Address _____

Date: _____
Attention: _____ (Target
Type of Editor)

Headline: Summarize Your Key Message:

_____

____
Sub-Headline: Optional:

_____

Location of the Firm and Date.

_____

369

Lead Paragraph: A summary of the newsworthy content.

Answers the questions:
Who:

What:

Where:

When:

Second Paragraph:
Expand upon the first paragraph and elaborate on the purpose of the Press Release.

Third Paragraph:
Further details with additional quotes from staff, industry experts or satisfied clients.

For Additional Information Contact:

About Your Expertise:
Presentation of your expert credentials

_____

_____

_____

_____

About Your Business:
Background company history on the firm and central offerings.

_____

_____

_____

Enclosures: Photographs, charts, brochures, etc.

Special Event Release Format   Notes

1. Type of Event
   _____

2. Sponsoring Organization
   _____

3. Contact Person Before the Event
   _____

4. Contact Person At the Event
   _____

5. Date and Time of the Event
   _____

6. Location of the Event
   _____

7. Length of Presentation Remarks
   _____

8. Presentation Topic
   _____

9. Question Session (Y/N)
   _____

10. Speaker or Panel
    _____

11. Event Background _____

12. Noteworthy Expected Attendees _____

13. Estimated Number of Attendees _____

14. Why readers s/b interested in event. _____

15. Specifics of the Event. _____

16. Biographies _____

Track Ad Return on Investment (ROI)

Objective: To invest in those marketing activities that generate the greatest return on invested funds.

Medium	Cost	Calls Received	Cost/Call	No. Act. New Clients	Cost/New Client
Formula:	A	B	A/B=C	D	A/D=E
Newspaper					

___ Classified Ads
_____

___ Yellow Pages
_____

___ Billboards
_____

___ Cable TV
_____

___ Magazine
_____

___ Flyers
_____

___ Posters
_____

___ Coupons
_____

___ Direct Mail
_____

___ Brochures
_____

___ Business Cards
_____

___
Seminars

_____

___
Demonstrations

_____

___
Sponsored Events

_____

___
Sign

_____

___
Radio

_____

___
Trade Shows

_____

___
Specialties

_____

___
Cold Calling

_____

___
Door Hangers

_____

___
T-shirts

_____

___
Coupon Books

_____

___
Transit Ads

_____

___
Press Releases

_____

___
Word-of-Mouth

_____

___

_____

_____

___
Totals:

_____

___

Advertising Tracking Form

Date　　　　Customer　Phone/　　Advertising　　Job?
Notes
　　　　　　　　　　　Email　　　　Source

_____
_____
_____
_____
_____
_____
_____
_____

Sample Thank-you and Referral Letter

Dear _____ (client name)

I wanted to take this opportunity to thank you for your business once again. If I can be of service to you in the future, I hope you will not hesitate to call.

In the meantime, I have enclosed a few business cards and referral cards. I would very much appreciate your passing them along to anyone in need of interior design services. As usual, I will mail you a referral fee for any business that comes my way from your efforts.

I have also enclosed a 'Customer Satisfaction Survey' with a self-addressed and stamped return envelope. Your feedback is invaluable in helping us to improve the services that we offer and we very much appreciate the time you will spend in completing the survey.

I hope you are enjoying your new surroundings and we look forward to serving you and your family in the future.

Please call me if I can be of any help. Thanks again.

Sincerely,

Top 20 Marketing Tips

The most important order you ever get from a customer is the second order.

In direct mailing, spend 10% of your budget on testing.

Understanding and adapting to consumer motivation and behavior is not an option. It is an absolute necessity for competitive survival.

A well-designed catalog mailed to a qualified response list will probably bring a one percent response.

Processing and fulfillment costs incurred from the time an order arrives until it is
shipped should be kept below $10 an order.

Know the power of repetition. Be sure your message is consistent.

The two most common mistakes companies make in using the phone is failing to track results and tracking the wrong thing.

Marketing activities should be designed to increase profits, not just sales.

It costs five times as much to sell a new customer as an existing customer.

Selling what your customers need, instead of what they want, can lead to failure.

Don't think that product superiority, technology, innovation or company size will sell itself.

Don't neglect or ignore your current customers while pursuing new ones.

People don't buy products, they buy the benefits and solutions they believe the
products provide.

Any decent direct mail campaign will cost $1.25 per piece.

The average business never hears from 96% of its dissatisfied customers.

Fifty percent of those customers who complain would do business with the company again if their complaints were handled satisfactorily.

It is estimated that customers are twice as likely to talk about their bad experiences as their good ones.

Marketing is everyone's business, regardless of title or position in the organization.

Exaggerated claims can produce inflated expectations that the product or service
cannot live up to, thereby resulting in dissatisfied customers.

Get to know your prime customers - the 20% of product users who account for 80% of the total consumption of that product class.

Classified Ad Worksheet

Ad Budget: _____

Ad Objective:　　　___ Go to Website　　___ Request More Info
___ Mail a Check
　　　　　　　　　　___ Introduce a new product/service　　___
Announce a Sale　　　　　　　　　　　　　___ Increase awareness
of product
　　　　　　　　　　___ Other

_____

Target Market:

_____

___

Target Market:
Demographics:
　　　- Age

_____

___

　　　- Gender

_____

___

　　　- Income

_____

___

　　　- Education

_____

___

　　　- Location

_____

___

Reading Interests:
　　　- Daily Newspapers

_____

　　　- Weekly Magazines

- Magazines
_____

- Trade Journals
_____

Product. Knowledge Level
_____

Purchase Motivators
_____

Best Category Heading
_____

Select Type of Message
    - Strong Offer with Best Value for Money
    _____

    - Point of Difference from Competitors
    _____

    - Listing the Benefits
    _____

Product Price: $_____

Ad Cost: $_____

Number of Responses: _____
Cost/Response: _____
Number of Sales: _____
Cost/Sales: _____

Marketing Plan   Month:

_____

Planned Accomplishments for month:
_____
_____

Describe target audience: _____

_____
_____
_____
_____

Success Measures:
Number of New Prospects   _____
Number of New Contacts to Referral Network
Sales Revenues of _____ by _____
Other measure: _____

Referral Network Action Plan:
We will attend the following events:
    Event   Date   Objective

_____
_____
_____

We will contact the following people in my network:
    Name   Date   Reason

_____
_____
_____

We will meet the following people in person:
    Name   Date   Reason

_____
_____
_____

We will keep in touch with the following people by sending them information, including articles and newspaper clippings:
    Name   Date   Information Type

_____
_____
_____

Past Client Action Plan:
We will contact the following past clients:
Method Options: In-person, Mail, email, phone.
    Name   Date   Reason
      Method

_____
_____
_____

Prospecting Action Plan:
Distribution Methods: Publications, Website, Organizations, Email, etc.

Method   Date   Subject
     Distribution

      Method
Article

_____
_____
Speech

_____
_____
Newsletter

_____
_____
Press Release

_____
_____

Other Activities:
    Activity Type   Date
    Target

_____
_____
_____

Sample Flyer Template

Company Name
Address
City, State, Zip code

Website
Main Phone:
Email Address

Service Area:

What We Do:

Products:

Services:

Specialties:

Associations:

Awards / Certifications:

Open Hours

Special Offer:

Additional Info:

Coupon:

$_____ Off Any _____ Service

Name: _____
Address: _____
Phone: _____
Problem: _____
Expiration Date: _____
Offer valid for 90 days from _____ (date) . Limit one (1) coupon per contract. Cannot be combined with any other offer. Not redeemable on minimum service charge. Coupon must be presented

at time of visit.

Referral Sales Letter

Dear _____ (customer)

_____ (company name) has come up with a great way to treat your friends and family as well as yourself.

Just give the coupon printed below to a friend, family member or business associate who has not yet tried our Liquor Store. Each coupon entitles the holder to a free _____ with the purchase of any _____. Now that's a great way to make loyal friends forever.

And there's more. Once a coupon is used by a new _____ (company name) guest, we will send you a voucher in return that's good for a half-price discount on any _____.

It's our way of thanking you for introducing your friends and associates to our Liquor Store. From the big screen High Definitions Television, to our friendly staff, your referrals are guaranteed to have a very enjoyable experience. And, you know from your own experience, that _____ (company name) is always ready to make everyone's visit a memorable event.

The attached coupon, which can only be used by someone other than yourself, is good through ____ (date). And the vouchers you receive in return are valid through ___ (date).

So tear off the coupon now and give it away.

Sincerely,

_____

Company Title
Detach Coupon:

Present this coupon for a special offer.
Exclusively for the friends and associates of:
Name: _____
Address: _____
Used by:
Name: _____
Address: _____

Redeem before _____ (date); only one coupon per person.
Does not apply with other offers or discounts. No coupon facsimiles accepted.

Sample Sales Letter Template

[Recipient's name],
[Recipient's designation],
[Recipient's company's name],
[Recipient's company's Address],
[Date]

Dear [Recipient's name],

We at _____ [company's name] believe that we can distinctly benefit your organization [Recipient's company's name] with our _____ products and services, if we are provided with an opportunity from your end. We excel in _____ [state the specific kind of product or service that our company provides. Mention our company's Unique Selling Proposition, and state how we can make difference to our client.]

We would like invite you to a special tour of our _____ (completed projects/ facilities) and a small session through which we will put forward why and how we are ahead of our competitors and how we can give you an edge over others. We can assure you that it will not be a waste of your precious time, as we value it ourselves.

Please kindly visit our website _____ [our website] to schedule an appointment.
We hope that you will render us a positive reply, so that we can each pursue a relationship through we can mutually benefit each other.

Thanking you
_____
[Your name/ title]
[Signature]
[Your designation],

[Our Company's name]
[Address]
[Email id]
[Web Site]
[Phone number]

Made in the USA
San Bernardino, CA
28 June 2017